RELIGIOUS LIBERTY
AND HUMAN RIGHTS

RELIGIOUS LIBERTY
AND HUMAN RIGHTS

Edited by
MARK HILL

UNIVERSITY OF WALES PRESS
CARDIFF
2002

© The Contributors, 2002

British Library Cataloguing-in-Publication Data.
A catalogue record for this book is available from the British Library.

ISBN 0-7083-1758-8

Typeset at University of Wales Press
Printed in Great Britain by Dinefwr Press, Llandybïe

Contents

Foreword

Since my appointment as Archbishop of Canterbury in 1991, it has been my pleasure to act as patron of the Ecclesiastical Law Society, jointly with successive Archbishops of York. The society, through its journal and conferences, has provided a forum for lawyers, theologians and historians to study the law of and about the church and has been one of the driving forces in the renaissance of ecclesiastical law as a discrete discipline.

Unsurprisingly, the Ecclesiastical Law Society took as its theme for its first residential conference of the new millennium the subject of religious liberty and human rights. The coming into force of the Human Rights Act in October 2000 gave topicality to the conference, while the tragic events of 11 September 2001 have given to this volume of essays an added poignancy.

The Archbishops' Council was pleased to be able to fund a research fellowship at the Centre for Law and Religion at Cardiff Law School to consider the effects for the Church of England of the Human Rights Act 1998. I am delighted that, in association with the Ecclesiastical Law Society, that fellowship concluded in the conference at Trinity Hall, Cambridge, at which the majority of the papers in this book were delivered. These, together with additional chapters especially commissioned to complement the theological and jurisprudential themes explored in the conference, create a volume which is informative, challenging and inspiring. It considers the practical working out of the emergent law in this country by reference to its theological origins and, in doing so, draws upon the experience of Europe and the United States of America.

This publication coincides with my retirement as Archbishop of Canterbury and President of the Anglican Communion worldwide. I congratulate the editor and publishers on producing a scholarly and provocative collection of essays which will inform and structure the dialogue in the coming years for my successor and for leaders of other faith communities.

+ George Cantuar:
Lambeth Palace

Preface
Human Rights: A Judicial Approach

STEPHEN SEDLEY

I have few if any qualifications for writing this preface. It is possible that the generous invitation to do so may have to do with my authorship not long ago of a judgment upholding the right of a group of evangelical preachers to warn passers-by that they would burn in hell if they failed to repent.[1] Whether the significant thing for the Ecclesiastical Law Society is that they were doing it from the steps of Wakefield cathedral I cannot say. It may also, however, have to do with my limited but rewarding role in helping to plan and deliver the Judicial Studies Board's most ambitious project to date, an intensive introduction to the Human Rights Act 1998 and the European Convention on Human Rights for the entire full-time and part-time judiciary of England and Wales. Scotland was of course ahead of us, both legally in the sense that the Scotland Act 1998 had already brought the Convention on stream in relation to devolution issues, which included criminal justice; and jurisprudentially in the sense that the Scottish courts early on showed a readiness to think the previously unthinkable in response to the new legal culture. And in one important sense Northern Ireland, though it is still struggling for the political settlement which will make the Northern Ireland Act 1998 a reality, has also for some years been ahead of us (at least, I would so regard it) in having a legal bar on unjustified discrimination on grounds of religion as well as of race, sex and disability.

Let me in any case first say a word about the Judicial Studies Board seminars, for we have recognized from the start that any judicial approach to the Act and the Convention must be a methodical and educated one. You cannot teach anyone, even a

---

[1] *Redmond-Bate v DPP* (2000) 7 BHRC 375, [1999] Crim LR 998.

judge, very much in a day, which was all that the system could afford; but what you can do, and what we set out to do, is demystify the new system and show judges through hands-on studies that if you approach issues methodically you can eliminate those to which the Convention contributes nothing and can resolve the others by an intelligent application of law and principle.

Three particular inputs, in addition to the hard work of the volunteer discussion group leaders, made the series special and – the evaluation questionnaires suggested – successful. One was the panel of sixty specialist academics and practitioners who in pairs delivered the opening lectures on the Act and the Convention. This was expertise which in the nature of things the judiciary lacked and had therefore to be found outside the judicial ranks. A second element was the deliberate collapsing of the judicial hierarchy. Law Lords sat down with deputy district judges to work on the same hypotheticals. It did no harm to anyone to realize that those at the foot of the ladder had as much to offer to the solution of the new problems as those at the top. Thirdly, a number of judges of the European Court of Human Rights made the journey over here to take part in the seminars, speaking briefly about their work, answering questions and sitting in on the case studies. I don't think it is possible to overestimate the beneficial effect they had on those seminars they were able to take part in. English and Welsh judges saw rapidly that, far from being invaders from another planet (not a complete parody of the view being advanced by segments of the press), these were fellow-judges facing similar problems to our own and sharing most of our concerns and ways of thinking. My single regret is that we were not able to have a Strasbourg judge on every seminar.

Of course the quality of the seminars and of the study-groups was not uniform; of course we could not achieve a great deal in a day; of course the written materials could have been improved upon; and of course there was the inevitable awkward squad whom nothing was going to persuade to change the way they did things. What was gratifying about the latter was that it was a far smaller element than we had anticipated, and that most of its members were approaching retirement.

Our planning was, however, predicated on an assumption which seemed uncontroversial at the time but which is starting to give serious concern. It was that the universities and law schools would by the time the Act came into force have reoriented their teaching to assimilate it, so that within a very few years we would have in our courts a new generation of lawyers to whom the Convention was second nature and with whose help the judiciary would continue their learning process. This is not happening. Anecdotal evidence, now confirmed by a survey conducted by Cardiff University, indicates that few law schools have planned collectively or centrally for a pervasive change. Individual law teachers, on whom the need to plan for change consequently falls, are responding unevenly and often negatively to the new need. It seems to me that the second of these phenomena is less open to blame than the first, though both are open to criticism. It is after all no easier for a law teacher than it is for a judge to re-educate him- or herself in a wholly new conceptual approach to a familiar subject. It is on the institutions in which they work that the essential responsibility must fall.

The Cardiff data, based on a good response rate of almost three-quarters, show that while nearly a quarter of universities have recruited new staff, a number of them at professorial level, to teach human rights, implementation is uneven and unsystematic. Almost a fifth of the responding universities were still not offering any undergraduate courses on human rights law. In the great majority of those which did, the course was optional. Only one responding university in five said that it had brought the Human Rights Act into all its courses. Most left it to individual course directors, sometimes with and sometimes without formal encouragement to make the change. Almost two-thirds said that their syllabus committee had considered and issued recommendations for the inclusion of the Act. But what, one needs to know, did they recommend, and what has been done to ensure that teachers are given the help they need, not simply in doing research but in changing what they teach? And how about the one-third of institutions who seem to have done nothing? How, you may wonder, can anyone teach evidence or procedure, to take only the two most obvious topics, without assimilating the Convention and its jurisprudence to their subject? It is a worry.

What, to our pleasant surprise, is proving not to be the worry we thought it would is the volume and character of human rights issues coming before the courts. Largely because of the deluge of cases which followed the coming into effect in 1985 of Canada's Charter of Rights and Freedoms, the Lord Chancellor's

Department's implementation working party, on which Lord Justice Brooke and I sat, planned for the worst-case scenario predicted by the more nervous; and the Lord Chancellor obtained from Parliament an increase in the permitted number of High Court judges to cope with the possible extra load. What has happened in the time since the Act came into force, however, indicates that it is settling in almost exactly as one would have wished it to.[2] It has certainly not proved to be the failure that the Canadian Bill of Rights 1960 was – a measure under which only one case of any significance was ever decided, establishing that a first-nation Canadian has as much right as a Canadian of European descent to be drunk in a saloon. Nor, however, does it show any sign of flooding our legal system. Human rights issues come up fairly steadily as extra elements in extant cases; few human rights cases are being launched which would not otherwise have been initiated. Some turn out, inevitably, to add nothing to the sum of received domestic jurisprudence; others are concentrating our minds beneficially on what we are or ought to be doing – for example in deciding whether it is reasonable, and now therefore Convention-compliant, to put someone out of their home or their job – without necessarily altering outcomes; and an important few are compelling us to rethink and reshape our law.

Quite why this benign pattern of experience, much closer to that of France than to that of Canada, seems to be characterizing our patriation of the Convention will deserve examination as time goes by. My own guess, for what it is worth, is that we would very probably have found ourselves travelling down the wide Canadian highway but for one thing: the existence of a ready-made body of case law at supranational level which has both limited the more ambitious practitioners' horizons and made it possible for them to predict outcomes in ways for which Canada possessed no analogue. There it has been the open season from day one. When in 1987 I took a sabbatical from the Bar and went to Canada to see how the Charter was working out in practice, I telephoned an old friend, by then a judge in Manitoba, and told him why I was there. 'Please don't ask me about the Charter;' he said, 'every two-bit criminal without a defence pleads the Charter. It's the worst thing

---

[2] See the evidence given by the Lord Chief Justice, the Master of the Rolls and the Senior Law Lord to the Parliamentary Joint Committee on Human Rights on 26 March 2001.

that's ever happened here'. I could see what he meant: in the same week a court had been asked to hold that a drunk driver, stopped by the Mounties in the middle of the night a hundred miles inside the Arctic Circle at 30 below freezing, was entitled to have his lawyer brought up from Whitehorse before they could make him blow into the bag. I do not believe that – much as we feared it – this kind of thing is happening here except perhaps on the smallest and most local scale. Occasionally, in fact, I worry that human rights points are not being spotted or are not being run for fear of a rebuff.

I have taken some time to discuss the settling in of the Act and Convention partly because my remit is the judicial angle, but mainly because I am in the company of authors whose knowledge of the substantive issues of ecclesiastical law as they are touched by questions of human rights is infinitely greater than mine. I was surprised some years ago to find that my jurisdiction as a judge of the High Court ran to the interpretation and enforcement of the Act of Uniformity as of all other primary public legislation. Where I agree with others whose papers are included in this volume, is in believing that so long as organizations, churches included, stay within the law, how they regulate their own affairs should not be the concern of the courts. The paradox for an established church, of course, is that it can never be wholly free of the law on which it depends for its nature and existence. I will come at the end of this preface to what may be a neglected example of this paradox. But first I offer a few thoughts about my proviso that an organized religion should be self-regulating so long as it stays within the law.

Until the passage of the Human Rights Act 1998 I do not imagine that this proposition was problematical. Nobody wanted the members or clergy of a church to be free to embezzle funds or commit assaults with some kind of benefit of clergy or other form of impunity. The concern which arose was whether section 6, by including the established church – as some considered inevitable – among the public authorities from whom it demanded observance of the Convention rights, would require the courts to take public charge of things which were domestic matters of faith and conscience. Here too it is worth pausing: is this always undesirable? If, as I have suggested, there would be no demur to the normal application of the criminal law within the church, we can probably agree that a member of the clergy who, albeit for understandable reasons, protected a co-religionist guilty of child sex abuse from detection would deserve neither moral nor legal exculpation. How, then, about the emotional abuse of vulnerable members of a religion or sect who want to leave it? It may not be a crime, but it can very well be a violation of the individual's Article 9 right to change his or her religion or belief. If such a violation were to be committed by a religious organization which has the legal status of a public authority, is there any reason why the remedies provided by the Human Rights Act should not be available to the victim? It may be inconceivable in the Church of England, but there are other state churches and religions where, I rather think, it is not. Recall that there are now forty-one states within Strasbourg's jurisdiction and more in the queue. Is there any reason why the privilege of public status should exempt an official organization, whatever its character, from the accompanying obligations recognized in the world's human rights instruments?

It was on account of less dramatic but analogous concerns that, as other contributors mention, what became section 13 of the Human Rights Act 1998 was introduced. It may well be that there was no need to worry and that nothing in the Bill was anyway going to force the church to celebrate same-sex marriages or enthrone women as bishops against its will. It may be, too, that section 13 – as is suggested in some of the following chapters – is of little substantive effect save as a reminder that the Convention is intended to protect, not to jeopardize, the collective practice of faiths. Whether the endeavour of section 13 to reassure congregations that they are on the individual, not the state, side of the Convention is workable in relation to a state church may have to be considered if the occasion arises. But I want to raise one or two more general issues about this provision and its sister provision in favour of the media in section 12.

The purpose of the Act is in a sense mechanical: it is designed not to create new law but to articulate with our constitution and legal system the principles and jurisprudence of the Convention. Of course that is an oversimplification, because the effects on our law will be and are meant to be profound; but it makes the necessary point that the Act is not a new Bill of Rights the contents of which have been fought over line by line in Parliament. It is the vehicle for an off-the-shelf Bill of Rights made fifty years ago in Rome in a form which, though very different from anything that would be drafted today, has shown itself capable of adaptation and growth in the hands of the European Court of Human Rights and comes to us in serviceable shape.

Unlike our law, which tends to be detailed and circumstantial and to take the form of rules, the Convention sets out broad principles. The Act has made it a form of superior law, though one which cannot override Parliament's clear commands. (The adjective 'unprecedented', which is frequently applied to the consequent power it reposes in the judiciary, would be better applied to the European Communities Act 1972, a true fundamental law.) But the way in which it operates is not to substitute one body of rules for another. It is to let the Convention permeate the fabric of the law, save where the law is prescriptively resistant to it, so as to modify rather than supplant it. This is why sections 12 and 13 are out of joint with the rest of the Act. They interpolate into the generalized machinery which the Act sets up a handful of special rules for special interests.

So far as I know, section 13 has not yet been the subject of judicial construction or application. Section 12, by contrast, has been. In the litigation brought by Michael Douglas, Catherine Zeta-Jones and their publisher *OK!* magazine against its rival *Hello!*, a Court of Appeal of which I was a member held it to be arguable that a right of privacy was now recognized by English law, which *Hello!*'s photographer had violated by gatecrashing the first two claimants' wedding; but that, the couple having sold the greater part of their privacy to *OK!* in the form of exclusive photo-story rights on the wedding, the injunction to stop *Hello!* publishing the unauthorized photographs would be discharged and the claimants left to their remedy in damages or an account of profits.[3] Not many days later the President of the Family Division enjoined the media against disclosing the whereabouts of the two boys who killed Jamie Bulger on their release from custody.[4] Both were private law cases, and in neither was the defendant a public authority. Yet in both cases the defendants relied on section 12(4) of the Human Rights Act 1998. It provides, as you will recall, that in any case potentially affecting the Convention right of freedom of expression the court must have particular regard to the importance

---

[3] *Douglas v Hello! Ltd* (2001) 9 BHRC 543, [2001] 2 WLR 992 CA.

[4] *Venables v News Group Newspapers Ltd* (2001) BHRC 587, [2001] 2 WLR 1038.

of that right. This provision bypasses the arguments about horizontality by laying down a special rule which in terms applies the Convention directly as between two private parties. When therefore you turn to the Convention, you see that the right to which particular regard is to be had, the right of free expression, is not absolute: it involves a proportionate regard for the rights of others. For Thompson and Venables, given the threats made against them, this meant among other things their right to life; for Douglas and Zeta-Jones it meant the right to respect for their private life. In other cases it may mean rights which are not in the Convention at all but which are still rights recognized by our law. I do not know if this is what the movers of the amendment which became section 12 meant to happen, but it is in my view now unquestionably a rule which conditions the application of the principles of the Convention in our domestic law, and perhaps not a bad one.

In other respects we may one day have to consider whether it is necessary to read section 12 or section 13 down, pursuant to section 3 of the Act itself, in order not to come into conflict with the Convention. There are two Articles in particular which may require this. Article 14 forbids unjustified discrimination in the enjoyment of Convention rights; and it is now supplemented by the new protocol, which the UK has not yet signed, enshrining a general right to be free of unjustified discrimination. There is also Article 17 which prevents the use of one right to stifle another and may be deployed to the same end. It may well be argued one day that to afford a special status to a party's Article 10 rights because it is a media organization, or to a party's Article 9 rights because it is a religious organization, is to discriminate unjustifiably if these rights are relied on to diminish the other party's enjoyment of its own Convention rights; and that section 12 or 13 needs accordingly to be read down, if necessary[5] to vanishing point. We shall see whether, in the face of such arguments, the protection by section 3 of unequivocal non-compliant primary legislation prevails and whether, if so, the Human Rights Act itself will suffer the ignominy of a declaration of incompatibility.

Those who think that none of this was necessary in the first place will find especially piquant the possibility of litigation –

---

[5] Cf. *Ashdown v Telegraph Group Ltd* [2001] 2 WLR 967, § 34, *per* Morritt V-C.

perhaps along the lines of the Moonies' litigation some years ago against the *Daily Mail* – in which one side relies on section 12 and the other on section 13. I offer no prediction of the outcome of such a postmodern contest, but there will be those who cannot resist mentioning something about the wind and the whirlwind to the originators of the two sections.

Let me mention finally an aspect of the substantive effect of the Human Rights Act 1998 which I suspect, from my limited reading, may have been overlooked or underestimated. This is the possible impact of the Act and Convention on religious schools. There is no doubt that the Convention protects the right of believers to have their children educated, if they wish to do so, in their own faith. It is equally clear that Article 2 of the First Protocol, while it guarantees no particular form or level of educational provision, forbids the state to deny anybody the right to education, especially – by virtue of Article 14 – if it does so by discriminating on grounds of religion. In this light there may be an important distinction between religious education, whether full-time or after-school, which parents arrange out of their own resources, and publicly funded education provided through a religious foundation. The former is plainly protected by the Convention. How about the latter if, as happens, it results in children being unable to get into the only decent school in their catchment area because their parents do not profess the necessary faith, not merely in theological but in denominational terms? I do not know the answer, but it seems to me to be a real problem in a country which, unlike others, both allows the state to fund sectarian education and integrates such education into the state system, yet for historical reasons does so without insisting in return that the schools be open to all eligible local children on an equal footing. Apart from the new problem of direct discrimination on religious grounds, there are parts of the country where the possibility already exists of indirect discrimination on racial grounds.

Equality of educational opportunity, it seems to me, may turn out to be the most fundamental of the questions posed for the churches by the Human Rights Act. It will require conscientious consideration of the effect of publicly funded sectarian schooling on the children of those who may not share their faith but do share their needs and, since 2 October 2000, their rights.

Acknowledgements

The editor and publishers are grateful to the Ecclesiastical Law Society for its assistance in the production of this volume. Drafts of chapters 3, 4, 5 and 6 were delivered at the Society's residential conference, 'Religious Liberty and Human Rights' held at Trinity Hall, Cambridge, on 30 March to 1 April 2001. They have each been updated and revised for publication herein together with chapters 1, 2, 7 and 8 which were commissioned subsequently from authors who had attended the conference and whose research interests complemented the themes explored. Particular thanks are due to Mr David Harte, the Reverend Stephen Pix and the Reverend Paul Benfield for their assistance in organizing the conference; to the Reverend Dr Robert Ombres OP, the Right Worshipful Sheila Cameron QC, the Honourable Mr Justice Gage and Mr Peter Collier QC who chaired the lectures and structured plenary discussion; and to Professor Norman Doe who acted as rapporteur. The contributions of Professor Simon Lee, Rector of Liverpool Hope University College, and the Right Reverend John Gladwin, Bishop of Guildford, added considerably to the conference, although their papers are not reproduced in this volume. Inquiries regarding membership of the Ecclesiastical Law Society should be addressed to 1 The Sanctuary, Westminster, London SW1P 3JT.

Thanks are also due to the Archbishops' Council of the General Synod of the Church of England for funding a Research Fellowship (to which the editor was appointed) at the Centre for Law and Religion at Cardiff University from 1998 to 2001 specifically to consider the impact for the Church of England of the Human Rights Act 1998, and to Professor Norman Doe, Director of the Centre, for the support and assistance which he has given to this project.

The chapter by Roger Ruston was researched and written with the aid of a grant from the Christendom Trust, which supports projects on Christian social teaching; that by Javier Martínez-Torrón was funded by project PB96-0633, granted by the Spanish Ministry of Education; and that by Ian Leigh had the support of the Arts and Humanities Research Board under its Research Leave Scheme.

As editor I would wish to thank Fr Robert Ombres OP, Miss Ruth Arlow and Mr Richard Tutt for their assistance in finalizing the manuscript; Mr Peter Moore for preparing the index; and my pupil James Rickards who showed a lofty disdain for the entire project but from whom I learnt much. Last, but by no means least, my thanks are due to Mr James Mannion for his contribution to this project and for his constant support in bringing it to fruition.

N.M.H.

Temple EC4
All Fools' Day, 2002

1

A New Dawn for Freedom of Religion: Grounding the Debate

MARK HILL

Certain dates will forever be imprinted on the lawyer's mind. One such is 2 October 2000. On this day the provisions of the Human Rights Act 1998 came fully into force in England.[1] The Act was part of the much-trumpeted package of legislation brought forth by New Labour in the euphoria of its electoral victory in 1997.[2] It was intended to symbolize the freedom of individuals, their investiture with tangible rights and liberties and the redrawing of the boundary between the citizen and the state. Those present at the Conference of the Cambridge Centre for Public Law in January 1999[3] may recall the comment of Lord Lester of Herne Hill QC, a driving force behind the incorporation into domestic law of the European Convention on Human Rights, eulogizing by borrowing from Wordsworth and applying it to the coming into force of the Act:

> Bliss was it in that dawn to be alive
> But to be young was very heaven![4]

With in excess of eighteen months having passed since that great dawn, a more reflective air now prevails in which the contributors to this volume – theologians, lawyers, judges and academics – can

---

[1] In relation to certain devolved powers, the Act had already been brought into force in Scotland, Wales and Northern Ireland. See Scotland Act 1998, Government of Wales Act 1998, and Northern Ireland Act 1998 respectively.

[2] It had been heralded in *Bringing Rights Home: Labour's Plans to Incorporate the European Convention on Human Rights* (Parliamentary Labour Party, London, 1996).

[3] 'The Human Rights Act and the Criminal Justice and Regulatory Process', University of Cambridge, Centre for Public Law, 9–10 January 1999.

[4] William Wordsworth, *French Revolution, as it Appeared to Enthusiasts* (1809) and *The Prelude*, bk xi, 1.108.

assess the degree to which the promise of the Act has been fulfilled, and its aspirations transformed into reality.

In his preface, Lord Justice Sedley has provided a personal perspective on the manner in which English judges have been groomed to deal with the jurisprudential revolution anticipated by the Act. The training of the judiciary – one reason for the long lead-time between the granting of royal assent in November 1998 and the coming into force of the Act – is symptomatic of the understanding that the change was not one of substance but of mindset. For indeed, as is explored in the following chapters, there is little novel, unique or startling about the Act. Its own short title makes plain that it is 'An Act to give *further effect* to the rights and freedoms guaranteed under the European Convention on Human Rights' (emphasis added). Rather than articulating a fresh and vital raft of rights for the birth of the third millennium, the government chose instead to buy into an international treaty half a century old. Though the first nation state of the Council of Europe to ratify the European Convention on Human Rights on 18 March 1951, and though permitting individual petition to the European Court in Strasbourg since 1966,[5] the United Kingdom had consistently declined to make the Convention part of domestic law.[6]

The Universality of Human Rights

In ratifying the Convention, and in giving further effect to it through the Human Rights Act, the United Kingdom engages more fully in the 'universal' corpus of human rights, variously described as neo-imperialism or cultural hegemony.[7] Tracing its history from the Universal Declaration on Human Rights in 1948[8] through to

---

[5] See generally A. Lester, 'Fundamental Rights: The United Kingdom Isolated' [1984] *Public Law* 47; and A. Lester, 'UK Acceptance of the Strasbourg Jurisdiction: What Really Went on in Whitehall in 1965' [1998] *Public Law* 237.

[6] For a discussion of the development of a rights-based culture in English common law, see A.W. B. Simpson, *Human Rights and the End of Empire: Britain and the Genesis of the European Convention* (Oxford, Oxford University Press, 2001), 14–41.

[7] See generally M. Evans, 'Human Rights, Religious Liberty, and the Universality Debate', in R. O'Dair and A. Lewis (eds), *Law and Religion*, Current Legal Issues 4 (Oxford, Oxford University Press, 2001), 205–26.

[8] UN General Assembly Res. 217A (III), 10 December 1948.

the Vienna Declaration and Programme for Action in 1993[9] via the International Covenant on Civil and Political Rights (1966) and the Declaration on the Elimination of All Forms of Intolerance and of Discrimination Based on Religion or Belief (1981),[10] such rights are differently articulated both in terms of their content and of their applicability. One distinguished commentator has stated:

> It is sometimes suggested that there can be no fully universal concept of human rights, for it is necessary to take into account the diverse cultures and political systems of the world. In my view this is a point advanced mostly by states, and by liberal scholars anxious not to impose the Western view on others. It is rarely advanced by the oppressed, who are only too anxious to benefit from perceived universal standards.[11]

The different formulations in international instruments of the right to religious freedom provide for more restrictive and more expansive meanings. It has been suggested that there is as yet no formulation of freedom of religion as an international human right that can properly be offered as having a universal legitimacy, although there is a predominantly accepted international *approach* that is subject to regional variation.[12]

The Historical and Theological Inheritance

A longer perspective, however, is helpful in order to appreciate the emergence and development of the post-war culture of human

[9] World Conference on Human Rights. For an overview of the proceedings and the Declaration text see (1993) 14 *Human Rights Law Journal* 346.

[10] UN General Assembly Res. 36/55, 25 November 1981. Note also Article 12 of the American Convention on Human Rights (1969); Article 8 of the African Charter on Human and Peoples' Rights (1986); Articles 26 and 27 of the Arab Charter on Human Rights (1994); and Article 10 of the Commonwealth of Independent States Convention on Human Rights and Fundamental Freedoms (1995).

[11] R. Higgins, *Problems and Process: International Law and How We Use It* (Oxford, Oxford University Press, 1994), 96.

[12] M. Evans, 'Human Rights', 219. Note however the criticisms made of the conflation of civil liberties with human rights in K. Ewing and C. Gearty, *The Struggle for Civil Liberties* (Oxford, Oxford University Press, 2001). The authors argue that such conflation is mistaken and that the main purpose of civil liberties is to develop an active political culture, that is, it is about freedom *to* rather that freedom *from*.

rights as evidenced in international documents and in the case law of domestic and pan-national courts. In Chapter 2, Roger Ruston shows that the theory of natural rights originated in the political theology of the Salamanca school of sixteenth-century Spain as a response to the moral crisis raised by colonization in the New World. The sources for the sixteenth-century natural rights theory were largely just war concepts, scripture and the tradition of natural freedom in canon law and the theology of Thomas Aquinas. The right of war discussed by Francisco de Vitoria established that indigenous people had natural rights of dominion in the form of ownership and self-government. The opposing humanist tradition of natural subjection came to the opposite conclusion on the basis of Aristotle's doctrine of natural slavery. Meanwhile the Dominican missionary bishop, Bartolomé de Las Casas, argued that authentic evangelization presupposes a natural, political liberty of all human beings, who are created in God's image. The gospel, considered as the law of life, can only be received by persons living in free communities. The humanist tradition was continued by Grotius and Locke. Grotius first made the crucial parallel between individuals in the state of nature and the international society of states, which gave rise to the idea of the sovereign individual with the right of self-preservation. Locke's account of natural rights uses the same biblical sources as that of the Spanish theologians, but is ambivalent, upholding the natural freedom of individuals and the right of property, while encouraging the dispossession of indigenous peoples in the American colonies.

With the discussion rooted in its historical context, Nicholas Sagovsky, in Chapter 3, develops this theme, indicating how, in the eighteenth and nineteenth centuries, the churches of the European establishment were deeply suspicious of notions of 'the rights of man' which were rightly seen to be subversive of the social order they supported and which supported them. His emphasis, however, is on the twentieth century and the emergence of a clearly articulated human rights culture in the international documents executed following the Second World War. Sagovsky points to some of the weaknesses of the contemporary understanding and application of human rights. The concept is seen as excessively individualistic, lacking a full account of what it means to be human, and is reliant on an inadequate sense of liberty – easily subverted to favour global capitalism. In considering 'divine justice', Christianity is sharply differentiated from the human rights tradition in that its concept of justice is located within the person of God. Sagovsky argues strongly that Christians should join in the public debate about the meaning and practice of freedom and justice. The human rights movement in many ways serves the cause of God's justice but there are real tensions for the Christian concerning the understanding of humanity, equality, impersonality and universality.

The American Dimension

Despite the commonality of both history and theology, the approach to religious liberty in the USA differs markedly from that in the United Kingdom and elsewhere in Europe. Mark Chopko, in Chapter 4, traces the divergent course plotted in America from the time of the first amendment to its new-born constitution in 1791. He considers the development and effect of the 'Religion Clauses' as continually revisited and reinterpreted by the American courts over the last two centuries. Such interpretations are of great value in considering the emergent English jurisprudence since they evidence the approach of a common law system to overarching constitutional provisions. At the same time, it illuminates, both empirically and anecdotally, the interface between the specificity of black-letter law and the generality of rights-based articulations of principle. It is of more than passing interest that in *Brown v Stott*,[13] Lord Steyn described the European Convention on Human Rights as 'our Bill of Rights'.[14] Whether the Judicial Committee will refashion itself more like the US Supreme Court and exercise a more overtly constitutional role remains to be seen.[15]

The Human Rights Act 1998

To assert that the Human Rights Act incorporated the Convention into English law is a convenient – although slightly misleading –

[13] [2001] 2 WLR 817.
[14] Ibid. at 839.
[15] See generally, N. Roberts, 'The Law Lords and Human Rights: The Experience of the Privy Council in Interpreting Bills of Rights' [2000] EHRLR 147.

shorthand.[16] The Act has two explicit purposes, and one pervasive effect. It is in the pursuit of these general purposes – and in the barely charted waters of the horizontal effect – that problems of definition and interpretation emerge, not least where religious liberty is concerned.

Interpretation of legislation

First, the Act requires the courts to interpret United Kingdom legislation so far as is possible in a manner compatible with Convention rights[17] and, in so doing, they must take into account – though not necessarily follow – the decisions of the European Court at Strasbourg.[18]

In R *(Alconbury Developments Limited) v Secretary of State for the Environment*,[19] an early decision on the Act by the House of Lords, the position was differently stated by two of the Law Lords. Lord Slynn observed that, 'in the absence of some special circumstances it seems to me that the court should follow any clear and constant jurisprudence of the European Court of Human Rights'.[20] Lord Hoffmann was not prepared to go so far:

> The House is not bound by the decisions of the European court and, if I thought that . . . they compelled a conclusion fundamentally at odds with the distribution of powers under the British constitution, I would have considerable doubt as to whether they should be followed.[21]

---

[16] A full discussion may be found in R. Clayton and H. Tomlinson, *The Law of Human Rights* (Oxford, Oxford University Press, 2000) and an insightful and thorough reflection on the first twelve months during which the Act has been in force is contained in the First Annual Updating Supplement.

[17] Section 3(1). In the event of there being an irreconcilable inconsistency, the domestic legislation prevails subject to a 'fast-track' system of executive action to bring English law into line with the Convention. See section 4 (declaration of incompatibility) and section 10 (remedial action).

[18] See section 2. This jurisprudence includes judgments, decisions, declarations and advisory opinions of the European Court of Human Rights, opinions and decisions of the Commission and decisions of the Committee of Ministers whenever made or given. The latter two ceased to produce such decisions and opinions as from 1 November 1998. A full discussion of the operation of the Strasbourg court is to be found in Chapter 5.

[19] [2001] 2 WLR 1389.

[20] Ibid., paragraph 26.

[21] Ibid., paragraph 76.

The Court of Appeal, in its unanimous judgment in *Aston Cantlow Parochial Church Council v Wallbank*,[22] put the matter with disarming simplicity: 'Our task is not to cast around in the European Human Rights Reports like black-letter lawyers seeking clues. In the light of section 2(1) of the Human Rights Act 1998 it is to draw out the broad principles which animate the Convention.'[23]

It must also be remembered that the procedures of Strasbourg are 'subsidiary to the national systems safeguarding human rights'.[24] It has been observed, 'by reason of their direct and continuous contact with the vital forces of their countries, the national authorities are in principle better placed than an international court to evaluate local needs and conditions'.[25] Thus not every Strasbourg decision is of direct application in the English courts. Equally, the Convention is a 'living instrument' and the jurisprudence which has emerged from Strasbourg falls to be carefully considered in the light of evolving social mores. The interpretation of the Convention by the Court, and until recently the Commission, reflects political and societal changes, as, for example, with the chastisement of children.[26] The functioning of the European Court of Human Rights is fully discussed by Javier Martínez-Torrón in Chapter 5. In addition he examines the major Strasbourg decisions on the subject of freedom of religion, pointing to a greater preparedness on the part of the Court to interfere to protect the right consequential upon the break-up of the Soviet bloc.

Since the Church of England legislates by Measure and since such Measures are classified under the Act as primary legislation,[27] they are to be interpreted, wherever possible, in a manner compatible with Convention rights. This applies also to subordinate legislation, such as Rules and Statutory Instruments.[28] Such a reading is to be adopted irrespective of when the relevant primary or subordinate legislation

---

[22] [2001] 2 All ER 363, *per* Morritt V-C, and Robert Walker and Sedley LJJ. Leave to appeal to the House of Lords was granted on 11 February 2002.

[23] Ibid., paragraph 44.

[24] This quotation is from *Handyside v United Kingdom* (1976) 1 EHRR 737 at 753, paragraph 48.

[25] *Buckley v United Kingdom* (1996) 23 EHRR 101 at 1299.

[26] See *A v United Kingdom* (1998) 27 EHRR 611, applied in the domestic courts in *R v H* [2001] EWCA Crim 1024 CA.

[27] See section 21.

[28] The interpretation section would seem to be sufficiently broadly drafted to include Canons as subordinate legislation being an 'other instrument' made under 'primary legislation', namely, the Synodical Government Measure 1969.

was enacted.[29] Commentators have suggested that the effect of this provision is significantly to change the common law principles of statutory interpretation.[30] Courts are obliged to use as the first guide to the construction of all primary and subordinate legislation not parliamentary intention[31] but compatibility with Convention rights. If no compatible reading of a piece of primary legislation is possible,[32] the court may make a declaration of incompatibility.[33] However, fast track remedial action by ministerial intervention is not available in respect of Church of England Measures[34] in the event that a competent court makes such a declaration.[35] Note also that the requirement for ministers to issue statements of compatibility for Bills during their passage through Parliament does not apply in relation to Church of England Measures.[36]

[29] See section 3(2)(a).

[30] See, for example, A. Smith, 'The Human Rights Act 1998: The Constitutional Context', a paper delivered at the University of Cambridge Centre of Public Law Conference, 'The Human Rights Act and the Criminal Justice and Regulatory Process', 9–10 January 1999.

[31] Note the extent of the search for legislative intent as discussed in *Pepper v Hart* [1993] AC 593 HL.

[32] A powerful indication has been given by the Judicial Committee of the House of Lords that courts will strain to find a compatible meaning even if that requires reading down the statutory provision. See *R v A (No. 2)* [2001] 2 WLR 1546 and, more particularly, *R v Lambert* [2001] 3 WLR 206.

[33] See section 4(4). At the time of writing there have been two declarations of incompatibility. In *R v Mental Health Review Tribunal ex p H* [2001] 3 WLR 512, certain provisions of the Mental Health Act 1983 were declared to be incompatible with Article 5. In *Wilson v First County Trust (No. 2)* [2001] 3 WLR 42, the bar to the enforcement of improperly executed consumer credit agreements under the Consumer Credit Act 1974 was declared to be incompatible with Article 1 of the First Protocol. In the latter case an appeal to the House of Lords is pending.

[34] See section 10(9).

[35] Competent courts include the High Court, the Court of Appeal, the House of Lords and the Privy Council. See section 4(5). The High Court has relevance for the Church of England in relation to committal for contempt and judicial review, as to which see M. Hill, 'Judicial Review of Ecclesiastical Courts', in N. Doe, M. Hill and R. Ombres (eds), *English Canon Law* (Cardiff, University of Wales Press, 1998), 104–14. The Privy Council is of more than theoretical importance. See, for example, *Cheesman and others v Church Commissioners* [2001] AC 19, (1999) 5 Ecc LJ 305.

[36] This is to be inferred from the silence in section 19 of the Act (where the provision for ministerial statements of compatibility is to be found) and the anomalous parliamentary procedures for legislating by Measure as discussed in M. Hill, *Ecclesiastical Law*, 2nd edn (Oxford, Oxford University Press, 2001) at paragraph 1.23. Compatibility with the Human Rights Act may become a matter for consideration by the Ecclesiastical Committee of Both Houses of Parliament: ibid. at paragraphs 2.06–2.07. Note however that statements of compatibility are

Regulation of public authorities

The second effect of the Act is to render unlawful any act by a public authority which is incompatible with a Convention right.[37] It also makes provision for compensation to be paid in the event of breach.[38] The thorny question, therefore, concerns the extent to which churches generally, and component institutions within them, may be classified as 'public authorities' for the purposes of section 6 of the Act.[39] The trend throughout Europe and in the USA has been to differentiate between the sacred sphere and the secular sphere. The American experience, as developed by Mark Chopko in Chapter 4, is of a distinct and impregnable wall of separation between church and state. Equally the jurisprudence of Strasbourg is suggestive of restraint and self-denial by national governments and courts in their involvement in religious affairs. As is ably identified by Javier Martínez-Torrón in Chapter 5, such holding back is identifiable as much in states where there is an established church or a concordat with one or more churches as where there is not. The experience of continental Europe and the jurisprudence of Strasbourg seem to indicate a reluctance on the part of the European Court and the Commission to enter into the internal affairs of religious organizations in member states whether established or not.[40] For example, the European Commission on Human Rights declined to entertain a claim arising out of clergy discipline procedure in the Church of England on the basis that the Commission did not consider the charge of conduct unbecoming a priest to be criminal under Article 6(1) of the Convention.[41] It also

---

no more than expressions of opinion by the minister concerned; they are not binding on the court nor do they have any persuasive authority: *R v A (No. 2)* [2001] 2 WLR 1546 at 1570, paragraph 69 *per* Lord Hope.

[37] See section 6.

[38] See section 8(2). In determining whether to make an award and how much to give, a court must take into account the principles applied by the European Court of Human Rights in relation to the award of compensation under Article 41 of the Convention. See section 8(4).

[39] See generally D. Oliver, 'The Frontiers of the State: Public Authorities and Public Functions under the Human Rights Act' [2001] *Public Law* 476. See also D. Oliver, 'Chancel Repairs and the Human Rights Act' [2001] *Public Law* 651.

[40] See also M. Hill, 'Church Autonomy in the United Kingdom', in G. Robbers (ed.), *Church Autonomy: A Comparative Study* (Frankfurt, 2001), 267–83.

[41] *Tyler v United Kingdom* (1994) 4 April, ECHR 21283/93. The Commission's decision is reproduced in M. Hill, *Ecclesiastical Law*, at 677–81.

considered the consistory court to be a sufficiently independent and impartial tribunal.

The Court of Appeal recently grappled with the 'public authority' concept in *Aston Cantlow and Wilmcote with Billesley Parochial Church Council v Wallbank*.[42] Ian Leigh in Chapter 6 discusses the judgment and its broader implications, finding little in the reasoning to commend itself, and much in the likely consequences to cause concern. Leigh further considers how and where the Human Rights Act will impact upon English law, examining the jurisprudence of Strasbourg from the perspective of the domestic law of the United Kingdom.

In Chapter 7 David Harte ventures some thoughts on how the law of employment and education might develop – willingly or unwillingly – in the light of the Human Rights Act. He concludes that change is inevitable and that it may not prove palatable to the Church of England.

The horizontal effect of the Act

Although the two explicit purposes of the Act are (i) to alter the principles of statutory interpretation exercised by the courts and (ii) to regulate the acts of public authorities, commentators have suggested that the Act will be more far-reaching. The so-called vertical effect is obvious – it concerns the hierarchical interaction between the citizen and emanations of the state. However, to the extent that a court is itself a public authority,[43] prohibited from acting in a way incompatible with convention rights,[44] such rights will fall to be considered in resolving private disputes between individual litigants. The development of the common law in this manner has been styled the 'privatization' of human rights.[45] Examples of this include the decision of the Court of Appeal in *Aston Cantlow*[46] and of the

---

[42] [2001] 3 WLR 1323. An appeal to the House of Lords is pending following the grant of leave on 11 February 2002.

[43] Section 6(3)(a).

[44] Section 6(1).

[45] See A. Clapham, 'The Privatisation of Human Rights' [1995] EHRLR 20 and A. Clapham, *Human Rights in the Public Sphere* (Oxford, 1993). See also A. Lester and D. Pannick, 'The Impact of the Human Rights Act on Private Law: The Knight's Move' 116 LQR 385; N. Bamforth, 'The True "Horizontal Effect" of the Human Rights Act 1998' 117 LQR 34; and D. Oliver, 'The Human Rights Act and the Public Law/Private Law Divide' [2000] EHRLR 343.

[46] See n. 42.

consistory court in *Re Durrington Cemetery*.[47] In the latter, Article 9 was engaged by the Jewish relatives of a man who had been buried several years earlier in the consecrated part of a municipal cemetery. The right of those relatives to manifest their religion by the observance of practices at Jewish burial grounds was an additional ground relied upon by the chancellor in granting a faculty for exhumation. Further examples of the operation of this principle of horizontality are to be found in the contributions of Ian Leigh and David Harte at Chapters 6 and 7 respectively.

Human Rights in the Spiritual Sphere

In Chapter 8, which concludes this discursus, Norman Doe returns the argument to its starting point. He seeks to discover, within the internal law and regulation of the component churches of the Anglican Communion, a concept of human rights. He finds certain traces both in the promotion of such rights in civil society and (though less so) in the functioning of the churches themselves. Such rights are fundamental to the dignity of the human person and are expressed by resolutions of the Lambeth Conference but not so much by component churches in communion with the See of Canterbury.

It is of interest that within the internal legal fora of member churches in the Anglican Communion – all of them, save perhaps the Church of England, being purely private organizations – canonical recognition is given, to a greater or lesser degree, to fundamental human rights of universal application. This is suggestive of a broad acceptance that there be submission – by Anglicans at least – to such universal principles. It may go further and pave the way to the wholesale adoption of the Human Rights Act by faith communities generally.

Such a course does not sit easily with the reluctance to interfere with the regulation of religious bodies as identified in the Strasbourg jurisprudence[48] and in the domestic courts.[49] Indeed the

---

[47] [2001] Fam 33 *per* Hill Ch. This was followed in *Re Crawley Green Road Cemetery, Luton* [2001] Fam 308 *per* Bursell Ch.

[48] See Chapters 6 and 7.

[49] See M. Hill, 'Judicial Approaches to Religious Disputes', in R. O'Dair and A. Lewis (eds), *Law and Religion*, Current Legal Issues 4 (Oxford, Oxford University Press, 2001), 409–20. See also M. Hill, 'Religious Liberty in the United Kingdom', 13 *Sri Lanka Journal of International Law* (2001), 1–15.

Human Rights Act 1998 seemed to put such deference onto a statutory footing. Section 13(1) of the Act provides:

> If a court's determination of any question arising under this Act might affect the exercise by a religious organisation (itself or its members collectively) of the Convention right to freedom of thought, conscience and religion, it must have particular regard to the importance of that right.

This would appear to create a spiritual sphere into which the courts will not trespass. This subsection has not so far been the subject of any reported decision. No mention was made of it in *Aston Cantlow*,[50] although in that case it was not Article 9 (freedom of religion) which was engaged, but Article 1 of the First Protocol (protection of property). However the courts have had occasion to comment on the twin provision in section 12 of the Act in which 'the court must have particular regard to the importance of the Convention right to freedom of expression'.[51] This section, however, despite its lofty language, mirroring that for freedom of religion, has been consistently read down by the courts.[52] In *Douglas v Hello! Limited*, Sedley LJ rejected the suggestion that there be a bland application of section 12(4) of the Act simply prioritizing the freedom to publish over other Convention rights. This was the case, amongst other things:

> because of the court's own obligation under section 3 of the Act to construe all legislation so far as possible compatibly with the Convention rights, an obligation which must include the interpretation of the Human Rights Act itself. The European Court of Human Rights has always recognised the high importance of free media of communication in a democracy, but its jurisprudence does not – and could not consistently with the Convention itself – give article 10(1) [freedom of expression] the presumptive priority which is given, for example, to the First Amendment in the jurisprudence of the Unites States' courts. Everything will ultimately depend on the proper balance between privacy and publicity in the situation facing the court.[53]

---

[50] See n. 42.
[51] Section 12(4).
[52] See *Venables v News Group* [2001] 2 WLR 1038; *Douglas v Hello! Limited* [2001] 2 WLR 992; *Ashdown v Telegraph Group* [2001] EWCA Civ 1142; *Beckham v MGN*, 28 June 2001 (Eady J); *A v B & C*, 30 April 2001 (Jack J).
[53] *Douglas v Hello! Limited* [2001] 2 WLR 992 at 1028, paragraph 135 *per* Sedley LJ.

It follows by analogy that the deference to religion articulated in section 13 is likely to be similarly illusory. It should however be remembered that what is envisaged in section 13 is not 'presumptive priority', but merely the having of 'particular regard' to the exercise of the Article 9 right to freedom of religion. This degree of mild – or not so mild – preference is entirely consistent with the approach hitherto adopted by the European Court in Strasbourg.[54] There may still be a prospect that creeping secularization will still stop short of the spiritual sphere.

Conclusion

Thus we find ourselves at a new dawn. It may not be as romantic or as revolutionary as presaged by the framers of the Human Rights Act but it is nonetheless real. The courts will find themselves looking at perennial questions but with new eyes. Grafting onto the common law concepts of fundamental freedoms, the violation of which is actionable, brings the courts more clearly into the political arena where policy arguments will be of greater significance.[55] Note, however, that in relation to mandatory powers concerning repossession of residential property under the Housing Act 1988, Lord Woolf has expressed the view that 'this is an area where, in our judgments, the courts must treat the decisions of Parliament as to what is the public interest with particular deference'.[56] Just as the Anglican Communion is seeking to express its own understanding of human rights, so the Church of England is under threat of compromising its spiritual identity by dint of interference from secular courts. The following chapters seek to examine the manner in which the concept of religious liberty will fall to be interpreted by the courts, to trace the course which has been followed to reach the present position and to venture some modest predictions for what lies ahead.

[54] See the discussion by Javier Martínez-Torrón in Chapter 5.
[55] See generally J. Laws, 'Meiklejohn, the First Amendment and Free Speech in English Law', in I. Loveland (ed.), *Importing the First Amendment* (Oxford, Hart, 1998); J. A. G. Griffiths, 'The Brave New World of Sir John Laws' (2000) 63 MLR 159; J. A. G. Griffiths, 'The Common Law and the Political Constitution' (2001) 117 LQR 42; and S. Sedley, 'The Common Law and the Political Constitution: A Reply' (2001) 117 LQR 68.
[56] *Poplar Housing and Regeneration Community Association Limited v Donoghue* [2001] 3 WLR 183 at 202, paragraph 69. Here it was Article 8 which was sought to be engaged.

2

Theologians, Humanists and Natural Rights

ROGER RUSTON*

Introduction

From the Christian standpoint there are things to be said for and against the idea of universal human rights. It appears both to harmonize and to clash with Christian traditions. On the positive side the universal scope of human rights expresses something that Christianity has always aimed for, that is, the unity of the human family, created by God and redeemed by Christ, sharing the earth as our common home and source of life. The command of Christ at the end of the gospel, to 'make disciples all nations' (Matthew 28: 19), implies this unity, and Paul's inclusion of Greek, Jew, barbarian, slave and free in Christ, who 'is all and in all' (Colossians 3: 11), is the theological epitome of it. Also, human rights provides a language of international justice across state boundaries – it gives a voice to the oppressed, the poor, the politically powerless of the world for whom the church has been traditionally concerned, by command of its founder (Matthew 25: 31–46). This is not only embodied in the list of social and economic rights, which in recent times the church has favoured, but is also implied in civil and political rights, since it is the poor who are disproportionately subject to such things as torture, false imprisonment, lack of privacy and due process of law. A similar identification between the cause of God and the cause of poor is shared by all the major religions.

On the negative side, however, the long association of rights with individualism seems contrary to the community ethos of the church. Classical Western human rights have always been

*This chapter was researched and written with the aid of a grant from the Christendom Trust, which supports projects on Christian social teaching.

associated with liberalism and liberalism has traditionally taken the abstract individual as its starting point for ethics, rather than the common good. Or rather, the common good is interpreted in such a way that it is morally neutral, simply a set of conditions that enable individuals to pursue their own separate goals.[1] Elevation of the individual over the collective results in a demotion of duties relative to rights. Moreover, precisely because of its traditional concern for the poor, the church has been highly critical of economic individualism with its freedom of contract and absolute property rights (see Catholic social teaching from *Rerum Novarum* (1889) onwards). Further, as the Catholic Bishops of England and Wales have recently pointed out, the tendency to reduce morality to a set of individual rights is bound to result in irresolvable conflicts – for example, between the right to life of an unborn child and the right to privacy in terminating a pregnancy.[2] Such conflicts cannot be resolved from within the discourse of rights itself, and we need other criteria in order to sort out competing claims. How do we find out what is *right* in such cases? Individual human rights cannot themselves constitute a morality, since they are invoked by people of widely different, even opposed moralities.

The contemporary discourse of human rights then is a multi-potent one, having widely different purposes and moral effects for different participants, often covering deep divisions of moral outlook and frequently representing only an illusory consensus.

Natural Freedom

I suggest that Christians might find their bearings in this maze by reconsidering the development of *natural rights* during the early modern period when the theological roots of the idea were much more obvious than they are now. Simplified ideas of their origins need to be questioned. It will become apparent that there have been radically divergent perspectives on rights from the outset.

Over a period of about 150 years, from Francisco de Vitoria's treatise *On the Indians of the New World* in 1539, to John Locke's

---

[1] See, for example, John Rawls, *A Theory of Justice* (Oxford, Oxford University Press, 1972), 246: 'The common good I think of as certain general conditions that are in an appropriate sense equally to everyone's advantage.'

[2] See *Human Rights and the Catholic Church* (1998), Catholic Information Service, available on the internet at *http://217.19.224.165/resource/hroi/index/htm.*

Two Treatises of Civil Government in 1689, political philosophers and theologians developed ideas of natural rights which were precursors of today's human rights. The writers involved were all Christians, and all accepted the biblical account of human origins – all had a 'theology'. They all belonged, moreover, to what the historian James Tully has called the 'natural freedom tradition'.[3] This had its roots in elements of Roman civil law, but was given greater significance and potential in the Christian context of medieval canon law. The foundational text is Gratian, *Decretum* Dist. 1 Cap. 7:

> Natural law (*jus naturale*) is common to all nations because it exists everywhere through natural instinct, not because of any enactment. For example: the union of men and women, the succession and rearing of children, the common possession of all things, *the identical liberty of all*, or the acquisition of things that are taken from the heavens, earth, or sea, as well as the return of a thing deposited or of money entrusted to one, and the repelling of violence by force. This, and anything similar, is never regarded as unjust, but is held to be natural and equitable.[4]

All men are born free, that is, they are not *by nature* subject to others. Aquinas gave it a theological interpretation: no man, having a rational nature, is ordained towards another person as to an end, but to God alone.[5] The political consequences of this doctrine are far-reaching: rulers govern by consent of the governed (even though all authority comes from God, according to Romans 13: 1); rulers are subject to the law, not above it; laws which conflict with the natural law which comes from the hand of God are not really laws at all; in extreme cases a tyrant may be deposed or killed. There are domestic consequences too: when discussing whether subjects are bound to obey their superiors in all things, Aquinas says that

> since by nature all men are equal, [a man] is not bound to obey another man in matters touching the nature of the body, for instance in those

---

[3] James Tully, *An Approach to Political Philosophy: Locke in Contexts* (Cambridge, Cambridge University Press, 1993), 17.

[4] Text from *Gratian, The Treatise on Laws with the Ordinary Gloss*, tr. Augustine Thompson OP (Washington, DC, Catholic University of America Press, 1993), 6; my emphasis.

[5] Aquinas, *Commentary on the Sentences of Peter Lombard*, 2. 44. 1. 3.

relating to the support of his body or the begetting of his children. Wherefore servants are not bound to obey their masters, nor children their parents, in the question of contracting marriage or of remaining in the state of virginity or the like.[6]

There are irreducible liberties belonging to every human being, which considerably modify any condition of servitude in which people might find themselves as a result of misfortune or punishment. No human being can be completely reduced to the state of being nothing but an instrument at the disposal of others.

Contrary to the natural freedom tradition, the alternative 'natural subjection' tradition traces all power back through a succession of absolute patriarchal rulers to the exclusive gift of God, denying any kind of participation by the people in government and giving superiors absolute powers over their subjects. The roots of such doctrines as the divine right of kings could also be found in medieval canon law – in such concepts as the *plenitudo potestatis*: the divine power of the pope transmitted through the monarchy.[7] But it was the natural freedom tradition that succeeded in the modern world and gave rise to various theories of natural rights.

The other essential ingredient of natural rights theories is the theory of war. The concept of justified warfare as a juridical process for the re-establishment of justice between states was one of the most important developments of medieval canon law. Its foundation was Augustine's concept of just war, as communicated in Gratian's *Decretum*. The intention of the lawyers was not to eliminate war altogether, but to 'establish limits within which war could justifiably be waged and to penalize participants in wars that transgressed those limits'.[8] The view that ultimately prevailed was that war was a law-bound activity which would be extremely costly to the public authority which fought for an unjust cause, or used unjust methods. The causes were restricted to the correction of an

---

[6] Aquinas, *Summa Theologiae*, IIa IIae, 104. 5c.

[7] See Kenneth Pennington, 'Bartolomé de Las Casas and the Tradition of Medieval Law', in *Popes, Canonists, and Texts 1150–1550* (Aldershot, Variorum, 1993), 2; also available on the internet at *http://classes.maxwell.syr.edu/His381/LasCasas2.htm*.

[8] James A. Brundage, 'The Limits of the War-Making Power: The Contribution of the Medieval Canonists', in *The Crusades, Holy War, and Canon Law* (London, Variorum, 1991), 69–85, p. 73.

injustice already received, including self-defence, and certain targets (for example, non-combatants), weapons (for example, cross-bows) and times (for example, Lent) were declared illegal.[9] As a consequence of this legal framework, many different kinds of rights were at stake: the right of a ruler to make war against another, the right of defence against attack, the property rights and damages resulting from a war, and rights of immunity. Unjust warfare forfeited such rights.

Right of War

It may seem remote from today's human rights debates to begin with the 'right of war' but this is the starting point for early modern natural rights. War, both international and civil, continues to be the experience of large numbers of people, providing circumstances in which human rights are most frequently and seriously violated. Moreover, the contemporary human rights movement came to birth immediately following the Second World War, and its first consequences – the war-crimes tribunals – addressed the crimes committed against humanity by the losing side in that conflict. Also, the international community is once again disposed to respond to certain cases of severe repression of human rights by wars of intervention. Of course, not all contemporary human rights questions have war as their background, but in early modern times – the sixteenth and seventeenth centuries – most of them did. It was in considering the so-called 'right of war' in the concrete circumstances of the time that other rights, including property rights, freedom from slavery and the right of self-government, received sharp definition and became the beginnings of modern human rights theory.

When in 1511 the first protests were made by Dominican missionaries at the inhuman treatment of the Indians of the Caribbean by Spanish conquistadors, the response from their unsympathetic superior in Spain was that 'these islands have been acquired by His Highness [King Ferdinand] *jure belli* [by right of war], and His Holiness [Pope Alexander VI] has made our Lord King a donation of the same, wherefore the servitude [of the

<hr />

[9] Ibid., 76.

Indians] is meet and just'.[10] Francisco de Vitoria's two major treatises on the subject, written nearly thirty years later, addressed the question of Spanish rights to make war against the Indians, with the recent conquest of Peru in the background. The second of them is entitled *De Jure Belli* (1539). This preoccupation with the 'right of war' continued well into the next century. In 1588 the Italian Protestant humanist teaching at Oxford, Alberico Gentili, a major influence on Thomas Hobbes and the English tradition, published his *De Jure Belli*, and in 1625 Hugo Grotius, who first clearly defined individual rights in the modern sense, did so within his most celebrated work *De Jure Belli ac Pacis*. An individualized 'right of war' features among the rights possessed by every man existing in a state of nature in the political philosophy of both Hobbes (*Leviathan*, 1.13) and Locke (*Two Treatises of Civil Government*, 2.19). The 'right' in question was not in the first instance meant in our familiar subjective sense, as in 'my rights', but it referred to the justice of war – 'what is just', or, as Grotius expressed it, 'what is not unjust'.[11] But out of this consideration emerged the first discussions of the natural rights possessed by individuals. The significance of the 'right of war' – or, as we refer to it, 'just war' – undergoes important changes but it is always present as part of the debates on natural rights, just as nowadays it is constantly associated with questions about human rights. At the present time many violations of human rights, for example, arbitrary arrest, imprisonment without trial, or trial by closed military tribunal, and torture, can be understood as *the con-tinuation of war by other means*. Exactly what part it plays in the discussion of natural rights differs significantly among these authors over the period of 150 years and the different ways in which they develop the theme reveal much about the real function of natural rights in their theories.

The aforesaid donation of the newly discovered lands across the Atlantic by the pope to the Spanish kings in 1493 expressed a doctrine widely held by medieval canonists that the papacy

---

[10] The words of the Dominican Provincial, Alonso de Loaysa, later Cardinal and head of the Council of the Indies, who held a very low opinion of the Indians and their capacity for Christianity. Gustavo Gutiérrez, *Las Casas* (New York, Maryknoll, 1993), 36.

[11] Hugo Grotius, *The Rights of War and Peace*, tr. A. C. Campbell (Washington, DC and London, 1901), 247.

possessed universal jurisdiction, and as a result could declare war against the enemies of the church and oblige Christian monarchs to take up arms against the infidel. The claim existed in different forms, the most extreme of which held that since the coming of Christ his followers had exclusive rights to the exercise of power and jurisdiction on this earth.[12] This power was, of course, concentrated in the papacy, since the pope was the vicar of Christ. Unbelievers were *de jure* and *de facto* subject to the church and had no just *dominium*, that is, no independent rights to their lands or possessions. For the thirteenth-century canonists Alanus Anglicus and Hostiensis, this had meant that 'unbelievers who do not recognize the dominion of the church may be lawfully invaded, according to the passage "All power is given to me in heaven and earth" (Matt. 28:18)'.[13] War of this kind would be not only just, but holy. In the early decades of the sixteenth century this was the doctrine held by influential Spanish canon lawyers[14] to justify the conquests: all legitimate secular power has been transferred to the Christian faithful. A less extreme version of the doctrine – that of the canonist Pope Innocent IV (1243–54) – held that unbelievers do exercise true *dominium*, and they may not be attacked unless they have done some wrong. In the latter case the pope holds authority over them *de jure*, and war can be declared against them to regain territories once Christian, or because they commit sins against the natural law. An important juridical consequence of this was that property, prisoners and land taken in such a war were acquired by just title.[15] The prisoners would become slaves, as an alternative to being justifiably killed for fighting in an unjust cause – the only justifiable source of slavery in the medieval canon law.

These arguments had been mostly deployed against Saracens and Moors to justify Crusades and wars of reconquest, as in Spain.

---

[12] James A. Brundage, 'Holy War and Medieval Lawyers', in Brundage, *The Crusades*, 122.

[13] This is Vitoria's reading of the canonists, see Vitoria, 'On Dietary Laws or Self-Restraint', in *Political Writings*, ed. Anthony Pagden and Jeremy Lawrance (Cambridge, Cambridge University Press, 1991), 225 (henceforward 'P & L').

[14] Matías de Paz and Juan Lopez de Palacios Rubios. The latter was responsible for the notorious *requerimiento*, a document to be read out to the Indians before attacking them, which solemnly informed them of their legal position with regard to the Christian authorities: see Pennington, 'Medieval Law', 3.

[15] Brundage, 'The Limits', 74.

At first, the same reasoning was applied by the lawyers to the Spanish conquest of the New World. But it soon became clear that this was an entirely different situation. These people had never been Christian or Muslim, and neither they nor their ancestors had ever done anything unjust to the Spaniards. So it looked as if they might be innocent victims of a war unjustly prosecuted by Christians. There was then an acute problem to be faced by the Spanish government concerning the moral and legal status of the conquest of the Americas. Since this government was staffed largely by churchmen, many of them with backgrounds in canon law, it is not surprising that a matter of foreign policy should be construed as a matter of justice and therefore a matter of conscience, with all the differences of interpretation you might expect among lawyers.

Theologians

Nearly fifty years after the discovery of the New World this problem was addressed by Vitoria, holder of the chair of theological jurisprudence at the University of Salamanca, in two celebrated long lectures he gave in 1539 on the subject of the wars against the Indians. It was in the course of the first of these, *On the Indians*, that he produced what was in effect the first politically engaged account of natural rights.

Vitoria was a scholastic, educated in Paris and with some leanings towards humanism. When he returned to Spain he became the centre of a Thomist revival, the first to lecture from the text of the *Summa Theologiae*, and the inspired teacher of a whole generation of 'theologian-jurists'. His field of expertise combines what we would call political theology and international law. Central to it was the just-war tradition to which I have already referred. He understood war as existing necessarily within the confines of a juridical process, governed by the civil law code. War could never be solely for the purpose of political glory or expansion of the state, but only for a just cause, that is, the punishment of a crime or correction of an injustice already received. Vitoria speaks of a global commonwealth, or *respublica*, competent to enact the law of nations. This law, which is partly a matter of universal custom and partly a result of pacts and agreements, is binding on individuals, including those engaged in war, and it is very close to natural law. But Vitoria also belonged to a Dominican tradition which rejected in principle any idea of worldwide authority – including Christian authority. This may perhaps be traceable to Aristotle's view of human nature being fully realized only in the *polis*, or city state, the small unit in which free men can participate in their own government.[16] This meant that, *on the natural level*, any properly constituted political community, whether Christian or not, must have real authority and jurisdiction and enjoy ownership of its goods and lands. There was no way in which the universal right of the pope or of a Christian emperor, such as the Habsburg Charles V, who was also king of Spain, could be assumed. Thomas de Vio, Cardinal Cajetan (1469–1534), master general of the Dominicans, set this doctrine out very clearly in his influential commentary on St Thomas, in time for it to have maximum effect on the debates surrounding the Spanish conquest of the Americas. Unbelievers do not fall under the temporal jurisdiction of Christian princes either *de facto* or *de jure*. 'No king, no emperor, not even the Church of Rome, is empowered to undertake war against them for the purpose of seizing their lands or reducing them to temporal subjection. Such an attempt would be based upon no just cause of war.' He points out that, in the Old Testament, from which many a holy-war enthusiast derived his justification for crusade against the infidel, 'war was never declared against any nation on the ground that it did not profess the true faith'. On the contrary, the only reasons were such offences as attacks on God's people or occupation of their land.[17] This meant that non-Christian rulers, whether Muslims or pagans, had a perfect right to their independence from the church, which had no right to judge them, let alone war against them.

In rejecting the medieval notion of the universal jurisdiction of the church, the Dominican theologians were putting in its place another kind of universalism, that of natural law.[18] The medieval order is being replaced with something recognizably modern: the

---

[16] Richard Tuck, *The Rights of War and Peace* (Oxford, Oxford University Press, 1999), 68.

[17] See translated passage in ibid., 70.

[18] See Hedley Bull, *The Anarchical Society* (London, Macmillan, 1977), 28.

international rule of law rather than the authority of persons with a divine mandate. The law of nations is a direct derivation of natural law, which applies to everyone, Christian or not. Moreover, it treated individual men as the ultimate bearers of rights and duties rather than states alone, which was the case with later international law.[19] It amounted to a desacralization of political power, since it put the whole question of unity of the human race on the natural level, where it is in principle intelligible to everyone on earth, rather than on the supernatural level, where it is intelligible only to Christians.

Dominium *and the Image of God*

But other arguments were brought against these pagans having true *dominium* (a term which meant both ownership and jurisdiction), designed to show that it was completely justified to take their lands off them and subject them to Christian rule. For example, it was said that they are sinners, and sinners cannot be true masters (according to a late medieval teaching made notorious by John Wyclif); they are unbelievers, that is, equivalent to heretics, and therefore their property can lawfully be confiscated by Christians; they are irrational barbarians, that is, like animals, and therefore can be hunted, as Aristotle says in his *Politics*; or they are like children, incapable of governing themselves. It would be interesting but time-consuming to relate what Vitoria wrote about each of these propositions. In various, hardly changed forms they have been constantly used by Europeans in subsequent centuries to justify taking over large regions of the world and displacing or killing the indigenous people. The basis of his refutations is that the foundation of all natural *dominium*, such as is enjoyed by the Indians, is the biblical revelation in Genesis 1:27, that 'all human beings are made in the image of God'. This is why, if the natives are to be considered in any sense as 'children', it is only a temporary condition and does not touch their capacity for true ownership and self-government: 'the foundation of dominion is the fact that we

---

[19] The contemporary human rights movement represents a return to the early modern dominance of individual persons and natural law rather than the states and treaties of nineteenth-century international law. Ibid., 39.

are formed in the image of God; and the child is already formed in the image of God.'[20] The traditional Thomist interpretation of this doctrine is that it refers to each person's endowment with reason and will, so that they are (unlike other earthly creatures) masters of their own actions and thus enabled to participate in God's own *dominium* over the world.[21] Assisting this argument was the wording of the Vulgate Bible, 'Subdue the earth, and have dominion over the fishes of the sea, the birds of the air and all living things which move upon the earth.' It is precisely the capacity for *dominium* that distinguishes human beings from beasts – it is not a distinction to be made *within* the human race. It belongs to every individual by *nature*, and so it cannot be affected by sin, religious belief or any other of the possibilities considered. This nature is universal and endows every people on earth, Christian or not, with the gift of God at creation: the right to own property, the right to live freely, the right to govern themselves. It is for this reason that – in the scholastic tradition – there is no general 'right of war' belonging to Christians against non-Christians, 'barbarians', unbelievers or however the outsiders are to be described; no right of war of the civilized against the uncivilized, the advanced against the backward. Right belongs by nature elsewhere – with the peoples themselves.

What was particularly wrong, according to the Thomist tradition to which Vitoria belonged, was the belief that pagans could be forced to accept the faith. There was already a well-established position on this question relating to the Jews and those Muslims who lived under Christian rule – permanent 'outsiders' in the Christian commonwealth. It is no accident that the question of just treatment of the Jews – toleration of their freedom of worship, their immunity from terror and forced conversion – became, in the writings of the Spanish theologians, one of the starting points for their consideration of natural rights.[22] In his commentary on Aquinas's question 'Should unbelievers be forcibly converted?', Vitoria invokes a canon *De Judaeis* in Gratian's *Decretum* (Dist. 45, Cap. 5). The Jews and Saracens are not to be forcibly baptized –

---

[20] Vitoria, 'On the American Indians', P & L, 249.

[21] For a full analysis of this Dominican teaching, the best account is that of Jaime Brufau Prats, *La escuela de Salamanca ante el descubrimiento de nuevo mundo* (Salamanca, 1989), 11–48.

[22] Vitoria, 'On the American Indians', P & L, 272, 341–51.

mainly because no one can receive faith against their will. He makes a guarded criticism of the religious policy of the Spanish Crown, by remarking that the forced conversion of the Moors has been a complete failure, as you would expect – 'they are as much Moors as ever they were'.[23] Vitoria adds that it is wrong 'because their liberty is taken away', making the striking parallel between forced conversion to Christianity and a shotgun marriage to a perfect wife, which, however much of a good thing in itself, would be a wrong done to the person (an *injuria*, denial of right). From a consideration of the rights of unbelievers *within* the state, Vitoria moves to unbelievers *outside* the state, that is, the American Indians, whose treatment is obviously the main goal of the argument. Even if no scandal were to ensue it would be wrong to convert them at sword-point, because it is a violation of their natural liberty, the king of Spain having no jurisdiction over them, any more than private citizens have over one another in Spain. And it would be an *injuria* to throw down their idols and destroy their temples.

So because of the existence of the Jews and the Muslims in the Christian commonwealth, the emergence of the concept of universal rights, based upon the idea of a natural unity of humankind across religious barriers, was always a latent possibility, and it only required the discovery of the millions of pagans across the oceans, who had never done any harm to Christians, to make it a reality. There were a small number of perceptive Christian thinkers – theologian-jurists and missionaries – who became aware of the moral demands of this event, and it was they who were best placed to develop the language of natural rights through the creative use of theology and canon law.

This brief account of what Vitoria had to say about natural rights would be misleading without also indicating that he developed the idea in another direction, asserting the freedom of Spaniards to travel in the New World, their right to trade there, preach the gospel, defend themselves against attack and rescue the innocent victims of human sacrifice. These are the so-called 'just titles', which all gave possible reasons for justifying the Spanish presence. They are the object of much controversy among modern

---

[23] Vitoria, 'Commentary on the *Summa Theologiae*, IIa IIae', 10.8, in P & L, 345.

scholars, as they were in Vitoria's own century. The question is whether Vitoria thought these were actual or hypothetical rights, that is, whether the Spanish conquest was actually justified by them, or whether it would have been justified by them if the Spaniards had come in peace rather than violent conquest.[24] He says that 'The Spaniards have the right to travel (*jus peregrinandi*) and dwell in those countries, so long as they do no harm to the barbarians, and cannot be prevented by them from doing so.'[25] This is a matter of the law of nations, which, he says, 'either is or derives from natural law'. It is the ancient law of hospitality to strangers, recognized by virtually every human society, and the Spaniards can insist on it. Vitoria's clever pupil, Melchor Cano, thought this was naïve. 'Who', he asked, 'would have described Alexander the Great as a traveller?'[26] These 'just titles' provided the beginnings of various rights of free movement across borders and fair treatment of aliens. Unfortunately, however, while it did establish certain rights of mobility in international law, it also enabled both sides in the dispute over Indian rights to use the authority of Vitoria. But there is no doubt that he established the main lines of argument for indigenous rights.

Humanists

In any case, the theologians did not have it all their own way. The right of Christians to make war against 'barbarians' was vigorously defended once again in 1550 by a Spanish humanist, Juan Gines de Sepúlveda. It comes as a surprise that humanists should be opposed to the idea of natural rights, but such was indeed the case. As Richard Tuck puts it, because of their contempt for untutored nature, outside of civil society, humanist lawyers 'found it virtually impossible to talk about natural rights, and extremely difficult to talk about rights *tout court*. What was important to them was not

---

[24] The latter was the interpretation of Las Casas, *Defense*, 341 (see n. 36 below). For a thorough discussion of this see Ramón Hernández, 'La Hipotesis de Francisco de Vitoria', in *Francisco de Vitoria y la escuela de Salamanca: La Etica en La Conquista de America,* Corpus Hispanorum de Pace, vol. 25 (Consejo Madrid Superior de Investigaciones Cientificas, 1984), 345–81.

[25] Vitoria, 'On the American Indians', P & L, 278.

[26] Pagden and Lawrance, Introduction to Vitoria, *Political Writings*, p. xvii.

natural law but humanly constructed law; not natural rights but civil remedies.'[27] In this respect, Sepúlveda, who received his humanist education in northern Italy, was 'an absolutely stereotypical humanist'.[28] The humanism of the Italian city-states had nothing to do with equality between individuals or between nations, and everything to do with the ascendancy of urban, civilized aristocrats over the illiterate, non-Latin speaking, uncultured people of the soil. Italian humanism was 'a program for the ruling classes', an ideology of power.[29] It was an aristocratic ideal. 'The highest humanist good resided with the happy few, with those who had the political rank for grand action or the virtues and economic resources for leisurely study.'[30] Looking back at the surviving literature of Greek and Roman cities, humanists identified with the ruling elites who had produced it and shared their ambitions and their disdain for uneducated peoples. 'They took for granted their affiliation with power . . . The opposite condition, powerlessness, led to barbarism and provincialism.'[31] Consequently, for at least some humanists, dominion over more benighted peoples, empire and the spread of 'civilization' were part of the programme.

It was Aristotle's account of 'natural slavery' in the *Politics* which gave the humanists their authority for this outlook. The restoration of the Greek text of Aristotle at the Renaissance gave rise to a new, non-scholastic, less theological approach to some of his doctrines. This is what he had written:

> One who is a human being belonging by nature not to himself but to another is by nature a slave, and a person is a human being belonging to another if being a man he is an article of property, and an article of property is an instrument for actions separable from its owner.[32]

The people who most fit this description are 'barbarians', and the primary method of acquiring such property is war, which in this sense is a species of hunting:

[27] Richard Tuck, *Natural Rights Theories* (Cambridge, Cambridge University Press, 1979), 33.
[28] Tuck, *War and Peace*, 43.
[29] Lauro Martines, *Power and Imagination: City-States in Renaissance Italy* (London, Allen Lane, 1980), 262.
[30] Ibid., 273.
[31] Ibid., 270.
[32] 1254ª15–18. tr. H. Rackham from the Loeb edn of the *Politics*.

the art of war will by nature be in a manner an art of acquisition (for the art of hunting is part of it) that is properly employed both against wild animals and against much of mankind as though designed by nature for subjection refuse to submit to it, for such war is naturally just.[33]

This passage from the Philosopher seems then to authorize slave-raiding, and ominously declares war waged against 'barbarians' to be naturally just. And it flatly contradicts the central tenet of the natural freedom tradition, which was why the Spanish scholastics, who accepted that tradition, and were also in some sense Aristotelians, had difficulties with it and resorted to some creative reinterpretations of Aristotle at this point, effectively nullifying the concept of natural slavery. They granted the existence of differences in levels of civilization, but denied it gave any right of war against those less advanced.[34] However, the humanists accepted it wholeheartedly, and tended to classify all those outside the Christian commonwealth as 'barbarians' – in the first place Turks and other Muslims, against whom even Erasmus urged perpetual war. They were quick to include in this category all the newly discovered peoples of America, total strangers as these were, of course, to classical civilization and the life of letters.

War against such people then would be a civilizing mission, all the more justified in that, once pacified, the barbarians could be taught the rudiments of Christianity and fulfil their natural role as servants to their European masters. Sepúlveda wrote:

> The Spaniards rule with perfect right over the barbarians, who, in prudence, talent, virtue and humanity are as inferior to the Spaniards as children to adults, women to men, the savage and cruel to the mild and gentle, the grossly intemperate to the continent, I might almost say as monkeys to men [*though this last phrase was omitted from the printed version of his book*].

This came dangerously near the heretical opinion – rejected by St Thomas and all reputable theologians, as well as by canon law – that faith could be communicated by force. This was probably the

---

[33] 1256ᵇ20–5.
[34] Vitoria, 'On the American Indians', P & L, 251.

reason why, in Spain, the Dominicans entirely disapproved of Sepúlveda, made it impossible for his book to be printed there, and ensured the defeat of his doctrines in the universities, but not before there had been a high-profile struggle between the two opposing sides.

The conquest of Peru, and destruction of the Incas in 1547, caused a crisis of conscience in Spain up to the highest level. Many influential figures, including the Dominican professors at Salamanca, were deeply opposed to the way it had been carried out. Consequently, in 1550, the emperor and the Council of the Indies called a halt to further expeditions and ordered the meeting of theologians and jurists at Valladolid to discuss 'how conquests may be conducted justly and with security of conscience'.[35] This was to be a debate between the champion of Indians rights, Bartolomé de Las Casas, the Dominican missionary and bishop of Chiapas in Mexico, and Sepúlveda the humanist. The contestants never met face to face, and where Sepúlveda took three hours to deliver his case to the learned *junta*, Las Casas took five days to read out his response, in effect a substantial book, now published in translation as *The Defense of the Indians*.[36] Fortunately, we have a succinct summary of the dispute made by one of the scholars at the meeting, the Dominican theologian Domingo de Soto, who was a friend of Las Casas and a colleague of Vitoria.

In Soto's words, the question to be disputed is

whether it is licit for your Majesty to make war against these Indians, before the Faith is preached to them in order to subject them to your rule so that afterwards they may be more easily taught and enlightened by the Gospel teaching in the knowledge of their errors and Christian truth.[37]

Sepúlveda has four reasons why this should be so. The first is the serious nature of the crimes of the Indians, notably 'idolatry and other sins they commit against nature'. The second is 'the

---

[35] Lewis Hanke, *All Mankind is One* (De Kalb, IL, Northern Illinois University Press, 1974), 66.

[36] Bartolomé de Las Casas, *In Defense of the Indians* (1552) [*Apologia*], tr. Stafford Poole, CM (DeKalb, IL, Northern Illinois University Press, 1992).

[37] Domingo de Soto, *Relecciones y Opusculos I*, intro., ed. and tr., Jaime Brufau Prats (Salamanca, Editorial San Estaban, 1995), 204.

primitiveness of their wits which is that of natural slaves and which
obliges them to serve those of more polished manners, as are the
Spaniards'. Thirdly, the preaching of the faith renders their
subjection convenient and expedient. Fourthly, their subjection to
Spain is deserved by the 'injury that some do to others, killing men
in order to sacrifice them and others so as to eat them'.[38] We have
met some these arguments already. My purpose for bringing them
up again is to show where the humanist way of thinking was
leading and to say something of Las Casas's distinctive replies.

Las Casas and Canon Law

Against these arguments Las Casas deploys a vast range of sources,
biblical, patristic, canonical and Thomist: sources he had explored
over a period of forty years' struggle on behalf of the Indians. But
for the most part he appealed to scripture and canon law.[39] Against
the doctrine of natural slavery he set Genesis 1:27:

> Again, if we want to be sons of Christ and followers of the truth of the
> gospel, we should consider that, even though these peoples may be
> completely barbaric, they are nevertheless *created in God's image*. They
> are not so forsaken by divine providence that they are incapable of
> attaining Christ's kingdom. They are our brothers, redeemed by
> Christ's most precious blood, no less than the wisest and most learned
> men in the whole world.[40]

He then cites Paul in Colossians 3:17, 'There is neither Greek nor
Jew', etc.

In the course of his long *Defense*, Las Casas asserts the following
rights of the Indians which countermand the supposed rights of war
of the Spaniards: the right of choosing their own rulers; the right of
possession (*dominium*); the right of self-defence; the right to worship God according to their own traditions until convinced of error;
the right to have the gospel communicated to them by peaceful,
rather than warlike means. These are natural-law rights; and what is

---

[38] Ibid., 205.
[39] See Pennington, 'Medieval Law'.
[40] Las Casas, *Defense*, 39; my emphasis.

most significant for our purposes, they are communal, rather than individual rights, although they will have individual consequences.

But the key natural right in Las Casas's writings is the right of liberty. Since liberty of some description is central to contemporary human rights ideas, and is generally given an individualist interpretation, it is worth attending to Las Casas's ideas on it, with a view to the differences between what the Spanish Catholic missionary bishop wrote and what Locke, the Protestant political thinker, wrote over one hundred years later. Las Casas's doctrine of liberty begins from the observation, based on Thomist principles, and backed by canon law, that if the gospel is to be communicated successfully to the indigenous people of the New World it must be done without force or threats. He brings forward a host of good reasons for this, including the prediction that violence will turn the Indians against the Christians, and therefore against their God and they will never find salvation. Only the non-violent method of evangelization, such as was used by Jesus, Paul and the other apostles, will have any chance of producing real Christians. Send in the soldiers first – as was too often the practice in Central America – and you have destroyed the new Christian people before it has come to birth. But there is a deeper reason: the faith can only be received by a free people, not by slaves. Las Casas understands the faith not as an individual possession, but in the biblical and medieval sense as the law of a free people under God (cf. James's 'law of perfect freedom', Jas. 1:25). One person on his own cannot keep a law, he has to belong to a community which is free. Consequently, the freedom he speaks about is a communal freedom, of the kind that is claimed even now by indigenous peoples throughout the countries of the world settled by Europeans during the colonial period. Reception of the gospel then requires the existence of a people, and that they remain free in a political sense at the moment of reception. If it is their right to hear the gospel and to have the choice of receiving it, it follows that it is their right to remain united and free in their communities, without which they cannot receive it. And they have a right to refuse it with impunity. This doctrine is an application of the Thomist principle that grace does not destroy nature, but perfects it. Evangelization absolutely requires a respect for natural liberty.

But the brutal policies of the conquest resulted in the break-up of native communities and families, the dissolution of their

structures of authority, and the scattering of the remaining
individuals to places dictated by the interests (largely material) of
their Christian overlords. This policy amounted to a violent
process of *individualization* – an effect of colonialism everywhere,
nowadays accelerated by its economic forms. Something like
human rights becomes a necessity under these circumstances, when
shared values are destroyed, an alien set of economic and cultural
goals are imposed on a people, and people are cast adrift from their
communities as individuals. Las Casas saw this happening at first
hand at its very earliest stages.[41]

The question remains as to whether Las Casas really understood
such rights as universal in the contemporary sense, or whether he
was only concerned with the specific rights of one group of people
– a preoccupation common enough in medieval law and not
necessarily linked with any idea of universal rights.[42] It is easy to
find remarks in his writings which appear to deny basic rights to

---

[41] Bartolomé de Las Casas, 'Octavo Remedio', *Obras Escogidas*, estudio critico
y edición por Juan Perez de Tudela Bueso (Madrid, Atlas, 1957–8), 5.75a.

[42] Las Casas is sometimes accused of being the first person to advocate the
transportation of African slaves to America to take the place of the Indians whom
he was so keen to liberate. If true without qualification this would be fatal to any
claim that Las Casas understood the meaning of universal natural rights. However,
this story is usually repeated without consulting the evidence or mentioning Las
Casas's repentance and retraction. In 1516, shortly after his conversion to the
Indian cause, he asked the king to send 'some twenty blacks or other slaves' to
work in the mines of Hispaniola. These were to come, not from Africa, but from
Castile where there were already many slaves of different origins. On several other
occasions over the next thirty years, he was to make similar requests for limited
numbers of black people from Spain. But he was not the first to suggest this, nor
did he call for transports from Africa or for fresh enslavement. Even so, his requests
were entirely wrong, as he eventually came to realize. He had simply gone along
with the universal and convenient assumption that the black people brought from
Africa by the Portuguese were Muslims captured in just wars who had been justly
enslaved as an alternative to being killed. Vitoria also accepted this and it appeared
not to trouble him – see his letter of 1546 in *Political Writings*, P & L, 334–5. There
was almost total insensitivity to this issue throughout Europe. But in 1547, on a
visit to Lisbon, Las Casas began to understand that this was a complete delusion
and that the Spaniards were benefiting from a massive and illegal trade carried on
by the Portuguese slavers. In passages added to his *History of the Indies* towards
the end of his life he says of himself, 'But after he found out, he would not have
proposed it for all the world, because blacks were enslaved unjustly, tyrannically,
right from the start, exactly as the Indians had been'; see Gutiérrez, *Las Casas*, 327.
He specifically includes the Moors in this retraction, and denounces the slave wars
in the strongest terms. Even those who have reservations about Las Casas admit
that this was the first such denunciation by a European.

the enemies of the church, particularly Muslims, and to heretics. Muslims, however, are accorded the right to be left alone in peace with their possessions when they are not actually attacking Christians or occupying their lands. Heretics and apostates are a special case: since at baptism they have made a solemn promise to God, the church can insist they keep it. There is no concept of religious pluralism, or individual freedom to change one's belief without temporal punishment. This kind of individual religious freedom – the freedom of individual dissent – was a very long time coming in Christian Europe, and Muslims still find it difficult to cope with. Religious freedom then, although universal in scope, in that it applies to all peoples, is not individualized in Las Casas's world and it does not persist once individuals have committed themselves. Las Casas would of course consider individuals who genuinely accept the gospel – as members of a free Christian people – to be free in a most profound sense already. Why should they throw away their freedom? However, apart from this major reservation, Las Casas did express a universalist outlook, for example, 'All the peoples of the world are humans and there is only one definition of all humans and of each one, that is that they are rational . . . Thus all the races of mankind are one.'[43] In his last work, *On the Power of Kings*, Las Casas puts forward what for that time and place was an advanced theory of democratic consent, in the course of which he states:

> So far as man is concerned, it is proved that since the beginning all human beings were born free. Since all men are of the same nature, God did not make any man a servant, but bestowed on all an identical freedom. And the reason is that rational nature absolutely is not ordained to another being, such as another man, as to its end (cf St Thomas *In Sent*. 44, 1. art 3 n. 5). Therefore liberty is a right (*libertas est jus*) necessarily inherent to man, as a principle of rational nature and is therefore a natural right.

He then quotes from the *Decretum* of Gratian the text I have already mentioned: 'Natural law is common to all nations because

[43] Las Casas, *Apologetica historia summaria II, Obras*, 7. 536–7, quoted by Brian Tierney, *The Idea of Natural Rights* (Grand Rapids/Cambridge, Eerdmans, 1997), 273.

it exists everywhere by natural instinct not because of any enactment. For example: the same liberty for all.'[44]

In another of his last works, *On the Treasures of Peru*, Las Casas made highly creative use of the legal maxim *Quod omnes tangit debet ab omnibus approbari*: what touches all must be approved by all. This had been used in medieval canon law to support the rights of the lesser clergy of a diocese or cathedral chapter to have a hand in the governing of the church, and had been important in the conciliar movement as well as in promoting the growth of parliaments.[45] Las Casas concluded from this principle that the pope cannot give the unbelievers a new king without their consent, which meant that he could not grant the Spanish king *dominium* in the New World without the consent of the indigenous people – a conclusion which owes more to the consensual aspects of medieval canon law than to modern ideas of popular democracy. But it is nonetheless liberating for that.

Sovereign Individuals

Access to colonial territories and the rights of war continued to play a crucial part in the evolution of natural rights doctrines throughout the sixteenth and seventeenth centuries. With the political philosophers of northern Europe, however, the rights in question were not those of the indigenous inhabitants, but those of the colonists. Understanding this important shift of interest helps us to understand the latent individualism of much of the later thinking about natural rights.[46] It is a development of the humanist tradition of which Sepúlveda was an early representative.

Whereas the scholastics, developing their doctrines from Augustine via canon law, saw war as a judicial process only to be resorted to in cases of actual injustice, the humanists were inclined to view it in the ancient Roman manner as an instrument of policy.

[44] Bartolomé de Las Casas, *De Regia Potestate o derecho de autodeterminación*, ed. L. Pereña, J. M. Pérez-Prendes, V. Abril and J. Azcárraga (Madrid, CSIC, 1969), 16.

[45] Pennington, 'Medieval Law', 5.

[46] The best accounts are given by Tuck in *War and Peace*, and James Tully, *An Approach to Political Philosophy: Locke in Contexts* (Cambridge, Cambridge University Press, 1993), 137–75.

It was essential for the preservation of the state and included the right of pre-emptive strike against peoples who might be a danger to the state at some time in the future. Alberico Gentili wrote in 1598 that

> No one ought to expose himself to danger. No one ought to wait to be struck, unless he is a fool. One ought to provide not only against an offence which is being committed, but also against one which may possibly be committed. Force must be repelled and kept aloof by force. Therefore one should not wait for it to come.[47]

He rejected the strictures of Vitoria: 'Let the theologians keep silence about a matter which is outside of their province.'[48] The key element in the humanists' justified wars is *self-preservation*, something that will profoundly influence the development of natural rights. But beyond defensive war, and also against the scholastic teaching, Gentili believed that states could go to war in order to punish people who lived in such a way that seriously violates natural law. Like Sepúlveda, he accepted that the Spaniards were right to make war upon the Indians for their supposed sins against nature – such as sodomy or cannibalism. 'Against such men . . . war is made as against brutes.' Gross violation of natural law makes men the enemies of the human race. Furthermore, 'no rights will be due to these men who have broken all human and divine laws and who, though joined with us by similarity of nature, have disgraced this union with abominable sins'.

The rights of the sovereign state issued from this basic necessity of self-preservation. A crucial role in this development was played by the Dutch Protestant scholar Hugo Grotius, a humanist by upbringing and conviction, writing in the first decades of the seventeenth century. The wars of religion were causing some profound rethinking about the role of the state. Upholding 'true' religion could no longer be accepted as the main function of the state since this was leading to enormous bloodshed and political instability. Grotius followed the humanist doctrine that the main function of war was the preservation of society, its citizens and their property,

---

[47] Alberico Gentili, *De Iure Belli Libri Tres*, tr. John C. Rolfe, Classics of International Law (Oxford, Clarendon Press, 1933), 2. 62.

[48] Gentili, *De Jure Belli*, 57.

and the upholding of religion became merely instrumental to this. As a consequence, the basic law of nature with regard to the state and each of its members was conceived as self-preservation rather than the propagation of a particular way of life.[49]

The first product of this reduction was the idea of the 'state of nature', which is the starting point for the reconstruction of political society in all the leading political philosophers of the seventeenth and eighteenth centuries.[50] The contract theory of the state holds that individual men in a state of nature, subject only to a natural law of self-preservation, realize that their best interests lie in renouncing their individual rights in this respect and investing them in a 'magistrate' or prince who would monopolize the powers of punishment and war and produce a state of civil peace in which all citizens could pursue their lives unharmed.

But Grotius's most important innovation was to identify the relationship between individuals in the state of nature with that of states in the international system.[51] International society was itself, in effect, a state of nature, there being no overall authority to govern it. Each state then has its own preservation and prosperity as its primary right and duty, along with a minimal set of obligations towards other states once its own existence has been secured. This is an observable fact about the world and Grotius boldly asserted that individuals are just like this. 'We can best understand the rights which individuals possess vis-à-vis one another . . . by looking at the rights which sovereign states seem to possess against one another.'[52] Individuals naturally possess all the natural rights that the state possesses, including the right of pre-emptive attack for the sake of the basic right of self-preservation. If they do not, how could they communicate them to the state?

The strong concept of state sovereignty which resulted from the break-up of the Christian commonwealth of Europe and the settlement which followed the wars of religion thereby gave rise to a strong concept of individual sovereignty, in which the individual – like the state – is the sole judge of his own best interests.[53]

---

[49] Tully, *Approach*, 26.

[50] Although the term 'state of nature' appears to have been the invention of Thomas Hobbes, the idea is clearly present in Grotius's *De Jure Belli et Pacis*.

[51] Grotius, *De Iure Praedae Commentarius*, 1, cited by Tuck, *War and Peace*, 82.

[52] Tuck, *War and Peace*, 85.

[53] See ibid., 82.

Whatever the other factors which gave rise to the liberal theory of the sovereign individual invested with a set of individual natural rights, this must be a very significant one.

According to Tuck, Grotius had political and mercantile objectives relating to the States of Holland and its trading companies in the East Indies and the Americas which need not detain us, except to remark that, like the Spanish Dominicans, but for very different ends, he develops a theory of individual rights against a background of colonial expansion and the ransacking of distant tropical lands for vast profit. This is confirmed by what Grotius has to say about the right of war against the native peoples of those lands. He adopted the humanist view that civilized, that is, Christian, people had the right to 'punish' barbarians and others who were guilty of violating the natural law. Writing specifically against the Spanish theologians, he held the view that there was a natural right to subdue the barbarians and bring them within the dominion of civilized, European rule.[54] As Tuck points out, this 'neatly legitimated a great deal of European action against native peoples around the world', and may be associated with the fact that the Dutch had begun to annex territory in the Far East and North America, as well as to trade there.[55] Relevant to this also is Grotius's assertion that there was a natural right to settle vacant or underused land and that, if the indigenous peoples occupying it refuse access, they may be punished by right of war, which every individual possesses against those who violate the laws of nature.

Much of this can be found in more developed form in Locke's *Two Treatises of Civil Government*, published in 1689. Since this is usually considered to be the foundation text for the liberal natural rights tradition, it is worth taking a careful look at some of Locke's arguments and what relation they bear to the natural rights theologians I have discussed.

Locke

John Locke, the English Protestant philosopher and Whig political activist, became a vigorous exponent of the natural freedom

---

[54] Hugo Grotius, *De Jure Belli et Pacis*, 2. 20. 40.
[55] Tuck, *War and Peace*, 103.

tradition, a fact which unites him in some sense with the Spanish
Catholic theologians I spoke of earlier, and which invites comparison between their natural light theories.

> To understand political power right, and derive it from its original, we
> must consider what state all men are naturally in, and that is, a state of
> perfect freedom to order their actions, and dispose of their possessions,
> and persons as they think fit, within the bounds of the law of nature,
> without asking leave, or depending upon the will of any other man.[56]

In the first of his *Two Treatises*, he refutes at tedious length the
opposing doctrine of natural subjection which had appeared a
generation previously in the work of the Tory theorist of the divine
right of kings, Sir Robert Filmer. Filmer argued that 'we are born
unfree and unequal, and that political society is not grounded in
the consent of the people, but in the ordination of God, as revealed
in the natural order of patriarchy. The original power of monarchs
lay in Adam's rights as father and husband'.[57] In the course of his
refutation, Locke offers an interpretation of Genesis 1:26–30 which
has much in common with that of Vitoria. Where Vitoria had to
dispose of the *plenitudo potestatis* of the pope and emperor, Locke
has to dispose of the patriarchal power of Adam for a similar
purpose: that is, to show that the power of dominion given at
creation is possessed by every member of the human race:

> God makes him 'in his own image after his own likeness', makes him an
> intellectual creature, and so capable of dominion. For wherein soever
> else the image of God consisted, the intellectual nature was certainly
> part of it, and belonged to the whole species, and enabled them to have
> dominion over the inferior creatures . . . (1.30)

> To conclude, this text is so far from proving Adam sole proprietor, that
> on the contrary, it is a confirmation of the original community of all
> things amongst the sons of men, which appearing from this donation of
> God; (1.40)

---

[56] *Two Treatises of Government* (Everyman edn, London, Dent, 1993), 2.4,
p. 116. References to the *Two Treatises* will be given in the text by treatise number
and paragraph number.
[57] Mark Goldie, Introduction to the Everyman edn, p. xviii.

This is followed by a startling passage on the social responsibilities of property which might have come from one of the Fathers of the Church, beginning:

> But we know that God hath not left one man so to the mercy of another, that he may starve him if he please: God the Lord and Father of all, has given to no one of his children such a property, in his peculiar portion of the things of this world, but that he has given his needy brother a right to the surplusage of his goods; so that it cannot justly be denied him, when his pressing wants call for it . . . (1.42)

As Goldie comments in his introduction to the *Two Treatises*, 'Locke exhibits [here] a doctrine of communal rights which have been called "use rights" or claim rights'.[58] The original common ownership bestowed in Genesis 1:26–30 was such that everybody had a right of access to use God's gifts. Locke puts forward a fairly strong doctrine of mutual respect, though it is to be noted that it is expressed in negative terms:

> The state of nature has a law of nature to govern it, which obliges everyone: and reason, which is that law, teaches all mankind, who will but consult it, that being all equal and independent, *no one ought to harm another in his life, health, liberty, or possessions.* For men being all the workmanship of one omnipotent, and infinitely wise Maker; all the servants of one sovereign master, sent into the world by his order and about his business, they are his property . . . made to last during his, not one another's pleasure. (2.6; my emphasis)

Although Locke is in most respects not a modern liberal, we can see here the familiar liberal doctrine of liberty as freedom from interference. It will make what he says about settlers' rights vis-à-vis the American Indians all the more difficult to account for.

The first conclusion from Locke's natural law of liberty is that 'all men may be restrained from invading others' rights, and from doing hurt to one another', and from violating the law of nature. To this end every man has the 'right to punish the transgressors of that law to such a degree, as may hinder its violation' (2.7). The explanation Locke offers is very similar to the one offered by the

---

[58] Ibid., p. xl.

humanists: that anyone who violates the law of nature is an enemy of humankind who 'declares himself to live by another rule, than that of reason and common equity, which is that measure God has set to the actions of men, for their mutual security'. He must therefore be destroyed. In his capacity of executioner of the law of nature, every man exercises his 'right to preserve mankind in general' (2.8). This Locke admits will seem 'a very strange doctrine' to some. By way of proof, he suggests that, if it were not true, then the magistrates of one country would not be able to punish 'an alien of another country' because in regard to them they are in a state of nature, governed only by natural law. 'Those who have the supreme power of making laws in England, France or Holland, are to an Indian, but like the rest of the world, men without authority' (2.9), implying that the 'Indian', that is, the native of America, is a fit subject for punishment by Europeans. This can only be so, of course, if the Indian does in fact violate the laws of nature. Locke implies this during his discourse on property.

Although treatment of the Indians is not the main theme of the treatise, it is still a very important element in Locke's general theory, demonstrating just what kind of individual rights he has in mind.[59] Locke was heavily involved with projects of colonization on the eastern seaboard of North America and had a professional and personal interest in the dispossession of native American peoples in those places which British colonists wanted to settle and cultivate. He was responsible for the *Fundamental Constitution of Carolina*, and had financial interests in companies involved in the slave trade.[60]

In answer to the objection that the state of nature is nowhere to be found, since everyone now lives in a political society, Locke says that there are two ways in which it continues to exist: 'all princes and rulers of independent governments throughout the world' are in this state of nature with regard to one another (just as Grotius had said); and so too are 'a Swiss and an Indian in the woods of America', striking bargains with one another. 'For truth and keeping faith belongs to men, as men, and not as members of society' (2.14). This indicates that Locke believes that the en-

---

[59] See Tuck, *War and Peace*, 167–81; Tully, *Approach*, 137–78.
[60] Tully, *Approach*, 140.

counter between Europeans and the indigenous peoples of colonial territories is governed by the law of nature alone, including the law which dictates personal punishment.

So the right of preservation gives every man in the state of nature an individualized version of the 'right of war' and even of pre-emptive strike ('I have a right to destroy that which threatens me with destruction', 2.16) that we previously encountered with the humanists. The offenders are to be dehumanized and killed: 'for the same reason that he may kill a wolf or a lion; because such men are not under the ties of the common law of reason . . . and so may be treated as beasts of prey'. One can only draw the conclusion that such men have lost their natural (that is, human) rights. It gives one a 'right of war, a liberty to kill the aggressor' (2.19). This is an ominous turn in the argument. It has normally been interpreted as referring to despotic rulers, but it obviously has other applications.

Locke shares with the theologians the traditional Christian starting point in Genesis 1:26–30 for the theory of property that 'God hath given the world to men in common' (2.26), a statement repeated many times in the chapter on property. The traditional question then is, if 'nobody has originally a private dominion exclusive of the rest of mankind', how come it is divided up between individuals? To be of benefit to any particular man it has to be appropriated by him. He removes it from the common by mixing his labour with it, that is, gathering or capturing it, 'thus the law of reason makes the deer, that Indian's who hath killed it; 'tis allowed to be his goods who hath bestowed his labour upon it' (2.30). The Indian lawfully possesses whatever he can take for his own consumption and that of his dependants.

However, the earth which God gave is not simply for the hunter-gatherer to roam about in, taking things for his immediate use. 'He gave it to the use of the industrious and rational' in order to cultivate for the benefit of humankind (2.34). When they do so, it becomes their property (2.32). In England land cannot be enclosed without the consent of other commoners, but originally, 'in the first peopling of the great common of the world, it was quite otherwise . . . And hence subduing or cultivating the earth and having dominion, we see are joined together' (2.35). It is quite clear from the frequent remarks Locke makes about the Indians and the vacant places of America that he believes them to be in a state close to this original state of the earth, waiting to be enclosed, that is, equivalent to an earlier stage of English land use, before 'the industrious and rational' got to work on it. 'Thus in the beginning, all the world was America' (2.49):

> For I ask whether in the wild woods and uncultivated waste of America left to nature, without any improvement, tillage or husbandry, a thousand acres will yield the needy and wretched inhabitants as many conveniences of life as ten acres of equally fertile land do in Devonshire where they are well cultivated? (2.37)

The implication is clear: the English settlers are perfectly justified in taking the land without the consent of the native inhabitants, who have no right to it, because they do not cultivate it. They live in a state of nature and consequently have a right only to what they can catch and eat (though that right comes to end once the land is enclosed for agriculture). If they resist the European settlement and cultivation they are in violation of natural law, become enemies of the human race, and the settlers have right to 'punish' them according to the principles set out earlier in the treatise. James Tully points out that the types of agriculture actually practised by the Indians of North America were simply ignored by the European settlers, probably because they were the work of women and not on the scale of European improved farming. Also ignored was the complex system of hunting rights, developed over millennia by the Indians, and their management of the land for that purpose. This was routinely dismissed by the settlers as indulgence in 'pastime', on the model of the aristocratic hunting estates of England.[61] Consequently, the land was 'vacant'. Their customary methods of land use do not correspond with what Locke defines as real property – they are only inhabiting the land without possessing it. This means that they are not using it as God intended, for the maximum benefit to humankind. The Europeans therefore have the natural right to occupy and cultivate it.

Locke clearly believed that these arguments were sufficient to justify the dispossession of the indigenous tribes of North America without their consent and to vindicate the superiority of European forms of political society and property established in the new

---

[61] Ibid., 150.

world.[62] Tully remarks that this is a departure from one of the fundamental principles of Western law, which we have already seen in use by Las Casas: *Quod omnes tangit* . . . 'What touches all must be approved by all'.[63] Moreover it contradicts Locke's own statements concerning individual liberty and the right of consent, for example, 'Men being . . . by nature, all free, equal and independent, no one can be put out of this estate, and subjected to the political power of another, without his own consent' (2.95).

Conclusions

This comparison of natural rights as they appeared in the writings of the theologians and the humanists illustrates their *dual path* in West European political history. Some authors appear to follow both paths, though unequally (both Vitoria and Locke in very different degrees): put crudely, it is a question of asserting the rights of the colonized or the rights of the colonizers. Of course, not all human rights questions now have to do with this relationship, but many of them still do. The two schools of thought show, at an early stage, some of the contradictory tendencies of human rights, often in the starkest terms, for example, rights of appropriation of natural resources versus rights of indigenous possession, or the rights of the free individual versus the rights of a community under threat. Many of the human rights issues that deserve the attention of Amnesty International and other human rights groups are the direct consequences of struggles between these different understandings of liberty. Such issues predominate in post-colonial areas of the globe such as Central America, where the issue of natural rights began its career 500 years ago. The fact that the rights of many people are violated by their own governments, rather than by foreign invaders, does not contradict these observations. It only serves to substantiate my suggestion that many violations of human rights are warfare continued by other means. The same forces are at work still, not only in post-colonial territories, but in Europe itself. Issues of the countryside and of agribusiness come to mind. They provoke us to ask the question 'In

[62] Ibid., 139.
[63] Ibid., 145.

whose interest are such rights being asserted?', often giving us clear enough answers in terms of people dispossessed or killed and profits made.

I have sketched the role of theology, canon law and scripture in all of this, and pointed out the central importance of the image of God. They are at the heart of the matter rather than the periphery. Although Christians need to talk to others about these things without using their own confessional language, it should at least be clear that the idea of human rights is not an alien import, but central to the very idea of evangelization. But even when human rights are loudly proclaimed, careful discrimination is needed as to whose interests are ultimately being served.

3

Human Rights, Divine Justice
and the Churches

NICHOLAS SAGOVSKY

Introduction

The development of a 'human rights culture' has been characteristic of the Western nations since the Second World War. The
emphasis on human rights in the UN Charter (June 1945), followed
by the Universal Declaration of Human Rights (1948), marked the
beginning of a new era. The Statute of the Council of Europe
(1949) made it clear that the upholding of human rights and
respect for the rule of law was to be a *condition* of membership of
the Council, which was being established as an instrument of
European unity. This embedding of respect for human rights in
international agreements and the creation of bodies such as the
European Commission of Human Rights and the European Court
of Human Rights to which the signatories would be accountable
was seen to be of vital importance in ensuring that the disasters
which had overtaken so many peoples in the world could not
happen in that way again. Thus, the Charter of the United Nations
speaks of the participating nations being determined

> to save succeeding generations from the scourge of war, which twice in
> our lifetime has brought untold sorrow to mankind, and to reaffirm
> faith in fundamental human rights, in the dignity and worth of the
> human person, in the equal rights of men and women and of nations
> large and small, and to establish conditions under which justice and
> respect for the obligations arising from treaties and other sources of
> international law can be maintained.

This emphasis on 'human rights' has been problematic for the
Christian churches as the notion does not arise directly from

sources within the Christian tradition. A line can certainly be traced from the notion of 'natural rights', which is found in Thomas Aquinas, and has been strongly developed in Roman Catholic thinking.[1] However, modern ideas of 'human rights' are descended more directly from sources that deployed the notion in *opposition* to the public practice of Christianity, against oppressive notions of divine order and 'divine justice'. This mixed lineage takes in the mythicized voyage of the Pilgrim Fathers (1620), the writings of Tom Paine (1737–1809), the Declaration of the Rights of Man and of the Citizen of the French Revolution (1789), and the United States Bill of Rights (1791) – which were all forms of protest against religiously inspired deprivations of liberty. The ambiguities of the situation should not be missed: Tom Paine was a secularist, but the (Protestant) religious roots of human rights thinking are evident in the works of Thomas Hobbes (1588–1679) and John Locke (1632–1704), founding fathers of modern liberalism. The largely Roman Catholic national churches of the European establishment were, however, in the eighteenth and nineteenth centuries deeply suspicious of notions of the 'rights of man', which were rightly seen to be subversive of the social order the Catholic Church supported. It was only in the later nineteenth century, with the publication in 1891 of *Rerum Novarum*, that the Roman Catholic Church began actively to promote such 'rights' as an expression of human dignity, and only after the Second World War, with the founding of the World Council of Churches in 1948, that the Protestant and Orthodox Churches found a common voice in support of human rights, a voice strengthened by the support of Pope John XXIII[2] and the teaching of the Second Vatican Council (1962–5).

This has not, however, been an easy convergence. The term 'human rights' does not appear in the scriptures of the Old or New

[1] See, for instance, John Finnis, *Natural Law and Natural Rights* (Oxford, Clarendon, 1980), especially pp. 198–230, for a major study in this tradition. Finnis's conviction that 'human rights' is 'a contemporary idiom for "natural rights"' (p. 198) fails to do justice to the complex aetiology of modern ideas about 'human rights'.

[2] *Pacem in Terris* (1963) was the first papal encyclical to endorse the term 'the rights of man' and to offer a list of such 'human rights' together with a corresponding list of 'human duties'. Significantly, it was addressed not just to Catholics but to 'all men of good will'. The text can be found, with other key documents of Catholic social teaching, in M. Walsh and B. Davies (eds), *Proclaiming Justice and Peace* (London, HarperCollins, 1991).

Testament, where the issue of what is 'right' for human beings is presented again and again as an issue of God's justice. There are serious questions the churches may want to put to what we may now call a 'human rights tradition' and there are serious questions that the 'human rights tradition' would wish to put to the churches about their understanding of divine justice. This is a vital dialogue, because it determines the extent to which Christians participate in the one secular, global movement that might in specific instances prove powerful enough successfully to resist global tyrannies, whether of socialism, fascism or capitalism. For the churches that have given their support to notions of 'human rights', the question is to what extent that support retains a theologically grounded critical detachment – or whether the churches' support of human rights in practice gives uncritical assent to an agenda set by secular liberalism.[3] To what extent can the human rights agenda of secular or pluralist policy be seen as an instrument of divine justice?

I shall first consider the notion of 'human rights', seeking to bring out some of the strengths and weaknesses in it. I shall then turn to 'divine justice', for a similar, critical discussion, before asking to what extent, on the basis of their understanding of divine justice, the churches can give their support to the movement for human rights, and how by so doing they may expect to modify understandings of human rights.

Human Rights

The incorporation of the European Convention on Human Rights into UK law in October 2000 epitomizes the change in legal philosophy that is being brought about by the developing human rights culture of our time. Though infringements of the European Convention were justiciable in the European Court of Human Rights at Strasbourg from the time that Britain ratified the Convention in 1951, there was no such redress in UK law. Where there were specific challenges that went to the European Court of

---

[3] Kieran Cronin comments, 'It is odd that Christianity has moved from a situation of hostility to this form of language, to one of almost naive and unquestioning acceptance.' *Rights and Christian Ethics* (Cambridge, Cambridge University Press, 1992), pp. xviii–xix.

Human Rights and Britain was found to be at fault, the legal process (which, of course, at this level continues as before) was both slow and expensive.

As yet there is no great body of UK human rights jurisprudence, so we do not know in much detail how the provisions of the Human Rights Act will work out, but it is already clear that a constitutional landshift has taken place. The legal system has shifted away from the confident presumption that the instruments of an unwritten constitution, formed out of monarchy, parliamentary democracy and the common law (and marinated in Anglicanism), could be trusted to defend the liberties of individual subjects. It has moved to the presumption that the rights of the citizen need to be preserved from administrative or legislative abuse by being spelt out and specifically protected in law. Writing of this change in culture, which can be traced back to the UN Charter, Robertson and Merrills say:

> Underlying the various systems [for the protection of human rights] which have been developed, and are developing, there is to be found a single philosophical impulse: the idea of the individual as a being of moral worth whose rights, whether in the civil and political sphere, or in the economic, social and cultural sphere, merit international protection.[4]

The question is now widely asked as to whether 'human rights' is in principle too individualistic a concept.[5] The overwhelming majority of expressions of human rights are indeed based on the trenchant affirmation of what both the UN Charter and the Universal Declaration of Human Rights call 'the dignity and worth of the human person'. This emphasis on the inalienable dignity of the individual, simply as a human being, is not based on any explicit religious or philosophical foundation but is taken as

---

[4] A. H. Robertson and J. G. Merrills, *Human Rights in Europe, a Study of the European Convention on Human Rights*, 4th edn (Manchester, Manchester University Press, 2001), 326.

[5] Francesca Klug refutes this strongly, speaking of 'a profound caricature of human rights as irredeemably egoistic and individualistic, with no capacity to recognise the common good'. *Values for a Godless Age* (London, Penguin, 2000), 14.

axiomatic.[6] What the UDHR expresses less consistently is the extent to which human beings only flourish as members of communities: the point Aristotle was making when he said that the human being is 'by nature a political animal' (and elsewhere 'an animal made for social participation (*koinonia*)').[7] Article 29, it should be noted, affirms: 'Everyone has duties to the community *in which alone* the free and full development of his personality is possible.' Again, the classic human rights documents only give hints of collective human rights.[8] For instance, the International Covenant on Civil and Political Rights (1966), when speaking of the rights of minorities, couches these in primarily individualist but also corporate terms:

> In those States in which ethnic, religious or linguistic minorities exist, persons belonging to such minorities shall not be denied the right, *in community with the other members of their group*, to enjoy their own culture, to profess and practise their own religion, or to use their own language. (Article 27)

The affirmation of the corporate rights of minorities has become increasingly important with the growing recognition of the past and present exploitation of indigenous peoples. It is not true that human rights are always expressed in purely individual terms, but the question must be raised as to whether the predominant emphasis on the individual means that social groups are seen as fundamentally aggregates of individuals. If so, the stance is anti-utilitarian: in a reaction to the appalling ways in which the power of the state has been used throughout the twentieth century as a tool of oppression, a principled stand has been made in defence of the conviction that the state is there to serve and protect each one of its members, not merely select groupings, and that it cannot be the role of the state to demand the involuntary sacrifice of the

---

[6] We might compare the careful balancing act between groundless assertion and theism in the drafting of the American Declaration of Independence: 'We hold these truths to be *self-evident*, that all men are *created* equal, [and] that they are endowed *by their Creator* with certain unalienable Rights.'

[7] Aristotle, *Politics* 1253ᵃ, *Eud. Eth.* 1242ᵃ.

[8] Conspicuous exceptions in this regard are the Conventions on Civil and Political Rights (1966) and Economic and Social Rights (1966), which talk of the rights of 'all peoples' and the African Charter on Human and People's Rights (1981).

individual's good for the good of the community, save in times of
extreme emergency. If the First World War made a mockery of the
adage *dulce et decorum est pro patria mori*,[9] the horrors of
Stalinism and the Holocaust graphically showed what it meant for
millions to die for someone else's conception of a Fatherland.
Implicit in the human rights movement is a Kantian conviction that
individuals can never be regarded by states as expendable means to
the state's ends, but must be seen as ends in themselves. In this
conviction there is an extraordinarily high valuation of the dignity
or worth of each individual, which necessitates a clear setting of
limits to state power over the individual. To this is added the conviction that all human beings must be included within some state
or other. The state that observes human rights is to be precluded
from drawing its boundaries tightly around some privileged ethnic
or national group. Nations who have signed up to contemporary
human rights instruments are accepting in principle a view of the
state that rejects ethnic exclusivism and affirms the ultimate
inviolability of each individual human being. Implicit in this is a
commitment to religious and cultural pluralism. The question the
churches have to face is whether this also implies a commitment to
secularism and, if so, whether they can conscientiously accept this
secular framework.

The criticism of the implicit individualism of 'human rights'
thinking can be pressed further to open out a debate about the
anthropology implicit in expressions of human rights. The very
notion of a 'human right' is an induction from what is thought to
be necessary for human flourishing, a transcendental condition of
what it is fully to enter into one's humanity. If human beings need
freedom from arbitrary arrest, freedom to practise their religion
without fear of persecution, security in tenure of their property,
these are 'rights' which it is the business of the state to protect.
'Human rights' are thus often spelt out in terms of the protections
that persons need in order to live and flourish as human beings.

Following the UDHR, the European Convention (1950) spells
out that 'Everyone's right to life shall be protected by law' (Article
2); 'No one shall be subjected to torture or to inhuman or

---

[9] It is a sweet and a proper thing to die for one's country. The poet Wilfrid
Owen wrote in '*Dulce et Decorum Est*' of 'the old Lie, *dulce et decorum est / pro
patria mori*'.

degrading treatment or punishment' (Article 3); 'No one shall be held in slavery or servitude' (Article 4); 'Everyone has the right to liberty and security of person' (Article 5); and so on. It is drafted as a framework document concentrating on civil and political rights which will be enforceable in law. There is, however, a definite shift away from the wider aspirations of the Universal Declaration, which is an aspirational document, not enforceable in law. Thus, the European Convention has no analogue to the Preamble of the UDHR which proclaims the Universal Declaration to be 'a common standard of achievement for all peoples and all nations', nor to the prescriptive note struck in Article 1: 'All human beings are born free and equal in dignity and rights. They are endowed with reason and conscience *and should act towards one another in a spirit of brotherhood.*'

The full title of the European Convention is the European Convention for the Protection of Human Rights and Fundamental Freedoms. It thus follows the practice of the UN in the division[10] that was made between the two Charters on Civil and Political Rights (1966) and Economic, Social and Cultural Rights (1966). The drafting of the European Convention was followed by that of the European Social Charter (1961), so the two together cover political or civil and social or economic rights, but the fracture between the two sorts of rights has been harmful. By contrast, the UDHR holds both together, and is cohesively prescriptive in both fields, the civil and political together with the economic and social, spelling out in a rounded way what human beings need. The obligation is laid not only upon states but upon members of states to promote this human provision for all of their members, in fact for all human beings. Not only is it prescribed that 'Everyone has the right to freedom of thought, conscience and religion' (Article 18); but also that

Everyone, as a member of society, has the right to social security and is entitled to realization, through national effort and international co-operation and in accordance with the organization and resources of

---

[10] Paul Sieghart sees this division as one which 'largely reflects the divisions of the cold war during which the UN Covenants were negotiated – and, regrettably, the continuing division between the world's two major ideologies which like to describe themselves respectively as "liberal" and "socialist" '. *The Lawful Rights of Mankind* (Oxford, Oxford University Press, 1985), 81–2.

each State, of the economic, social and cultural rights indispensable for his dignity and the free development of his personality. (Article 22)

Everyone who works has the right to just and favourable remuneration ensuring for himself and his family an existence worthy of human dignity, and supplemented, if necessary, by other means of social protection. (Article 23.3)

Everyone has the right to a standard of living adequate for the health and well-being of himself and of his family, including food, clothing, housing and medical care and necessary social services, and the right to security in the event of sickness, disability, widowhood, old age or other lack of livelihood in circumstances beyond his control. (Article 25.1)

Motherhood and childhood are entitled to special care and assistance. (Article 25.2)

Article 27 prescribes that 'Everyone has the right freely to participate in the cultural life of the community, to enjoy the arts and to share in scientific advancement and its benefits', and Article 28 largely asserts: 'Everyone is entitled to a social and international order in which the rights and freedoms set forth in this Declaration can be fully realized'; finally, Article 29 speaks of correlative duties: 'Everyone has duties to the community in which alone the free and full development of his personality is possible.'[11]

Between the UDHR and the European Convention on Human Rights, to which one might also add the European Social Charter, there is a shift away from an enumeration of human rights based upon a teleological, normative and integrated account of human flourishing, towards one based on a more formal, less dynamic, less integrated, 'thinner' induction. The UDHR is more Aristotelian in tone; the EDHR and European Social Charter are more Kantian (though without the Kantian emphasis on duty). Thus, it is striking that Article 28 of the UDHR recognizes the need for a social and international order in which human rights can be realized. If this is put together with what is said about a just wage and the right to a

---

[11] Compare the American Convention on Human Rights (1969) which also makes mention of human duties, and the African Charter on Human and Peoples' Rights (1981), which has the heading for Part I 'Rights and Duties', and enumerates in Articles 27–9 a number of specific duties.

standard of living adequate to the well-being of the individual and their family, it is clear that the UDHR is calling for human rights to be embedded in a humane social and international order. There cannot be the one without the other. This goes far beyond the formal advocacy of democracy, or the uncritical acceptance of global capitalism, which is often associated with the human rights movement.

The UDHR was a document of high-minded aspiration; the European Convention comprises treaty obligations drafted in such a way as to be justiciable. The aspiration in the Preamble to the UDHR towards a social and economic order that will support the development of the rights and freedoms it enumerates is reduced in the EDHR to talk of 'the Governments of European countries which are likeminded and have a common heritage of political traditions, ideals, freedom and the rule of law'. The focus is narrowed from an integrating vision of a social, economic and political order that will engender human flourishing to a shared rule of law by which the civil and political liberties of individuals are to be protected. Though there is a system of monitoring compliance with the European Social Charter, it does not have behind it the same legal clout. In effect, and specifically by the incorporation of the European Convention into UK law, 'human rights' has predominantly come to mean civil and political rights.

The problem with this reduced concept of human rights is that the concept of liberty to which it makes appeal is not the product of a sufficiently 'thick' understanding of humanity. It has a thin moral content; the implication that liberty itself must be *practised* in political, economic and social interaction with other free human beings is not followed through; the suggestion that the consistent practice of liberty which engenders liberty for others must entail the voluntary curtailment of personal freedoms, and must be thought through in economic and social terms (as every parent knows), has no obvious place in much popular 'human rights' thinking. Nor is there any clear means of arbitration between differing conceptions of human rights, and so of justice, based on differing anthropologies: in practice the 'right to life' is not extended to the aborted foetus; the right not to be deprived of liberty under the European Convention explicitly excludes 'persons of unsound mind, alcoholics or drug addicts, or vagrants'; the 'right to just and favourable remuneration' and the 'right to a social and international order in which the rights and freedoms set out in the UDHR can be fully realized' are not seen as making the exploitative practice of global capitalism, the payment of less than a living wage, or the failure to remit the debts of chronically indebted nations, offences against human rights.

The problem here is the problem to which attention has been drawn by Alasdair MacIntyre.[12] The Enlightenment project was an attempt to think through what it meant to be human, applying critical reason to every aspect of received tradition and possible scientific experiment, to provide understandings which were in principle universal. The Enlightenment split, identified by Weber, between rationally established facts and subsequently applied values, still lurks behind the modern concepts of human rights. Increasingly, human rights have come to be seen as 'the facts' about what is needed to flourish as a human being in the world, the values they engender being the values brought to bear in the promotion of human rights: toleration, respect for the law, promotion of democracy, with religious faith as an optional extra. Francesca Klug's recently published book on the Human Rights Act exemplifies this when she calls it *Values for a Godless Age*.[13] This potential division between facts and values, the potential lack of an integral sense of 'human rights' and a 'thick' induction of what it is to be a human being, is what makes the movement for human rights so vulnerable to ideological subversion. What is missing in the many discourses about human rights is a consistent critique of the economic and political order that sustains the policing of human rights. Increasingly, the 'human rights' agenda has become confused with a construal of human rights that is favourable to global capitalism: the 'right' to free trade in the service of the agenda set by the needs of the developed nations; the 'right' of free speech that does not curb the power of the media, including

---

[12] See especially A. MacIntyre, *Whose Justice? Which Rationality?* (London, Duckworth, 1988).

[13] In *Values for a Godless Age*, Francesca Klug accepts this construal with evangelical zeal, arguing that the Human Rights Act 1998 is 'the only vehicle I am aware of which has the potential to provide in a diverse society the common set of values that [people] seek' (p. 200) and that, 'If human rights defenders are not to be as irrelevant by the end of the twenty-first century as Christian missionaries became by the end of the twentieth (*sic*), they are going to have to engage more fully with the rest of the population on these questions, and in terms which relate to people's lives' (p. 215).

advertising and the internet; the 'right' to increasing prosperity for the rich nations regardless of the depletion of the world's resources and the damage to the environment. Within the classic statements of human rights, references to 'the right to work' and the 'right to a just wage' (neither of which is included within the European Convention of Human Rights) stick out as relics of an older conception of human rights, which preceded the ideological interpretations of global capitalism. Unless there is developed a deeper critique of the ideological abuse of the discourse of human rights, the permanent and irretrievable devaluation of the currency is assured and its value as an international benchmark for human flourishing seriously diminished. This is why the fragmented discourse of human rights needs to be brought into engagement with some wider discourse of justice.[14]

Divine Justice

If the language of human rights is problematic, so too is the language of justice. One of the reasons for the prevalence of the language of human rights in the public discourse of contemporary societies is because it is thought to be clearer and sharper than the language of justice, which has often been reduced to or confused with criminal justice. Justice is rightly seen as an 'essentially contested concept',[15] that is, a concept the proper use of which inevitably calls up continuing and ultimately unresolvable debates. What 'justice' is taken to mean depends on who is using the term, in what context and for what purpose. The question, 'Whose justice?' was well put.

[14] This paragraph was drafted before 11 September 2001. Since that date the ideological discourse about 'human rights' used by the West, especially the United States, has largely been overtaken by talk of the 'war against terrorism', which is even less accountable to a 'thick' induction of what it means to flourish as a human being, and in practice (for example, in talk of 'collateral damage' meaning civilian casualties) represents a reversion to the kind of utilitarianism against which much 'human rights' thinking has been developed. Inasmuch as 'the war against terrorism' represents a claim to 'justice' it shows that notions of justice, no less than notions of such a 'war', and of 'human rights', need careful, critical analysis.

[15] The term is that of the philosopher W. B. Gallie. See 'Essentially Contested Concepts', in *Philosophy and Historical Understanding* (London, Chatto & Windus, 1964), 157–91. Gallie specifically chooses 'social justice' as an example of an 'essentially' contested concept' (pp. 181–2).

Within the Christian tradition, based on scripture, 'God's justice' is central. The justice that human beings practise, inasmuch as it is just justice, is understood to be an expression of the justice of God. For those who work with the texts of the Judaeo Christian tradition, God's justice is taken to be justice exercised personally, according to the situation, in a manner that is appropriate to the individual or community. This contrasts sharply with notions of human rights which are exercised impersonally (that is, according to an impersonal, legal framework of 'right'), regardless of the situation and in a manner which protects the individual or community but does not actually restore a situation. There are, however, convergences because the exercise of justice can never be truly impersonal: the defence of human rights in the lawcourts depends upon the skilled judgment of individual judges (sometimes called 'justices' because of the way in which they personify justice). The development of jurisprudence is an exercise in *prudentia*, that is, of practical reason, and of 'equity', which is judgement 'appropriate' to the situation.

Christianity is sharply differentiated from the human rights tradition in that its concept of justice is ultimately located within the person of God. To speak of justice is to speak of the exercise of God's word and God's will, which are two ways of speaking about the activity of God. What God says and what God does are all of a piece. It is this conviction which grounds the Christian concept of a 'natural order', a concept developed with the help of impersonal Stoic conceptuality. Only in the scientific revolution did the idea of 'natural order' lose its personal connotations as the direct product of the creative, ordering activity of the personal God. It is because of this disjunction that 'human rights' may now be seen as 'obviously' grounded within the natural order and as an expression of the dignity of human beings, but without there being any sense that this depends upon the creative, ordering activity of a personal God. Through the seventeenth and eighteenth centuries the direct attribution to God of the 'natural rights' of man became increasingly attenuated. In the works of Locke, Rousseau and Kant the mediating understanding of a 'social contract' obscured the strong sense of natural law and natural rights which were directly and immediately attributable to the shaping hand of the Creator. By the twentieth century, with the magisterial revival of social contract thinking in the work of John Rawls, all reference to God disappeared absolutely.[16] The question for Christians has now become how an impersonal and secular theory of human rights, whether grounded in some form of social contract theory or presented as an a priori affirmation of the dignity of human beings, can be related to the personal understanding of justice derived from the scriptures.

Within the Hebrew scriptures, it is striking that the practice of justice is attributed first and foremost to God:

> For the Lord your God is God of gods and Lord of lords, the great, the mighty, and the terrible God, who is not partial and takes no bribe. He executes justice for the fatherless and the widow, and loves the sojourner, giving him food and clothing. Love the sojourner therefore. (Deut. 10:17–18)

The judgments of God (that is, God's edicts) are the basis of the justice that is known in the world. It is by God's active edict that creation itself has been called into being and, similarly, by God's active edict that Israel has become a people. There is a direct analogy between the two. What God does in *establishing creation* is just and what God does *within creation* is just, and if God elects to enter into covenant with one nation from all the nations and to establish that nation in its own land by fulfilment of divine promise that is also an expression of justice.

Simply to enunciate this line of thinking today is to raise questions about the partiality of God, the expulsion of the Canaanites from the land they inhabited, about Zionism, the *intifada* and the future for the Middle East. The Judeo-Christian tradition appears indefensible in the light of Enlightenment presuppositions about equality and even-handedness. It takes a further critical leap to subject Enlightenment presuppositions to a deeper historical critique and suggest that they themselves were the product of a Christian reading of the Hebrew scriptures which extended ideas of the election of Israel towards a universal horizon. It is now well understood that, in the formation of the

---

[16] Rawls posits an 'original position' in which actors divested of all knowledge of what might be their position in life, and so their vested interests, seek disinterestedly to work out principles of justice which ensure 'fairness' for all. See *A Theory of Justice*, 2nd edn (Oxford, Oxford University Press, 1999), especially pp. 10–15.

Hebrew Bible, the narrative of the Exodus and the Covenant at Sinai preceded the narrative of the Creation, so that the Creation narrative can itself be seen as predicated on Covenant-belief. Creation is seen as covenantal *fiat*: a calling into relation with God. Jürgen Moltmann writes:

> In the Old Testament, theological thought begins with Yahweh's liberation-history with Israel in the Exodus and only afterward, and on this basis, comes to the confession that this God of liberation is the Creator of all things and the Redeemer of all people.[17]

'Human rights', which represent that which is 'right' for all people by virtue of their creation, must then be seen theologically in the context of human liberation.

This insight has, of course, been picked up particularly strongly in liberation theology, which emphasizes that the justice of God is exercised in support of those who are socially marginalized. The widows, the orphans, the sojourners, and the poor stand for those who are most vulnerable in society and who are most likely to suffer from economically driven failures of justice. Throughout the Deuteronomic and prophetic literature there are constant warnings against the exploitation and social exclusion of the poor and an emphasis upon mechanisms of reintegration for the marginalized. To us, the provision in the Torah (the Law) for the forgiveness of debt, whether on a seven-year or a fifty-year cycle is a striking ideal. The Deuteronomic vision contains the affirmation (in the context of provision for debt release) 'There will be no poor among you (for the Lord will bless you in the land which the Lord your God gives you for an inheritance to possess)' (Deut. 15: 4). The blessing of God is seen to integrate the people and consolidate their fruitful possession of the land. Within Deuteronomic theology, it is the failure to keep to the path of God's justice, clearly mapped in the Torah, which leads to exile and dispossession. Hence the emphasis in Deuteronomy on keeping the 'statutes and ordinances' which have been given to the people by God.

---

[17] See J. Moltmann, 'The Original Study Paper: A Theological Basis of Human Rights and of the Liberation of Human Beings', in A. O. Miller (ed.), *A Christian Declaration on Human Rights* (Grand Rapids, MI, Eerdmans, 1977), 31.

Both in Deuteronomy and, to some extent, in the Books of Samuel and Kings, there is a triumphalistic note about the theme of the establishment of justice in Israel. The establishing of justice is achieved through great prophets and leaders like Moses and Joshua, through judges at the local level and the judges who are charismatic leaders, through the Levitical priesthood, and then through the monarchy. These are the agents and mediators of God's justice.[18] Walter Brueggemann writes:

> In the context of Israel's completed testimony, it is difficult to overstate the pivotal importance . . . of . . . the commitment of Yahweh (and of Israel) to justice. If we consider in turn the prophetic, psalmic, sapiential, and apocalyptic texts, it seems evident that Israel, everywhere and without exhaustion, is preoccupied with the agenda of justice that is rooted in the character and resolve of Yahweh. This justice rooted in Yahweh, moreover, is to be enacted and implemented concretely in human practice.[19]

The ideology of the kingly mediation of justice is made very clear in Psalm 72:

> Give the king thy justice, O God,
>   and thy righteousness to the royal son!
> May he judge thy people with righteousness
>   and thy poor with justice!
> Let the mountains bear prosperity for the people,
>   and the hills, in righteousness!
> May he defend the cause of the poor of the people,
>   give deliverance to the needy,
>   and crush the oppressor!

Here, we are in a completely different world from that of human rights thinking. This is the world of ancient monarchy and what is being depicted is the good king whose rule is beneficial to his people both internally and externally, who comes to be recognized

---

[18] This is brought out very strongly in W. Brueggemann, *Theology of the Old Testament* (Minneapolis, Fortress Press, 1997), especially part IV, 'Israel's Embodied Testimony', pp. 567–704.

[19] Ibid., 736.

for his just rule even beyond the borders of his own land. The successful and just reign of the good king on earth reflects and participates in the kingly rule of God: 'Give the king thy justice, O God.' It is perpetuated in the royal dynasty: 'and thy righteousness to the royal son!'

The sub-theme of the prosperity of the land links with another major theme in Hebrew notions of divine justice: God provides *enough* to meet the needs of everyone and so everyone's needs should be met. The paradigmatic image of this is the provision of the water, the manna and the quails in the wilderness. With the manna particularly, it is clear that there was to be no hoarding: 'He that gathered much had nothing over, and he that gathered little had no lack; each gathered according to what he could eat' (Exod. 16: 18). Each is instructed to gather enough for one day's needs, with special provision being made for the sabbath (Exod. 16: 22–30). The gift comes demonstrably from God; it is to sustain God's people on their journey. The lesson they are to learn before they come into the fertile Promised Land is that God's provision is adequate for all. Hence the prophets' fulminations against hoarding and against oppression of the needy. In this under-standing of justice, wealth is to be enjoyed but not at the expense of the poor. Where the poor lack basic necessities the wealthy should provide for them out of their surplus.

The practice of God's justice was by no means universally welcomed in Israel. Israel's rejection of God's justice is made apparent in the Deuteronomic history, in the destiny of individuals like Jeremiah and in the depiction of the enigmatic servant figure of Deutero-Isaiah. The costly vocation of the servant to justice is made very clear:

> Behold my servant, whom I uphold,
>   my chosen, in whom my soul delights;
> I have put my Spirit upon him,
>   he will bring forth justice to the nations . . .
> He will not fail or be discouraged till he has
>   established justice in the earth;
>   and the coastlands wait for his law.
>   (Isaiah 42:1–4)

Later, the vocation of the servant to suffering is made equally clear:

> He was despised and rejected by men;
>   a man of sorrows and acquainted with grief;
>   and as one from whom men hide their faces
>   he was despised, and we esteemed him not.
>
>   (Isaiah 53:3)

In the post-Exilic scriptures, it is the sheer cost of doing justice that comes to the fore. The notion of divine justice does not change; what does change is the understanding of the mediation of divine justice through individuals who make this their priority above all else. God 'shall see the fruit of the travail of his soul and be satisfied', writes Isaiah (53: 11).

This is a sketch of the background to the understanding of Jesus in the New Testament. In Matthew's Gospel, Jesus is a new Moses, preaching once again the Deuteronomic message of fidelity to God and to the Law, the good news of God's generous provision to meet human need, and of the divine kingship. In Luke's Gospel and in Acts, Jesus is the one who reaches out to the marginalized and reintegrates them within the community that celebrates God's jubilee. The 'Kingdom of God' is the kingly rule of God who establishes his justice through the 'Son' anointed with the Spirit. The early Christians saw in the death of Jesus his costly submission to earthly injustice, and the public vindication of Jesus as the agent of God's justice:

> He committed no sin; no guile was found on his lips. When he was reviled, he did not revile in return; when he suffered, he did not threaten; but he trusted to him who judges justly. He himself bore our sins in his body on the tree, that we might die to sin and live to righteousness (*dikaiosune*: justice). By his wounds you have been healed. (1 Peter 2:22–4)

Reference to the one who 'judges justly' brings in another dimension which distinguishes the Judeo-Christian notion of divine justice from timeless ideas of human rights. God's judgment takes place both outside and within time. Within the Christian tradition, the incarnation and the resurrection are taken to be divine acts, initiated outside time, but enacted within time to establish justice upon earth. The hope of future action by God definitively to establish justice is characteristic of Christian teaching. Thus, so long as there is time, God's justice is always in process of being realized on earth, and where there are situations of appalling and agonizing injustice there is always the hope of future justice. It is this conviction amongst the Jews that was tested, for many to destruction, by the Holocaust and which for Christians is enacted in the death and resurrection of Christ. When the hope of justice is put together with the testimony to the human mediation of justice by God's servants, the centrality of the conviction that *justice* must be enacted by the church can readily be understood.

Within this overarching theological understanding of justice as yet only partially realized and justice hoped-for, two convictions are of particular significance for establishing a convergence with secular understandings of human rights.

The first is that of the *dignity* of each human being, simply through their creation by God. Moltmann writes, 'The dignity of the human being is not in itself a human right but a source and ground for all human rights.'[20] This is to be linked with the conviction that humans are made in the 'image of God', and that the 'image of God' is evident in male and female together (Genesis 1:27). The churches have readily affirmed the dignity of each human being, and of human beings together ('male and female') made in the image of God, and therefore never to be regarded as expendable by other humans in the service of some human project. Since the Second Vatican Council, Roman Catholic theology has made much of these themes:

> There is a growing awareness of the sublime dignity of the human person, who stands above all things and whose rights and duties are universal and inviolable. He [sic] ought, therefore, to have ready access to all that is necessary for living a genuinely human life: for example, food, clothing, housing, the right freely to choose his state of life and set up a family, the right to education, work, to his good name, to respect, to proper knowledge, the right to act according to the dictates of conscience and to safeguard his privacy, and rightful freedom even in matters of religion.[21]

---

[20] J. Moltmann, *On Human Dignity* (London, SCM, 1984), 9.
[21] Pastoral Constitution on the Church in the Modern World (*Gaudium et Spes*) (1965), 26.

The unqualified affirmation of the right to religious freedom, deriving from the freedom now seen to be implicit in human dignity,[22] represented a major shift in Catholic thinking – a recognition of the cogency of the critique that had been so powerfully levelled against the church throughout the previous century.

A second strand drawing Christian understanding close to the developing human rights consensus, and contributing to it, is that of *liberation*. The contribution of liberation theologians has been to see liberation in the broadest sense, political, economic and spiritual, as characteristic of the action of God for humanity and constitutive of full human being in the world.[23] If the enumeration of human rights offers a standard against which the need for liberation can be judged, a dynamic approach to liberation means that human rights are always seen as in process of realization. Within the Christian tradition there is an acceptance that the full realization of the 'right' for humans individually and for humanity as a whole, can only come about through the action of God, but in the interim action for human rights is action that accords with the liberative purposes of God. The justice of God is understood not only as the ultimate, and hoped-for, horizon to all human action for justice, but as a dynamic within history in which humans participate when they engage in action which brings about human liberation.

Nevertheless, the language with which Christians are likely to remain most comfortable is the language of *justice*, precisely because it has such deep roots within the Christian tradition. Just as Israel was constituted by the Exodus, and the Exodus was

[22] This may also be linked with the 'right to life', which in some recent Roman Catholic teaching (especially under John Paul II) has been seen as fundamental. Thus the Bishops of England and Wales wrote in 1996: 'Individuals have a claim on each other and on society for certain basic minimum conditions without which the value of human life is diminished or even negated . . . In Catholic terms those rights derive from the nature of the human person made in the image of God . . . These rights are universal. The study of the evolution of the idea of human rights shows that they all flow from this one fundamental right: the right to life'. *The Common Good* (Manchester, Gabriel Communications, 1996), 36.

[23] Liberation theologians have largely followed writers of the left in their suspicion that human rights language falls short of the imperatives generated by the need for freedom from oppression. One exception is G. Gutierrez, who draws attention to the prophetic use of the term 'human rights' by Bartolome de Las Casas (1484–1566). See G. Gutierrez, *Las Casas, In Search of the Poor of Jesus Christ* (Maryknoll, NY, Orbis, 1993), 594.

confirmed in the giving of the Law, so for Christians the church of God is constituted by God's just action in the resurrection of Jesus Christ and confirmed in the giving of the Spirit. The church of God exists to enact the kingly rule of God, which is the rule of justice. If the horizon of the church is universal, its horizon for justice must be universal. It exists to enact God's justice in its internal dealings and to be the agent of God's justice in society – which will entail both the affirmation of that which is seen to be in accord with God's will and resistance to that which is counter to God's will. This of course brings into focus the point at issue: the relation between the church and the movement for human rights.

Divine Justice, the Movement for Human Rights and the Challenge to the Churches

There are Christian thinkers who argue strongly that the church has no business to preach universal justice. Stanley Hauerwas includes in his book *After Christendom? How the Church is to Behave if Freedom, Justice and a Christian Nation are Bad Ideas* an essay on 'Why Justice is a Bad Idea for Christians'. He is concerned lest, 'in the interest of working for justice, Christians allow their imaginations to be captured by concepts of justice determined by the presuppositions of liberal societies'.[24] Surprisingly, Hauerwas does not have an essay on why 'human rights' is a bad idea for Christians, though one might have expected this from him. Christians have no specific *theory* of justice, but they are, as Hauerwas stresses, committed to the practice of justice in accord with the will of God. We have seen that there are certain characteristics of such practice: it is personally mediated and enacted; it is concerned with the overcoming of social exclusion (we might add that it is hospitable); it is concerned with the re-establishment and reintegration of the other (that is, it is actively concerned with reconciliation); it is concerned with division of resources to the extent that everyone (including future generations) have enough. We have shown that it is linked with the assertion of human dignity and the imperative for human liberation from dehumanizing oppression.

[24] S. Hauerwas, *After Christendom? How the Church is to Behave if Freedom, Justice and a Christian Nation are Bad Ideas* (Nashville, TN, Abingdon Press, 1991), 68.

This by no means adds up to a theory of justice. Some would say it is a spirituality of justice. For others, like myself, it is enough to establish broad parameters from which a critique of any theory of justice and its enactment in terms of human rights can be brought to bear. There is bound to be, as we have seen, a continuing tension between religious and secular ideas of human rights because the world's religions offer normative accounts of human flourishing which do not conform to the pluralist, secular paradigm. Where Jews or Muslims or Christians become involved in the struggle for human rights, this is *de facto* to accept and even to promote the right of members of other religions to practise their religion freely and publicly, and thus to make their contribution in a pluralist society. It is liberal secularism which continues to force upon the religions an ideology of peaceful coexistence, but it is the religions which have the resources to continue to challenge liberal secularism wherever it operates with reduced ('thin') and ultimately dehumanizing accounts of human flourishing. What the religious dynamic offers in critical solidarity with the human rights movement is a dynamic way of living in confrontation with injustice, of bringing the cry for justice to God, of turning the pain of injustice into a cry on behalf of humanity to a God who is the fount of this same agonized longing for justice. Turning away from the movement for human rights in the service of a purer spiritual ideal (which can so easily become repressive) seems to me little short of a betrayal of humanity in the name of religion, and the irony of the human rights movement as far as the Christian churches are concerned is that it is from outside the religious encampment that this movement in its modern form, which in so many ways serves the cause of God's justice, has arisen. However, there are real tensions for the Christian between the notions of humanity, equality, impersonality and universality in the human rights movement and the theological grounding in divinity, personality and particularity that undergirds the churches' understanding of God's justice. Nevertheless, the churches must be prepared to forgo the certainties of ring-fenced theological positions, to debate the ambiguities of the human rights movement (and their own practice) with its practitioners and theorists; to act as critical participants in this worldwide movement for human dignity and liberation, looking not so much for the resolution of the inevitable tensions between religious ideas of divine justice and secular ideas of human rights, but rather for the

establishment of God's justice through God's agents working for
human rights both within and without the community of the
churches.

4

The Challenge of Liberty for Religions in the USA

MARK CHOPKO*

In 1791, the United States amended its two-year-old Constitution to adopt a series of assurances that the new federal government would respect the rights of its citizens. The first sixteen words of the first of these amendments address the concern of this conference: 'Congress shall make no law respecting an Establishment of Religion, or prohibiting the Free Exercise thereof . . .' It was a proud achievement for this new democracy. It was hoped that, by refusing a central government any power over religion, the ability of the republic to survive would be enhanced. More than 200 years later, with the fall of totalitarian regimes in Europe, one of the proudest exports of the United States has been its tradition of strong civil liberties, especially freedom of religion. As a representative of the largest religious denomination in the United States, it falls to me to address both the promise and the reality of the constitutional assurances.

In many respects, the promise of the American constitutional experiment has borne great fruit for all religions. Religion and its institutions have thrived. Religion does not enjoy the financial support of government for evangelization and proselytization, and its internal operations are generally free of governmental scrutiny. However, as in any relationship between parties, there are tensions. The fear that some cooperative venture may result in an establishment of religion, as that term has been broadly interpreted over the last fifty years, has harmed much-needed efforts to build better collaborative relationships between the institutions of government and institutions of religion addressing the real needs of society.

*The opinions expressed in this chapter are the author's and are not necessarily those of the United States Conference of Catholic Bishops or any of its bishop members.

Similarly, the interpretation of the Free Exercise provision has removed much of the restraint on the administrative powers of government, and has not vigorously protected the rights of religious individuals, much less institutions. The growth of a complex, secular, regulatory society has strengthened the power of government to interfere in the operations and missions of religious institutions in ways unimaginable at the dawn of the republic. The growth in the twentieth century of jurisprudence that emphasized personal individual freedom over the rights of groups has meant that the rights of institutions are more often sacrificed in the face of countervailing demands of individuals. I contend that much-needed balance in the law and society would follow the strengthening of clear legal protections for religious institutions.

Historical Background

To place this review in context one must examine briefly the history and intentions of the drafters of the Religion Clauses.[1] The Supreme Court has regularly insisted that history and experience form the only reliable guide to the interpretation and application of the Establishment Clause.[2] Unfortunately, consideration of history and experience often produces as many disagreements on the Court as does how to test the constitutionality of a law or arrangement.[3]

[1] Some commentators contend there is but one Religion Clause – a singular sixteen-word phrase adopted at the same time by the same Congress. For example, Stephen Carter, *God's Name in Vain* (New York, Basic Books, 2000), 217 n. 21. Most have accepted there are two provisions, as does the US Supreme Court. I will accept the Court's convention here and do not express an opinion on which view is correct.

[2] For example, *Lynch v Donnelly*, 465 US 668, 673–6 (1984). The convention in citing US Court opinions is Vol., Court, page (year). Virtually all of the decisions cited might now be found on the internet at commercial venues such as *westlaw.com* or free sites such as Cornell University's Legal Information Institute, *www.law.cornell.edu*.

[3] Compare Justice Souter's opinion in *Agostini v Felton*, 521 US 203, 243 et seq. (1997) with Chief Justice Rehnquist's opinion in *Wallace v Jaffree*, 472 US 38, 91 et seq. (1985). Forty years ago, Justice Brennan concluded that 'the historical record is at best ambiguous, and statements can readily be found to support either side of the proposition. The ambiguity of history is understandable if we recall the nature of the problems uppermost in the thinking of the statesmen who fashioned the religious guarantees; they were concerned with far more flagrant intrusions of government into the realm of religion than any that our century has witnessed.' *Abington Twp. v Schempp*, 374 US 203, 237 (1963) (concurring).

Although these disagreements do not decide cases, they show the Supreme Court struggling with meaning and intentions, rather than simply incanting language by statesmen such as Thomas Jefferson or James Madison, or elevating a metaphor about 'separation of church and state' – a phrase that does not appear in the Constitution – into a constitutional talisman.[4] Forgotten in disputes about the interpretation of the Religion Clauses is that the clauses themselves were political compromises forged by persons of different cultural, religious and regional experiences. No one view in fact predominated.[5] Although it is beyond the scope of this paper to recite in detail the history of the drafting and negotiations that led to the wording of the Religion Clauses,[6] some 'legislative history,' such as it is, may be illuminating for the present discussion.

A hallmark of the American experiment in democracy was the creation of a limited central government. The new government was considered by the separate states a necessary evil and its scope, reach, rights, obligations and duties were therefore circumscribed in the constitutional text. Real power resided in the states and in the people. Concerned about the potential power and intrusion of the new government, those who created it referred to it as 'federal', not 'national'.[7] The architects of this regime, the 'Federalists', students of the Enlightenment, clung to the view that, if a power was not enumerated, it was not included.[8] One of the architects of the Constitution, James Madison of Virginia, when asked about the

[4] Jefferson's reference to a 'wall of separation' between religion and government is one such example.

[5] The variety of state statutes was succinctly catalogued by Sanford H. Cobb in *The Rise of Religious Liberty in America* (New York, Macmillan, 1902), 507. The first amendment, ratified by representatives and conventions of eleven states by 1791, was the product of differing state preferences.

[6] That history is found, for example, in Chester J. Antieau, *Freedom from Federal Establishment: Formation and Early History of the First Amendment Religion Clauses* (Milwaukee, Bruce Publishing, 1964), cited and relied on by an eight-justice majority in the US Supreme Court. For example, *Walz v Tax Commission*, 397 US 664, 668 (1970), and in Thomas Curry, *The First Freedoms: Church and State in America to the Passage of the First Amendment* (New York, Oxford University Press, 1989).

[7] A national government might seek to increase its power at the expense of those who created it. The 'federal' government denoted a federation of power centres, the states, deriving their powers from the consent of the people.

[8] For example, the Constitution provides that there shall be no religious tests for public office. Art. VI, cl. 3. Some of the framers of the constitutional text thought that meant that the central government would have no power over religion.

absence of protection for religion under the Constitution replied that
he thought that the absence of any express power for the government
was clear and the religious diversity of the country made preferences
politically untenable.[9] This was certainly a departure from the
expected powers of government in Western history.[10]

There remained serious opposition to the potential reach of the
new government by citizens and some states. Five states – New
Hampshire, New York, North Carolina, Rhode Island and Virginia
– indicated a need to address freedom of religion.[11] James
Madison, threatened with opposition from Baptist ministers in his
bid for re-election, changed his mind about the need for a
constitutional amendment on religion and agreed to support such
an amendment. The process of compromise that resulted in the
Establishment Clause seems to indicate that it was designed to
prevent Congress from establishing or favouring a *national* religion
and to prevent Congress from interfering with state policies concerning religion.[12] The first version of what became the Religion
Clauses was among a group of amendments introduced by James
Madison on 8 June 1789.

During debate on 15 August the House considered the amendment. Madison explained its meaning to be 'that Congress should
not establish a religion, and enforce the legal observation of it by
law, nor compel men to worship God in any manner contrary to
their conscience'.[13] He also observed that the amendment had been
required by some state conventions which feared the Constitution
might have given the Congress authority to make laws that infringe
the rights of conscience or establish a national religion; 'to prevent

[9] For Madison's views, see *Debates on the Adoption of the Federal
Constitution* (2nd edn, ed. J. Elliott, 1836), 3. 330.

[10] At the end of the Revolution, Benjamin Franklin, the United States
representative to France, was asked by the papal nuncio about the selection of a
resident bishop for Catholics in the United States. Mr Franklin replied that the
church could exercise governance over Catholics in any way it saw fit. In his view,
the new government had no power to dictate the governance of religious
organizations. Anson Stokes, *Church and State in the United States* (New York,
Harper Brothers, 1950), 1. 477–8.

[11] Four (New Hampshire excepted) raised a need for a no-Establishment Clause.
Debates on the Adoption of the Federal Constitution, 1. 328 (New York); 334
(Rhode Island); 3. 659 (Virginia); 4. 244 (North Carolina).

[12] *Annals of Congress*, ed. Gales and Seaton (1789), 1 (record of First US
Congress).

[13] Ibid., at 730; *Jaffree*, (see n. 3) 472 US at 95–6 (Rehnquist, J., dissenting).

these effects he presumed the amendment was intended'.[14] If anything, the proposed text ('No religion shall be established by law
. . .') evoked limited concern that it might be construed *adversely* to
religion.[15] But the language passed the House. The amendment was
intended as a warning sign to government, not a roadblock to the
influence of religion. As the current US Chief Justice has
emphasized:[16]

> None of the other Members of Congress who spoke during the August
> 15 debate expressed the slightest indication that they thought the
> language before them from the Select Committee, or the evil to be
> aimed at, would require that the Government be absolutely neutral as
> between religion and irreligion.

The subsequent adoption of the amendment by the representatives
and conventions of eleven states reflects broader concerns than
simply a restatement of a viewpoint of a particular state or person.

As part of the Bill of Rights, the Establishment and Free Exercise
Clauses were intended by the framers to be complementary and
comprehensive protections for religious liberty. '[T]he Religion
Clauses had specifically and firmly fixed the right to free exercise
of religious beliefs, and buttressing this fundamental right was an
equally firm, even if less explicit, prohibition against the establishment of any religion by government.'[17] The framers of the Constitution 'had no fear or jealousy of religion itself, nor did they
wish to see us as an irreligious people'.[18]

History and experience indicate that, although the Establishment Clause was intended to prohibit the preference of one
religion over another, it did not forbid any assistance, regulation or
other interaction between religion and government.[19] The Religion

---

[14] Ibid.

[15] *Annals*, 1. 729–30.

[16] *Jaffree*, 472 US at 99 (Rehnquist, J., dissenting).

[17] *Wisconsin v Yoder*, 406 US 205, 214 (1972).

[18] Senate Report No. 376, 32nd Cong. 2d Sess. 4 (1853) (Appointment and Compensation of Legislative Chaplains); see also *Zorach v Clauson*, 343 US 313 (1952).

[19] The examples are well known. The framers of the Religion Clauses in the
First Congress allowed state involvement with religion, including payment for
chaplains (*Marsh v Chambers*, 463 US 783, 788 (1983)), the Thanksgiving Holiday
(ibid., at 788) and the inclusion of churches in land grants in the Northwest
Territories. See *Wallace v Jaffree,* 472 US at 100 (Rehnquist, J., dissenting).

Clauses reflect the experience of their framers that an officially preferred or nationally established religion (and actions that tend towards that result) generates religious intolerance and infringes upon religious liberty.[20] However, the Establishment Clause was not meant to drive a wedge between religion and government, but to avoid relationships between the two that pose a realistic threat of impairing religious liberty.[21] Both Clauses were intended to work together to foster religious freedom. While one of the purposes of the Religion Clauses is to protect personal religious liberty,[22] it would also seem well established that another was to preserve the integrity of religious and governmental institutions.[23] The federal constitutional structure protects governmental and religious organizations from interfering with each other.[24] However, they also must be able to collaborate because together they share important responsibilities with deep roots in our national traditions. Assuring collaboration without loss of institutional and personal freedoms remains a difficult and continuing conundrum.

New Applications – New Problems

In contemporary US society, many of the difficulties experienced by religious institutions are summed up in one question: by what right do we seek to participate, to be exempt from the burdens of government, to speak strongly and prophetically about moral issues in public policy, etc.? The articulation of a constitutional basis on which to answer this question in all its permutations, for the protection of institutional rights, separate and apart from the protection of individual rights, has become the daily task of

[20] See, for example, *Abington Township*, 374 US at 221–31, and at 228 (Douglas, J., concurring); *Torcaso v Watkins*, 367 US 488, 490 (1961).

[21] See, for example, *Lynch*, 465 US at 683.

[22] Stokes, *Church and State*, 1. 556 (clauses added as protection *for* religion, not *from* religion).

[23] See *Abington Township*, 374 US at 222. In an article by the same name as his thesis, Carl Esbeck argues that the Establishment Clause was intended as a structural barrier to the exercise of governmental power over religion. 84 *Iowa L. Rev.* 1 (1998).

[24] Government neutrality in matters of religion prevents the fusion of government and religious functions, *and* protects the freedom of religious observance from state compulsion, *Everson v Board of Education*, 330 US 1, 15 (1947).

religious institutions in the United States. In articulating principles of free exercise of religious conscience and limited authority of government over religion, the framers intended, even if they did not write in detail, strong protection of the rights of religious groups (as groups).[25] The implications of the constitutional text are at the root of debates and events that have not always benefited institutions of religion, as separate from their members. That is the challenge of liberty for religion in the United States.

Historical Intent and Contemporary Interpretations Diverge

The Religion Clauses of the First Amendment set out a general allocation of power and its limitations, but as a promise left to future generations to interpret and apply. Certainly, at the time of its framing, the behaviour of the new government and the new leaders reflected the preferred and respected place of religion in American life. In early encounters between religious institutions and the courts in the United States, religion and the claims of those who lead it were often treated with some deference. For example, the courts of the United States respected title of the Anglican Church in the United States to its lands over claims that the Revolution had extinguished land grants.[26] One hundred years later, when the Rector of Trinity Church in New York City called an English pastor to assume leadership of the parish, the Supreme Court of United States rejected a claim that the immigration laws of United States barred the entry of the new pastor. The Court was of the view that, unless the Congress specifically included religious institutions within the ambit of the statute, religion was simply not to be subject to such mundane regulation.[27] Religious groups could 'call' whoever they thought best to pastor them without restriction by the

---

[25] In contrast, commentator Sophie van Bijsterveld has noted in European law that, while there is a tendency to place religion in a private sphere and describe it in individual terms, the social (and hence) legal reality is different. She notes that the European Commission on Human Rights, for example, protects institutional rights from attack by individuals. 'Religion, International Law and Policy in the Wider European Arena', in R. Ahdar (ed.), *Law and Religion* (Aldershot, Ashgate, 2000), 165–9.

[26] *Terrett v Taylor*, 13 US 43 (1815).

[27] *Rector of the Holy Trinity Church v United States*, 143 US 467, 516 (1892). However, when the matter in question implicated what was seen as a matter of public welfare or morals, for example, the practice of polygamy by members of the Mormon Church, the public need trumped religious rights. *Reynolds v United States*, 98 US 145 (1878).

government. Individual rights, such as they were, were sometimes subordinated to the needs of the wider community.[28]

Independent judicial review is one of the strengths of the US system. It is part of the 'democracy' the United States regularly seeks to export to developing parts of the world and to the new democracies in Eastern and Central Europe. Independent judicial review has created its own body of law separate and apart from the legislative history of a constitutional text that courts interpret. Most scholars agree that the contemporary history of the Religion Clauses dates from the 1940s. Until then, there had been very little opportunity for the courts, especially the United States Supreme Court, to interpret and apply the Religion Clauses.[29]

In 1940, the Free Exercise Clause of the First Amendment was applied against the efforts of the State of Connecticut to restrict the ability of Jehovah's Witnesses to proselytize and solicit support door-to-door. Except in cases of fraud, and other substantial interests directly impacting the common good, the Court held that the power of the states simply did not extend to such restraint on religious action.[30] The Court erected a high barrier against such actions. In 1947, the Court applied the no-Establishment Clause to the states. In that case, the Court upheld the efforts of the State of New Jersey to assist school parents in bus transportation, including in the programme parents who chose to send their children to religious schools.[31] Neither case relied on a complete review of the history of the constitutional text, sparking the debate that continues today.

Although the Supreme Court has regularly insisted that history is its touchstone in applying and interpreting the Religious Clauses of the First Amendment, the enduring problem of constitutional litigation in the United States has been how to keep faith with the values embodied in constitutional text while responding to problems that were simply beyond the contemplation of the generation that

---

[28] For example, the Supreme Court in *Jacobson v Massachusetts*, 197 US 11 (1905) sustained a state's refusal to honour a religious objection to vaccination laws. Public health concerns were deemed compelling and a community's needs lifted over an individual's.

[29] For example, Phillip Johnson, 'Concepts and Compromise in First Amendment Religious Doctrine', 72 *Cal. L. Rev.* 817 (1984) ('scholars know that the present doctrinal approach stems from post-World War II Supreme Court decisions').

[30] *Cantwell v Connecticut*, 310 US 296 (1940).

[31] *Everson v Board of Education* (see n. 24).

framed it. During our colonial period, the great institutions of public welfare – schools, hospitals, charity – were almost exclusively in the hands of religious institutions. Government simply did not have the size or the resources to provide the services. For the public welfare to be promoted during this period, plainly, the institutions of government and religion needed to cooperate. Respectful cooperation could not have been intended to be unconstitutional.

As I see it, government and religion, as institutions, have complementary but separate missions. Government is to provide for the common defence and security, the protection of civic rights, and the orderly relations between persons. Religion aspires to higher purposes and, from that motivation, addresses the moral dimensions of public and private life and seeks to improve the lot of all the people of God. Those who view government and religion as two entirely separate spheres, communicating over a void, are mistaken. The spheres of government and religion rather intersect. The space described by the intersection indicates that these institutions share interests in promoting the public good. Although the motivation (and missions) of the institutions are entirely different, the actions undertaken by these institutions are often indistinguishable from the perspective of the beneficiaries. Most of the constitutional adjudication in the last fifty years, indeed, much of the fighting in the public arena over the proper roles of religion and government, has to do with drawing appropriate lines to protect the autonomy of the institutions of government and institutions of religion in this area where their interests intersect. The need for line drawing has further complicated the process of providing a true basis of constitutional interpretation that properly and authentically reflects its history.[32]

---

[32] The 'Lemon' test has roots in *Lemon v Kurtzman*, 403 US 602 (1971), which invalidated laws of two states providing salary supplements and other assistance to religious schools. The Court said there for a law to be constitutional it must have a secular purpose, not have the primary effect of advancing or inhibiting religion, and not 'excessively entangle' government in religion. In explaining a companion case approving government grants to Catholic colleges, *Tilton v Richardson*, 403 US 672 (1971), the Court said that the colleges were not 'pervasively sectarian', meaning that they were not incapable of separating religious from secular matter. *Hunt v McNair*, 413 US 734, 743–4 (1973). Many of us in religious institutions find the phrase and its lineage a most bigoted and insulting expression. Richard Baer, 'The Supreme Court's Discriminatory Use of the Term "Pervasively Sectarian"', 6 *Journal of Law and Politics* 449, 453 (1990). See discussion of *Mitchell v Helms* (n. 33).

In my view, perhaps a majority of the Supreme Court recognizes that its judicial interpretations of the Religion Clauses simply went too far in the direction of excluding religion from realistic collaboration with government in ways that penalized the greater society. Rules of decision which suspiciously scrutinized every collaborative relationship and presumptively disqualified those institutions that took their religion seriously had the effect of systematically stripping religious influences and institutions from public life. There is some sense that as a society we may have moved too far, too fast, and that antiseptically treating religious expression leaves us worse off as a people. In the last few years, the Court has begun to revise its case law governing the relationship between religion and government.[33] Nonetheless, religion is still regarded by some with suspicion and seen as a force to be kept at arm's length in relationships with government. Rather than respect the place of religion, the courts force religion to justify, to an extent not placed on other institutions in society, why secular rules that govern a for-profit workplace should not apply to it. Rather than seeing religion as something special, to be subjected to the most 'delicate and sensitive' touch,[34] religion is simply treated as 'everything else'. Particular aspects of this phenomenon are treated below.

The Privatization of Religion

As an institution, religion was routinely given preferred treatment in colonial society. Perhaps for that reason, the framers of the constitutional text thought it unnecessary to express institutional rights plainly. On the other hand, the rights of persons and the limits on government were new ideas, and the framers, students of the Enlightenment, described powers of a limited government and

[33] In *Agostini v Felton*, (see n. 3), the Court rewrote the *Lemon* test to make its application less doctrinaire and more nuanced, folding 'excessive entanglement' into the test for primary effect. 521 US at 233–43. In *Mitchell v Helms*, 530 US 793, 828–9 (2000), a plurality of four justices abandoned 'pervasively sectarian' as a basis for disqualification of religious institutions, focusing instead on what the institution did with government assistance. Two justices concurred in the judgment but did not join in the opinion depriving the plurality of a majority. Ibid., 836 et seq. (opinion of O'Connor and Breyer). There are sympathetic references in the concurrence, however. Ibid., 840–1.

[34] Annals, 1. 730 (Remarks of Daniel Carroll); *James Madison, Memorial and Remonstrance Against Religious Assessments* (1785), reprinted in *Everson* (see n. 24), 330 US at 63–72.

rights of persons, but not institutions, qua institutions. So it was with religion – described as a personal affair. The idea that one's relationship with one's God is entirely private was an under-standable reaction to the world in which religious and govern-mental powers were united, often to the detriment of both believers and dissenters. If religion belongs to the person alone, then no earthly authority – religious or governmental – can mediate one's salvation or regulate one's citizenship on the basis of religious identity. If, however, religion were a public matter, then worship, financial support and other conduct are subject to external authority, including punishment in proper circumstances. This was the world in which framers of the US Constitution lived.

The dominant Protestant culture in the United States shaped institutions of government, through the law and by public opinion. The privatization of religious expression was part of this culture.[35] I do not suggest a theological critique of this phenomenon but rather a legal and cultural critique of some negative aspects of this phenomenon. I highlight three in particular.

First, although no religion was to be 'preferred,' for purposes of law and public opinion, those religions which were organized in more 'democratic' fashion were seen more favourably than those that appeared autocratic or hierarchical, such as the Catholic Church. Church institutions, professing spiritual allegiance to a pope in Rome and whose ranks swelled with the arrival of millions of immigrants, were regarded as un-American. The dominant American culture attempted forcibly to assimilate immigrant populations, especially through common schools. The Catholic bishops, for their part, reassuring their fellow citizens that they, too, were Americans, sought the protection of US law to engage in cooperative ventures with government, but yet to preserve the autonomy of their institutions against efforts to prohibit, limit or assimilate them.[36] US law did not know how to deal with these structures. To assert institutional rights created competition. The first efforts of United States Supreme Court to explain religious

---

[35] Michael McConnell, 'Singling Out Religion', 50 *DePaul L.Rev.* 1, 27 (2000). See Frederick Gedicks, 'Democracy, Autonomy, and Values', 60 *So. Cal. L. Rev.* 1579, 1582–5 (1987).

[36] Mark Chopko, 'American and Catholic', *DePaul University Centennial Series* (forthcoming 2002).

institutions utilized a 'free association' model.[37] The model, in which an association is the sum of its parts, would not adequately explain the polity and practices of an institution like the Catholic Church.

Second, the privatization of religion, based as it is on a strong protection for individual conscience set in juxtaposition with governmental authority, does not adequately reflect the basis on which religious voices – institutional voices – engage moral aspects of public policy questions. Because religious institutions were not always understood as possessing rights in and of themselves, it was easy to see how institutional claims of right could simply be ignored. When religious voices are raised in public debate, and those voices are the voices of leadership, there are often contrary noises seeking their exclusion. The byword of these noises is that religious institutions are seeking to 'impose' their views on the citizenry. Although the constitutional text not only does not exclude religious voices from public debate, but would protect them, religious institutions in US society waste much effort arguing with their own people and their critics (sometimes the same group) about the right to speak to the moral aspects of important public policy questions. I will deal with this problem in detail in the next section.

Third, a philosophy that defends the primacy of individual conscience over contrary and competing communal demands creates conflict in interpreting the legal relationships between the institutions of religion and government. In contemporary US society, every religious institution reports increased efforts by disagreeing voices in their own communities to seek judicial relief, through the secular courts, over doctrine, structure and temporal matters. Rather than seek to resolve these matters within the churches, or simply seeking a more amenable religious community,

---

[37] In *Watson v Jones*, 80 US 679 (1871), the Court disallowed attempts by a pro-slavery faction of the Presbyterian Church to use the secular courts to contest revision of the Church's doctrine by, and wrest control of the church's property from, an anti-slavery majority. The Court said it must defer to the decision by the highest church authority, and so must the members. Having joined the church and thereby consented to its rules and discipline by their association, the members could not seek judicial relief for a doctrinal dispute, for then such 'consent' would be 'vain' and subvert the religious body to the state. Ibid., 729.

Americans have expressed their dissatisfaction through litigation. It has always been so in our history. The ambiguous basis on which the protection of the institution of religion rests, as distinct from the rights in interest of believers, fuels this behaviour, both on the part of individual believers and on the part of the courts. This phenomenon will be examined in some detail below.

Efforts to Limit Religious Voices in Public Debate
Americans might seem schizophrenic on the question of religious participation in public life. On the one hand, Americans express confidence that religion has great power to ameliorate the worst aspects of our culture and society. At the same time, we seem to adhere to the view that religious leaders should keep out of political matters altogether. Save our culture but stay out of debates about its direction. Confusion starts with the terminology 'political matters,' which embraces two issues. First, public policy issues have moral aspects. The process by which public policy is made, through legislatures and administrative action, is in some measure 'political'. Second, electoral politics involving the choice of candidates for public office is also an aspect of this question. In my view, it is absolutely essential that religious leaders participate in the former, but not the latter. Indeed, a leading US commentator suggests that religious leaders who link their voices to candidates undermine the prophetic voice of religion in society and exacerbate the trend to treat religion as just another interest group.

Those who urge religion to stay away from the moral aspects of issues in public policy debates do not understand either the nature of religion or their own constitutional history. Religious voices have had a long and mostly distinguished history of influencing choices on matters affecting the public good. Even the very First Amendment of the Constitution was a result of a 'political' meeting between James Madison and Baptist ministers in his congressional district. As noted above, Madison had expressed the view in the Continental Congress that there was no need for an amendment on religion. In his view, and the view of many Federalists, the Constitution already denied any power to the new federal government over religious matters, which would remain the proper venue of the states. The anti-Federalists, nonetheless afraid of the potential power of the new government, sought an amendment primarily as a means of assuring limitations on the new

government. These Baptist ministers shared that view. In their
encounter with Madison, at a place still revered by Baptists, the
ministers explained to him that they would oppose his candidacy
for re-election to the Congress (from the pulpit) unless he agreed to
support an amendment strengthening protection for religion.[38]
Madison was re-elected to Congress in Philadelphia after providing
suitable assurances to these ministers, and in turn he championed
the cause of amending the Constitution to include words very
similar to what is now the First Amendment.

American leaders such as George Washington recognized that
religion and morality are essential conditions to the maintenance
of democracy.[39] The separation of church and state, as an idea, was
intended to protect the institutional autonomy of the mediating
structures of religion and government. In this way, it would also
serve to preserve individual and institutional religious liberty.[40]
Separation of church and state, correctly understood, was not
separation of religious and moral influences from the national life
and especially from the formation of public policy. Efforts to
exclude religion from public debate on moral issues would send the
wrong message at a critical time in the nation's journey. It would
send a message that religion has nothing to do with the big
questions of life that must be asked and answered along the way.[41]
That has never been the story of religion in the United States.

Religious leaders have served in the forefront of all of the vital
human rights struggles in our history. Leadership for the abolition
of slavery came principally from ministers in the North who

[38] Michael McConnell, 'Taking Religion Seriously', *First Things* (May 1990).

[39] George Washington, Farewell Address, reprinted annually in the Congressional Record on his birthday. See, for example, 147 Congressional Record, S1543
(26 Feb. 2001).

[40] 'Separation of Church and State' grew from a metaphor used by Thomas
Jefferson explaining to the Danbury (Connecticut) Baptists Association why he
would not proclaim a day of 'thanksgiving', a religious exercise he thought beyond
the constitutional competence of government. He referred to the Religion Clauses
as building a 'wall of separation between Church and State'. The letter was a
political statement designed to respond to his critics who vilified him as an atheist
in the presidential election of 1800. Daniel Dreisbach, 'Another Look at Jefferson's
Wall of Separation', *Witherspoon Lectures*, 10 (Washington, DC, Family Research
Council, 1 August 2000).

[41] That fear has been expressed repeatedly about the sometimes ruthless
exclusion of religious influences from public life. See American Council on Education, *The Function of the Public Schools in Dealing with Religion* (Washington,
DC, 1953).

campaigned against that great evil. Evangelical fervour created the temperance movement, which led to an ill-fated experiment with prohibition. The champions of the civil rights movement were principally African-American clergy and the leadership of every major denomination in the United States. In the 1980s, at the height of Ronald Reagan's attempts to bring down the Soviet Union, the Catholic bishops of the United States started a public debate over the legitimacy of the possession and use of nuclear weapons.[42] It is difficult to conceive of any issue of public policy, great or small, that does not have a moral dimension on which religious voices are vital for complete understanding of the complexities of the matter. The former Dean of the Harvard Divinity School has suggested that we should not ordain clergy who do not understand how to read a budget.[43] He was not concerned about the ability of pastors to conduct temporal matters. Rather, he was more concerned with the moral implications of budgets, especially national budgets: it is there the society sets its priorities by fixing the amount of money it is willing to spend on every aspect of the national life.

Religious institutions have the same 'rights' to speak as any group in US society. We are protected by the Free Speech Clause of the First Amendment.[44] We also have rights, although less securely recognized, under the Free Exercise Clause. In fact, religious organizations, as tax-exempt, non-profit entities, address issues in public debate in less pervasive ways than for-profit corporations. Not only do non-profit and religious entities have limited resources available to them, but they are denied political action committees and other devices that are permitted to their for-profit corporate cousins. Under the tax laws of United States, tax-exempt entities – which, by definition, includes religious organizations – are limited in the amount of certain kinds of speech they may freely engage in without losing their tax exemption.[45] The tax laws provide that, in

---

[42] Carter, *God's Name in Vain*, at 4, 12. See, generally, James Reichley, *Religion in American Public Life* (Washington, DC, Brookings, 1985), chapter 5, 'Churches and Political Action: 1790–1963'.

[43] Revd J. Bryan Hehir, 'The Church, Politics and the Law', *Proceedings of the Diocesan Attorneys Association*, 12 (1988; private print). Father Hehir at this time is President of Catholic Charities – USA, a national association in service to individual diocesan charities agencies.

[44] *Rosenberger v Board of Rectors*, 515 US 819 (1995).

[45] Internal Revenue Code, section 501(c)(3), 26 USC §501(c)(3).

order to preserve exemption from taxation and the deductibility of contributions to donors, an entity may not engage in 'substantial' lobbying.[46] In addition, there is an *absolute* ban on any kind of action which endorses or supports candidates for election.[47]

The fact that religious organizations broadly engage issues in public debate does not mean that they have the same latitude to address the merits (or lack thereof) of candidates. That kind of political action implicates both theological and legal issues. For its part, the Second Vatican Council said that the Catholic Church must not tie itself to any political party or movement.[48] The bishops correctly recognized that the church would lose its prophetic ability to speak for the common good of all by linking its future fortunes to the success or failure of a political movement. It would also violate the tax exemption laws, as noted above. The penalty for the loss of tax exemption would mean the institution is subject to taxation, and the contributions of individual donors would not be deductible from gross income for purposes of figuring their own tax liabilities. There are those who counter that religion must be free when it discerns the need to speak without fearing the tax laws and the caprice of regulators. Although there is merit in that argument, one must exercise care that such 'political' involvement does not lower respect for religion or blunt its voice.[49]

Religious organizations, addressing matters in public debate, even those with small size and limited resources, may still be as a threat to the rich and powerful. Religion has a prophetic voice in US society, often urging a different path to the one chosen by government. The fact remains that religions must often educate their own people about the need (and the right) to speak to issues on public agendas.

Participation of Religious Entities in Public Initiatives
Based on the history of United States, one would expect that religious organizations would be regular partners of government in promoting the common good. Plainly, most of the public initiatives undertaken by government to promote the public welfare fall into

---

[46] There is no definition of 'substantial', although regulatory experience places it at between 5 and 15 per cent of an entity's resources.

[47] 'Absolute' means 'complete – no exceptions'.

[48] Second Vatican Council, *Gaudium et Spes*, paragraph 76 (1965).

[49] Carter, *God's Name in Vain*, 55–8 (Politics! Not Elections).

the area of interests that are shared with religious organizations. Whether these are in education, health care, public welfare or related initiatives, religious organizations, although from a different perspective, share an interest in advancing the public good. But such participation is regularly criticized, politicized and litigated. I understand (and there is no serious dispute) that the government may not directly finance proselytization, worship and religious instruction. But when the actions are in education, health or welfare, religious motivation should not be penalized, nor should religious entities sacrifice their unique character in order to serve the people and society.

In practical terms, a religious organization may participate in public initiatives in one of three ways. It may be a contractor, as part of larger government programmes, to deliver services in the name of the government. It may also be a recipient of direct grant assistance, with or without conditions, to promote a shared interest. Finally, under some programmes, a religious organization may simply be a provider of a service that is purchased by an individual citizen through a government-supplied certificate, voucher or scholarship. In brief, there is no constitutional rule against participation of religious organizations in public programmes on the same footing as their non-religious counterparts.[50] However, the government's ability to set conditions on participation or use participation as a trigger for extensive regulation may be a reason for a religious organization *not* to participate in a programme.[51]

When religious organizations serve as government contractors, they are serving within the four corners of a government programme. In the nineteenth century, our Supreme Court refused to disqualify a Catholic hospital on account of affiliation, and has said the government may even employ a cleric to carry out a government programme. The cleric (or in that case the Sisters of Providence Hospital) was doing the government's work (to fight contagious diseases).[52] Since the 1980s, the US Congress has explored ways to mobilize local community resources, including

[50] *Bowen v Kendrick*, 487 US 589 (1988).

[51] *Rust v Sullivan*, 500 US 173 (1990).

[52] *Bradfield v Roberts*, 175 US 291 (1899). See *Roemer v Maryland Public Works Board*, 426 US 736, at 746 (1976) (the state may send a cleric, even a clerical order, to perform a wholly secular task, citing *Bradfield*).

religious organizations 'as appropriate', to solve social problems. The proposed inclusion of religious groups in a federal family planning programme that would explore the validity of abstinence education among teenagers was immediately challenged by the American Civil Liberties Union and others as authorizing government funding for the distribution of religious messages to 'vulnerable young people'.[53] The Supreme Court held the involvement of religious organizations on the same terms and conditions as their secular counterparts, as part of a larger community-based strategy to address the problem of teenage pregnancy, did not necessarily involve unconstitutional assistance to religion.[54]

When a religious institution has been set to receive direct financial assistance from the government, most of these administrative and legislative devices have generally been ruled unconstitutional.[55] Some thirty years ago, a substantial majority of the Court endorsed the view that the First Amendment was to be designed to prevent the 'sponsorship, financial support, and active involvement of the sovereign in religious activity'.[56] Although the present Supreme Court appears to be deeply and irreconcilably divided over how to define what these terms mean,[57] it seems safe to say that a majority of the court would bar direct and unrestricted cash assistance to religious organizations without some tie to a secular public programme.[58]

In recent years the nature of the analysis has changed from one in which religious organizations are presumptively disqualified (under the rubric 'pervasively sectarian'), to one in which the religious identity of the recipient is but the first step in further analysis.[59] Writing for a four-justice plurality in June 2000, Clarence Thomas indicated that the genesis of the term 'pervasively sectarian' was in anti-Catholic rhetoric, unworthy of the

---

[53] Adolescent Family Life Act, 42 USC §300z–5(a)(21)(B).

[54] *Bowen v Kendrick*, 487 US at 611–15.

[55] *Lemon v Kurtzman* (see n. 32); *Rosenberger*, 515 US at 846–7 (O'Connor, J. concurring).

[56] *Walz v Tax Commission*, 397 US at 668 (eight justice majority).

[57] See *Board of Education v Mergens*, 496 US 226 (1990), compare 249 (O'Connor) with 260 (Kennedy) (competing opinions divide on methodology, not result).

[58] But see *Comm. on Public Education v Regan*, 444 US 646 (1980) (reimbursement of educational expenses).

[59] *Mitchell v Helms* (see n. 33).

Court or the country.[60] Although his opinion was not a majority, it is an important legal development.[61] For purposes of judging the involvement of religious organizations, it appears that the Court views more realistically the needed partnership of religious organizations with the government. The end of the legal rules that presumptively disqualify religious institutions means that the Supreme Court must consider new and better analytical devices that more authentically allow courts to interpret and apply the constitutional text, based on what actions are performed, not who performs them.

A further development in this area of the national life is the question of vouchers or certificates used by citizens to purchase services from public and private (including religious) entities. A recent decision of the US Supreme Court upholds the constitutionality of a voucher-funded service that includes religious providers, if the programme is properly designed.[62] It seems clear that the Court will sustain other voucher initiatives that provide a public service to a broad range of recipients, identified by non-religious criteria, in which the assistance does not create incentives for citizens to choose for or against religious providers (in other words, if the programme is religiously neutral). The holding was based on a series of Supreme Court cases validating programmes offering tax deductions for educational expenses (including expenses at religiously affiliated schools),[63] scholarship assistance to disabled individuals (including education at a Bible school),[64] and the provision of a deaf interpreter to a student at a Catholic high school.[65] A certificate is already a part of a federal childcare development programme.[66] Generally, however, citizens have been wary of voucher programmes that have been proposed for consideration in legislatures and on the ballot. Previous efforts to expand the range of educational choice to include religious schools through voucher and other programmes have met with mixed

---

[60] Ibid., at 828.

[61] There remains the problem of educating the inferior courts about this shift. For example, *Steele v Industrial Development Board*, 117 F.Supp. 2d 693, 706–7 (M.D. Tenn. 2000) (reversed on appeal on other grounds: 2002 WL 1858636, 14 August 2002).

[62] *Zelman v Simmons-Harris*, 122 S.Ct. 2460 (2002).

[63] *Mueller v Allen*, 463 US 388 (1983).

[64] *Witters v Washington Comm'n for the Blind*, 474 US 481 (1986).

[65] *Zobrest v Catalina Foothills School District*, 501 US 1 (1993).

[66] Child Care and Development Block Grant, 42 USC §9858n(2).

success and failure.[67] The favourable decision by the US Supreme Court in the Cleveland, Ohio voucher case will renew the political debate.[68]

Against this background, religious organizations are now very much in the forefront of national debate on the question of 'charitable choice' and partnerships between government and 'faith-based organizations'. This programme continues to be discussed as a centrepiece of the Bush Administration's social policy. It has been documented in the social science literature that religious organizations can be among the most successful at resolving problems that plague the public good.[69] Yet close connection between government policy and religious actors has rekindled suspicion about the ability of religion to act in a religiously neutral manner with respect to the beneficiaries of its assistance.[70] Similarly, there are other voices in society that urge the institutional recipients of public assistance to conform their conduct, not to religious ideology, but to secular ideology or forfeit their ability to participate in public programmes. Both of these issues go to the heart of the current controversy.

---

[67] Such a programme was upheld in Milwaukee, Wisconsin in *Jackson v Benson*, 578 NW 2d 602 (Wisc.), cert denied, 525 US 997 (1998), but rejected in Cleveland, Ohio in *Simmons-Harris v Zelman*, 234 F.3d 945 (6th Cir. 2000) (reversed on appeal). Ballot initiatives recently failed with voters in California and Michigan.

[68] Already, *Zelman* has been applied to reject state laws that disqualify students in theology programmes from scholarship assistance. *Davey v Locke*, F.3d (9th Cir. 2002) (2002 WL 1578831).

[69] Stuart Taylor writing in the *Legal Times* of Washington says, 'Bush's initiative has great promise if designed with care, skill and restraint. It could harness the enormous altruistic energies that are fostered by faith, thereby extending the benefits of faith-based programs to countless thousands who have not been helped by existing government programs and secular charities. The risk of inadvertently subsidizing some religious activity seems a small price to pay for the hope of improving the services and augmenting the resources available to help the homeless, the hungry, drug addicts, alcoholics, the mentally ill, victims of domestic violence, prisoners and their families, and others.' *Legal Times* (5 Feb. 2001), 50. It has been noted that a faith-based experiment in managing a Texas correctional facility has reduced recidivism rates by 80 per cent. *Legal Times* (5 Feb. 2001), 10.

[70] 'Jewish Leaders Criticize "Faith-Based" Initiatives', *Washington Post* (27 Feb. 2001); links and articles collected at *www.pewforum.org*. The programme is being criticized by the left as too religious, and by some evangelical Christian leaders as too governmental. 'Bush Aide Tells of Plan to Aid Work by Churches', *New York Times* (8 March 2001), A10.

As to the first issue, the ability of religion to live up to its promises not to direct government funds for religious instruction or proselytization, there are two answers. If a religious organiza- tion certifies that it will not use government funds for prohibited purposes, then suspicion to the contrary rests on the supposition that religion cannot be trusted to honour its own word. For that assertion to be true, religious administrators must lie (something that still violates one of the Ten Commandments!) to the govern- ment, about what it will *really* do in a programme. Not only has the Supreme Court rejected such an assertion, it was unwilling to remake it into a constitutional rule.[71] In addition, the vindication of important federal interests in non-discrimination does not rely on absolute assurances from potential grantees that there will never be a problem. Rather, enforcement occurs after the fact. Requiring prospective recipients to promise that there will never be a discriminatory issue in the workplace in order to obtain the grant would mean that there would never be any federal programmes.[72]

As to the second issue, under the concept of 'charitable choice', religious entities are not required to forgo their religious identities in order to participate. The point was to expand the range of service providers beyond government-inspired homogeneity into a more realistic mix. Moreover, the government has the obligation to provide non-religious alternatives to the delivery of the services.[73] Charitable choice rests on a fundamental proposition that the delivery of social services in the society is more effective when it respects the religious diversity of the population.[74] The ability of the government, however, to attempt to condition the participation of religious entities on conformance with secular principles remains a matter of substantial debate.

The Power to Remake Religion in a Person's Image
Increasingly, adherents choose not to abandon their religious institutions over disagreements of faith, doctrine or practice. Nor

---

[71] *Mitchell v Helms*, 530 US at 833 (plurality) and 859 (concurrence).

[72] *Mitchell v Helms*: Brief Amicus Curiae of United States Catholic Conference at 28, n.19 citing 20 USC §1681 et seq. (sex discrimination in education).

[73] 42 USC §604a(e)(1).

[74] Executive Order 13199, Establishing White House Office of Faith-Based Community Initiatives, §1 (29 Jan. 2001); 42 USC § 604a(d)(2). The first federal 'charitable choice' programme offering assistance to needy families states clearly religious entities 'retain' their religiosity.

do they seek to engage the normal processes by which these questions can be examined and resolved within religious institutions. Rather, they have chosen to seek redress for their grievances with the government and in the courts.[75] The liabilities claimed threaten to breach centuries-old barriers protecting the autonomy of religious institutions and their internal affairs from the long arm and power of the government. Nothing would be more of an affront to the constitutional scheme erected more than two centuries ago. Unfortunately, numerous examples abound.

It is black-letter law that ministry personnel may not litigate, in the civil courts, the terms and conditions of their ministry. This rule of law is known as the 'ministerial exception' which acts as a barrier to the adjudication of claims arising out of ministry service.[76] The vast majority of courts have construed this exemption broadly and have extended it to the full array of federal anti-discrimination statutes.[77] In doing so, the courts recognize that the failure to give an exemption could entangle the civil courts in the adjudication of religious matters, including interpretation of doctrine, policy, polity and pastoral practices, and that such entanglement is unconstitutional.[78] In addition, under federal employment law, religious organizations may exercise a 'preference' for members of the faith community.[79] Yet the number of claims involving the demands and grievances of ministry personnel continues to rise. The persistence of these claims and the compelling nature of some fact situations act as pressure on the courts, not only to accept jurisdiction of these cases, but to grant relief.

Under state law, however, religious organizations are not always fully immunized. In one case, a Catholic employee persisted in wearing monk's robes into his place of employment, a Catholic

[75] *Bouldin v Alexander*, 82 US 131 (1872); *O'Connor v Diocese of Honolulu*, 884 P. 2d 361 (Haw. 1994) (contesting excommunication).

[76] *McClure v Salvation Army*, 460 F. 2d 553 (5th Cir. 1972), cert. denied, 409 US 896 (1972).

[77] *Starkman v Evans*, 198 F. 3d 173 (5th Cir. 1999) (bar to adjudicating disability discrimination claim by choir director). There are recent pressures to narrow the exception to religiously required conduct or where the underlying conflict necessarily involves a religious question. See *McKelvey v Pierce*, 173 NJ 26 (2002).

[78] *EEOC v Catholic University of America*, 83 F. 3d 455 (DC Cir. 1996) (applying ministry exception to professor of canon law); *Starkman v Evans* (see n. 77).

[79] Title VII of the Civil Rights Act of 1964 exempts religious institutions from provisions of federal law barring discrimination in religious hiring and employment practices. 42 USC 2000e–1(a).

parish, in violation of the orders of the diocesan bishop and the pastor. When terminated, he sued in civil court and won, on the theory of religious discrimination under state law.[80] He indicated that he no longer considered himself a Catholic and therefore was not subject to the discipline of the bishop. One would assume, therefore, under this theory, that a non-Catholic employee could choose to dress as the Holy Father and be immune from discipline for these actions. Even in states where there are statutory exemptions for religious organizations, the courts have flirted with limiting exceptions. In one recent case, a non-Catholic employee was dismissed for evangelizing his co-workers on the premises of his Catholic employer. The lower court found a 'public policy' in the provisions of a state constitution barring discrimination on religious matters that would apply to give relief for the termination. The State Supreme Court reversed this, relying on other provisions of the state constitution guaranteeing the freedom and autonomy of religious institutions.[81] These cases are exceptional. However, exceptions cultivate the hope of relief in similar situations.

Religious institutions in United States are liable for the consequences of their contracts, torts and indebtedness, to the same extent as any other institution in society. Barring a statute allowing for some form of 'charitable immunity', now virtually abolished in the US, religious institutions may not plead their charitable status to avoid the consequences of their own actions and the actions of those authorized to act in their names.[82] Nonetheless, there are three trends evident in the reported decisions which give one pause in examining the consequences of litigation against religious institutions.

First, in tort litigation, litigants are not satisfied alleging secular torts based on actual knowledge of persons in charge of religious institutions. They tend to push the boundaries of litigation and seek to impose, through the tort system, secular supervision standards on

---

[80] *Ward v Hengle*, 76 Fair Empl. Practices Cases (BNA) 36 (Ohio, Summit County, 1997).

[81] *Silo v Catholic Healthcare West*, 103 Cal. Rptr. 2d 825 (App. 2001), reversed, 119 Cal. Rptr. 2d 698, 705 (2002).

[82] Mark E. Chopko, 'Ascending Liability of Religious Entities for the Actions of Others', 17 *Amer. J. of Trial Advocacy* 289 (1993).

religious organizations that, for centuries, have operated according to biblical principles and pastoral practices. The concepts of reconciliation, personal penance, restitution and reform, at the heart of the religious experience, are alien in secular litigation involving the misdeeds of ministers. To litigants, and the secular press, this looks like a cover-up. The tension between pastoral practice and secular standards creates challenges for religious institutions both in the press and in the courts. The results have been, in a word, 'uneven'.[83]

Second, there have been efforts to force liability on entire religious institutions for their alleged failure to act as a 'reasonably prudent' religion. Such a claim, in those terms literally, was made against the Conference of Bishops in the United States. Our objections to this litigation on constitutional grounds were on the threshold of a hearing in a state supreme court when the plaintiffs dismissed the Conference of Bishops from the underlying litigation in order to avoid a likely adverse precedent. Nonetheless, there are examples involving many religious denominations in which the failure of some minister or some ecclesiastical superior in one region is alleged to be a problem for which every member and every institution of the ecclesiastical community must answer. With one discredited exception, all of these claims have been, quite properly, rejected.[84]

Third, some religious communities find the concept of state incorporation anathema based on their own self-understanding of the commands of the Bible. The liability system has forced these communities to choose between their self-understanding of what the Bible commanded with respect to state benefits (incorporation) or the consequences of an adverse decision that could reach a member's assets.[85]

It should be clear that one cannot remake the polity of a church in one's image.[86] Plainly, injuries deserve compensation and

---

[83] There is a division in the cases whether a tort remedy for alleged negligent supervision of an ecclesiastical supervisor for the sexual assaults of a cleric within his church discipline is constitutionally viable: *Pritzlaff v Archdiocese of Milwaukee*, 533 NW 2d 780 (Wis. 1995) (no); *Jones v Trane*, 591 NYS 2d 927 (N.Y. Cty. 1992) (yes); *Gibson v Brewer*, 952 SW 2d 239 (Mo. 1997) (sometimes).

[84] *N.H. v Presbyterian Church*, 998 P. 2d 592 (Okla. 1999) (resolved on common law grounds). Cases collected in Chopko, 'Ascending Liability', 337–41.

[85] *Cox v Thee Evergreen Church*, 804 SW 2d 190, 193 (Tx. Ct. App. 1991).

[86] In *Weaver v Wood*, 680 NE 2d 918 (Mass. 1997), The First Church of Christ, Scientist was sued by dissenters over the growth of evangelization efforts from print media to electronic media. The dissenters claimed that they were simply

ministry personnel deserve to be treated with respect. However, as noted above, Americans show their dissatisfaction by litigation and would rather seek the power of the courts to try to compel a religious institution to reform rather than utilize church processes to bring about distributive justice.

Governmental Power to Remake Religion in the Government's Image

One of the biggest dangers to religion in the United States today is not overt discrimination, but calcified indifference.[87] The tensions that this has created for religious organizations cannot be underestimated. Creeping governmental power tends to treat religion like everything else, and any demand for any exception to any rule as an inconvenience. Administrative power is insensitive to the ways in which the governmental demand for uniformity creates burdens and difficulties for religious communities, which by their very natures are diverse and different from each other. Government that is entirely indifferent to the legitimate needs of religious communities does not serve well the needs of religious citizens.

A major factor that has exacerbated the situation for religious organizations was the decision of the US Supreme Court in 1990 in *Employment Division v Smith*.[88] In that case, Native Americans who belonged to a religion in which the drug peyote was ingested were terminated from their jobs as drug counsellors in a state programme. They contested the terminations on religious grounds arguing that the failure to accommodate their practices violated their rights under the US Constitution's Free Exercise Clause. Not surprisingly, given the use of drugs by drug counsellors, they lost. What was surprising was that a majority of the Court took this

enforcing the terms of the foundress's trust. Other churches cried 'foul', noting that the means of evangelization and the spreading of the gospel message by churches is simply a power that is beyond the authority of the government to circumscribe or regulate in any way. For example, *United States v Ballard*, 322 US 78, 86 (1944). The state Supreme Court ruled not that constitutional autonomy of religion required dismissal, but state trust law. It said that the enforcement of the trust was the exclusive domain of the state Attorney General, opening the door to possible future action by the state.

[87] It is well documented that those churches who are in distinct minorities and communities tend to fare less well than the larger and better-known religious communities. Von Keetch, 'The Need for Legislation to Enshrine Free Exercise in the Land Use Context', 32 *U.C. Davis L.Rev.* 735, 743 (1999).

[88] 494 US 872 (1990).

opportunity, with no notice or opportunity for briefing and argument, to rewrite the substantive rules applicable to the Free Exercise Clause. Prior to this decision, a valid Free Exercise claim could be trumped if the government showed (1) that it had a compelling reason to limit or prohibit the activity and (2) that the means chosen were the narrowest way in which the interest could be accomplished. After *Smith*, any rule which was facially neutral and did not discriminate on the basis of religion would no longer have to be defended by the government under this 'compelling interest analysis'. Rather, the burden would shift to the religious adherents to show why the government acted irrationally. As practitioners know, the burdens of proof and going forward (and the degrees of difficulty associated with them) often determine the outcome before the case is filed. The new burden on religious adherents was steep.

The reaction from the religious community was swift and furious condemnation. It was seen as adding fuel to an already difficult situation faced by religious organizations dealing with the creeping power of an indifferent government. Although the twists and turns of the reaction to *Smith* are far beyond the paper,[89] a brief summary is needed. At the request of religious and civil liberties groups, the Congress passed and the President signed the Religious Freedom Restoration Act in 1993.[90] Although the RFRA in fact only created new statutory procedural rules and a cause of action for religious adherents, the unfortunate choice of the word 'restoration' in the title meant that the courts could see this as an effort by the Congress to invade the constitutional authority of the Supreme Court to interpret constitutional law. The Supreme Court indeed saw RFRA as an excuse for a constitutional 'food fight'. In 1997, the Court declared the RFRA unconstitutional as applied to the states in a case brought by the archbishop of San Antonio, Texas, challenging the refusal of a local city to approve a church renovation to allow the rapidly growing faith community a suitable place to worship.[91] Congress then proceeded to consider a Religious Liberty Protection Act. In summer 2000, a Bill was

---

[89] See, for example, the collection of papers in 56 *University of Montana Law Review* (1995). See also, the testimony before the House and Senate Committee hearings on religious freedom after *Smith* in the 105th Congress.

[90] 42 USC 2000bb, et seq. (1994).

[91] *City of Boerne v Flores*, 521 US 507 (1997).

passed by an overwhelming margin in the US House of Representatives. It was stalled in the Senate where civil rights groups, responding in part to the call of homosexual rights organizations, demanded that the Bill be amended (among several reasons) so as not to allow religious organizations to use the Act as a source of protection against local and state civil rights ordinances.[92] To break the impasse, in August 2000, the Congress passed and, in September 2000, the President signed the Religious Land Use and Institutionalized Persons Act, which provided that local and state governments and prison authorities alone would have to answer for a limited but important number of clashes between religion and public authorities.[93]

Indeed, land use authorities were the major source of complaint by religious organizations. In some parts of the United States, land use authorities attempt to protect historic religious properties from demolition or renovation.[94] In parts of the United States that are rapidly growing, land use authorities act to restrain growth of all entities, including churches and church schools, through limited hours of operation, limiting the numbers of worshippers, controlling the size of parking and other similar restrictions. These rules, stated broadly and neutrally, usually do not single out religious organizations for disparate treatment. Yet, plainly, a rule that permits organizations to operate from 8 a.m. until 10 p.m. means that religious organizations could only have sunrise services or midnight mass at their peril.[95] A limit on the number of worshippers is especially offensive as people could be turned away from public worship because of the administrative convenience of regulators.[96] Unfortunately, these are real examples. Other rules have a disparate impact on religious organizations because of the nature of the physical space they occupied. A rule taxing rainwater

---

[92] See information collected at *www.atheists.org/flash.line/rlpa29.htm*.

[93] 42 USC § 2000cc, et seq.

[94] *Keeler v City of Cumberland*, 940 F.Supp. 879 (D. Md. 1996).

[95] The legislative background of the RLUIPA, including statements by both houses of Congress and a legislative report with numerous examples (for the support of the earlier RLPA) is provided in detail at *www.becketfund.org*. See also Testimony of Mark Chopko on need for federal legislation, *www.house.gov/judiciary/222353.htm* (March, 1998).

[96] Re: Sunnyside Centenary United Methodist Church No. LUR 99–00768 CU EN, Part IV (Portland, Oregon, 14 Jan. 2000) (no more than 70 persons allowed for worship).

drainage by the linear foot would tax a for-profit skyscraper a much smaller amount than a religious property which had extensive parking around several low rise buildings.[97]

In situations that are not covered under the rubrics of the law of land use or institutionalized persons, religious organizations are now relying on Free Speech and Free Association rights under the First Amendment, as opposed to a robust Free Exercise right. A refusal, for example, to allow a student publication offering a religious perspective on campus events to be funded in the same way as non-religious publications, was invalidated under the Free Speech clause.[98] A similar result occurred in a case in which a school district allowed non-religious community organizations to have access to school facilities, but not religious organizations.[99] Under the *Smith* rule, the Supreme Court majority said the religious organizations seeking exemption or accommodation should find relief in the political, not the judicial, process. What happened to RFRA is evidence of the weakness of that approach.

As a result, there is increasing pressure to use the agencies of government to force religion to conform to personal or secular standards and preferences. The death of the Religious Liberty Protection Act in the United States Senate, when religious organizations refused to submit to secular levelling, shows that this conflict is serious and possibly not reconcilable. The pressure on religious organizations is significant. As noted above, for example, part of the controversy surrounding charitable choice initiatives is a demand that, if faith-based organizations participate in government programmes, they must surrender their religious exemption under the federal employment statute. Claims have been filed with the federal Equal Employment Opportunity Commission to force religious organizations to choose between secular principles and their own pastoral needs. For example, it is generally thought that the ministry exception applies to the selection of faculty in seminaries (including a determination by religious authorities

---

[97] One could make a similar set of observations about limitations on religious activity in prison. For example, cancellation of prisoner activities at Christmas included cancelling religious services, which were considered to be just another 'activity'.

[98] *Rosenberger v Board of Rectors* (see n. 44).

[99] *Lamb's Chapel v Center Moriches School Dist.*, 508 US 384 (1993); see *Good News Club v Milford School Dist.*, 533 US 98 (2001).

alone who is most suitable to educate new clergy). That rule is not accepted by some administrators and was disregarded in a recent administrative case involving a Lutheran seminary.[100]

Disgruntled adherents are resorting to governmental administrative power to enforce a kind of creeping 'pervasive secularization' on religious organizations. Government contends that it has the power to define religion and the power to define, of course, is a power to confine. In some states, there are efforts by state employment administrators to limit exceptions and accommodations to those job positions that are 'purely religious'.[101] The government, of course, will tell the religious organization which positions are so qualified.

A broader initiative aimed at Catholic institutions is the campaign being conducted to eliminate statutes designed to protect the conscientious objections of Catholic employers to the broader secular culture that accepts contraception and abortion. Until recently, it was beyond question that government and the larger society would accommodate Catholic health care and other community outreach organizations in a sincere effort to respect differing religious traditions. No more. In at least twenty states there have been efforts, at times secret and swift, to amend state insurance laws requiring that, if an employer provides prescription drug coverage, the employer must provide coverage for approved contraceptives.[102] When confronted, the proponents offer a very narrow exemption designed to accommodate only those religious organizations that are serving members of their own community, employ numbers of their own community *and* engage in the inculcation of religion. If one is promoting the social gospel, in other words, that entity is not entitled to protection. There are even comments made that Catholic agencies providing welfare and health care are 'secular' anyway. The Catholic Bishops of

---

[100] Action by Philadelphia District EEOC Office against Gettysburg Theological College in *Steenhuisen v ELCA*, Charge No. 170960799 (21 Oct. 1997).

[101] Montgomery County, Maryland Human Rights Ordinance, § 27–19(d)(2) (that county is home to the international headquarters of the Seventh-day Adventist Church, which has only hired Adventists since the nineteenth century). That provision was declared unconstitutional in *Montrose Christian School v Walsh*, 770 A.2d 111, 128, 129 (Maryland 2001).

[102] In addition, there are thirteen states where the issue is being introduced *www.covermypills.org/facts/states.asp*. Some states have no religious exemption; some only a narrow one.

California have challenged that state's law in a very important lawsuit designed to test whether government has the power to define and confine religion under a broader secular mandate.[103] Religious organizations that do not share the views of the Catholic Church on contraception and abortion have rallied to the Catholic bishops' cause, recognizing that this case presents a paradigm example of the clash between religious autonomy and the need to protect, as a matter of constitutional principle, the rights of religious institutions on the one hand, and the pervasive and levelling authority of government on the other.

In restating the problem, the answer is suggested. There is a need for vigorous and complete Free Exercise protection, not only of individuals, but of institutions. One of the main benefits of the *Smith* opinion is a reference in the majority opinion that the Court did not intend to remake the free exercise law protecting the internal autonomy of religious organizations against government scrutiny.[104] If so, perhaps the *Smith* rule suggests both an end to and for itself.

Final Observations

The United States Constitution described not detailed rules but broader goals. Its aim was civic peace intended to last over centuries, guiding those who would lead the new republic and its citizens towards principles that, if followed, would protect them from internal strife. As directed by the Religion Clauses of the First Amendment, the new federal government was formally disentangled from institutions of religion and individual conscience was formally protected. It is clear that the framing principles did not allow individuals (or groups) to threaten the public good. Neither did it alter the reality, both in that society and in the present one, that the institutions of religion and government, while separate, must collaborate to build the public good. These principles,

---

[103] *Catholic Charities of Sacramento v Superior Court*, No. C037025 (filed 20 Nov. 2000) (statute stayed pending oral argument). Subsequently, the California Court of Appeal rejected the constitutional arguments. 109 Cal. Rptr. 2d 176 (App. 2001). Review has been granted by the California Supreme Court and a decision is expected by early 2003. 112 Cal. Rptr. 2d 258 (S.Ct. 2001).

[104] *Smith*, 494 US at 877 (citing associational rights and autonomy cases).

however well intended, were not clearly followed. They have been applied and refined in the crucible of judicial review, mostly in the last fifty or so years, in litigation. The society, as it has grown and changed and become more diverse, has trusted more the power of the state rather than the inherent value of religion.

Common law judicial review has lifted the power of the state over religion in dangerous ways, as the purveyor of benefits, the grantor of exemptions and the allocator of programmatic solutions. Liability systems, inherent in the process of judicial review, have been pressed by aggrieved citizens to impose secular standards on religious organizations. It is my thesis that the absence of clear, well-articulated protection for the institutional rights of religion exacerbates this situation. Such a power resides in the Religion Clauses, implicit, among other examples, in the behaviour of the framing generation that placed religion in an exalted place and explicit in the autonomy and neutrality principles that limited government. The institutions of religion were firmly in charge of the engines of social welfare – education, health care and relief. While the United States Supreme Court has made plain the civil courts lack the competence to adjudicate cases involving the internal affairs of religious organizations, the actions of subordinate courts and government agencies at all levels test those limits. The protection of institutional rights is inherent in the development of constitutional rights in the United States, recognizing first the right of individual conscience against any power of government and the right of like-minded believers to bind themselves together by common, religious principles. But the protection of the group is far more than the assertion of some aggregation of individual rights. The institution itself has rights deserving protection, and its leaders have the right and ability to speak to important questions affecting the common good of the country.

Because the judicial philosophy of contemporary society enhances both the power of government and the rights of individuals, the equally and historically compelling case for the rights of mediating institutions, such as religion, tends to be left behind, along with the sense that the public good must serve as the benchmark against which demands of individual right or governmental power must be evaluated. Plainly, the Constitution can and must serve to protect personal rights, but it must also protect the integrity of religious institutions. The power of government must be carefully circumscribed by workable principles lest the good, uniqueness and diversity of religion be lost to the levelling engine of government. As Baptist scholar James Woods has said, when we lose the right to be different, we lose the right to be free. As countries experiment with ways in which to enhance the protection of individual rights, they should be aware, looking to the US experience, that protection of individual rights must be in careful balance against the legitimate and compelling needs of government and the integrity of those mediating structures that have served to support, nourish and preserve the lives and welfare of every individual and added stability and morality to the state.

5

Religious Liberty in European Jurisprudence

JAVIER MARTÍNEZ-TORRÓN

The European Court of Human Rights and Religion

The protection of religious freedom in the international sphere has gone hand in hand with the general instruments aimed at the safeguarding of human rights.[1] In that sphere,[2] the European system is

[1] See generally C. Evans, *Freedom of Religion under the European Convention on Human Rights* (Oxford, Oxford University Press, 2001); M. D. Evans, *Religious Liberty and International Law in Europe* (Cambridge, Cambridge University Press, 1997); L. M. Hammer, *The International Human Right to Freedom of Conscience* (Burlington, Ashgate, 2001); J. Martínez-Torrón and R. Navarro-Valls, 'The Protection of Religious Freedom in the System of the Council of Europe', in B. Tahzib-Lie, C. Durham and T. Lindholm (eds), *Freedom of Religion and Belief: A Desk Book* (Dordrecht, Martinus Nijhoff, forthcoming); J. Martínez-Torrón, 'La protección internacional de la libertad religiosa', in *Tratado de Derecho Eclesiástico* (Pamplona, Eunsa, 1994), 141–239; B. G. Tahzib, *Freedom of Religion or Belief: Ensuring Effective International Legal Protection* (Dordrecht, Martinus Nijhoff, 1995). For a summary of the concept of religious freedom in international documents, see J. Duffar, 'La Liberté religieuse dans les textes internationaux', in *La libertad religiosa: Memoria del IX Congreso Internacional de Derecho Canónico* (Mexico City, UNAM, 1996), 471–97. For the purposes of this essay, I have preferred to focus on the case law of the European Court of Human Rights and reduce the bibliographical references to a minimum; further references can be found in the works previously cited.

[2] It is well known that the first decisive step towards the international protection of human rights was the Universal Declaration of Human Rights in 1948. After it there have been two main milestones in the history of UN efforts to encourage respect for religious liberty around the world. The first is the 1966 International Covenant on Civil and Political Rights (Art. 18). The second is the 1981 Declaration on the Elimination of All Forms of Intolerance and of Discrimination Based on Religion or Belief. There are other initiatives adopted by international organizations with a more limited geographical reach. It is worth mentioning here: the 1969 American Convention on Human Rights (Art. 12); the 1981 African Charter on Human and Peoples' Rights (Art. 12); and some of the documents produced by the Organization (formerly Conference) for Security and Cooperation in Europe (OSCE), in particular the Vienna Concluding Document of 1989 (especially principles 16–17).

usually considered the most successful one, a model of efficiency. The reason is that the European Convention on Human Rights is the only international convention whose provisions are enforced by a specific judicial machinery: the European Court of Human Rights, located in Strasbourg (hereinafter ECtHR or 'the Court').

The European Convention on Human Rights (hereinafter ECHR or 'the Convention'), signed in 1950[3] and successively amended by several protocols, is the first and principal achievement of the Council of Europe.[4] The ECHR created a specific judicial body to guarantee an efficient protection of the rights and freedoms recognized in the text. This has made of the Convention a unique instrument for the advancement of human rights in the international sphere. The ECHR effectively functions as a 'Bill of Rights' for democratic Europe and the ECtHR works as its constitutional court. Within the Council of Europe system, only the decisions of the Court have binding force on member states.

The ECtHR began its activities in 1959. Its structure and procedure have been substantially changed by Protocol 11 to the Convention, which came into force in November 1998.[5] One of the most interesting and important modifications introduced by Protocol 11 is that individuals have been granted the right of direct

---

[3] The European Convention was signed in Rome on 4 November 1950 and came into force on 3 September 1953.

[4] The Council of Europe was founded in 1949. Its prevalent aim was to gather the European democratic countries and reinforce the respect for human rights. Initially the Council of Europe counted ten member states (Belgium, Denmark, France, Ireland, Italy, Luxembourg, the Netherlands, Norway, the United Kingdom and Sweden). Membership has expanded as democracy has spread throughout Europe. Today there are forty-three member states. The most recent ones to be accepted are Armenia and Azerbaijan, 25 January 2001. Information about the Council of Europe, its organization, activities, documentation, etc. can be obtained on line at *http://www.coe.int/*.

[5] The ECtHR functions now on a permanent basis. It has as many judges as there are states who have signed the ECHR and consequently accepted the jurisdiction of the Court. The judges are elected by the Parliamentary Assembly of the Council of Europe from a list of three candidates presented by the state. They serve for a term of six years. The full text of the ECHR as amended by Protocol 11, and the rest of the basic texts of the Convention, can be obtained on the website of the ECtHR: *http://www.echr.coe.int/* (visited February 2002). All the decisions of the Court are now available on the same web pages.

access to the Court.[6] Today, the ECtHR may receive applications directly from any person, non-governmental organization or group of individuals. After an application has been declared admissible, a chamber or a grand-chamber decides on the merits.[7] The ECtHR, following the text of the Convention, has been traditionally inclined to facilitate a friendly settlement between the parties, provided that human rights are duly respected.[8] If this is not possible, the Court will follow its ordinary judicial procedures and deliver a judgment that is final and has binding force for the State concerned. The experience of more than forty years reveals that member states normally accept and execute the decisions of the Court.[9]

As in every other comprehensive international document concerning human rights, religious freedom is one of the rights included in the Convention and is therefore placed under the protective umbrella of the ECtHR. Three provisions of the

[6] Before 1998, they were entitled only to file an application before the European Commission of Human Rights, claiming that a member state had infringed the Convention. The Commission was not a judicial body, but acted as a filter. It decided which applications were admissible and deserved an examination on the merits. These were transmitted to the Court, accompanied by a report on the merits of the case. Commonly these decisions were based upon legal reasoning more expansive and complex than what one might expect from a non-judicial body. In practice the Commission often acted as a court rather than an administrative auxiliary body. Thus there is a type of case law of the Commission which parallels that of the Court and which includes the reports on the merits elaborated in the few cases declared admissible. Protocol 11 eliminated the Commission. The filter function previously performed by the Commission is now undertaken by committees of three judges.

[7] All applications are first examined by a committee of three judges. A committee may declare an individual application inadmissible by a unanimous vote, either for procedural reasons or because it considers the application 'manifestly ill-founded'. Otherwise, a chamber of seven judges will decide on the admissibility and merits of the case. The Court may also sit in a grand chamber of seventeen judges if a case raises an issue of general importance – especially when a serious question concerning the interpretation of the Convention is involved, or when the decision of a chamber might have been inconsistent with the case law of the Court. In chambers as well as in the grand chamber there shall sit as an *ex-officio* member the judge elected in respect of the State Party concerned by the application. The composition and procedure of the Court are regulated in section II ECHR, Arts. 19–51.

[8] See Arts. 38–9 ECHR.

[9] If the Court finds that there has been a violation of the Convention, the party injured may be afforded a just satisfaction. The Committee of Ministers of the Council of Europe supervise the execution of the judgment. See Arts. 41 and 46 ECHR.

Convention deal with religion. Freedom of thought, conscience and religion is recognized in Article 9 ECHR.[10] Article 14 enshrines the principle of equality and prohibits discrimination based on religion.[11] Article 2 of the First Protocol (1952) endorses the rights of parents to choose the religious or ideological orientation of their children's education.[12]

Before 1993, the ECtHR did not take much interest in questions raised by the exercise of religious freedom.[13] Apparently, the Strasbourg jurisdiction was persuaded that there was no need to intervene in that sort of conflict, as if it were an implied application of the 'margin of appreciation' doctrine whereby national authorities had a reasonable margin to interpret the rights and freedoms included in the Convention, adapting them to the relevant domestic law. The reality is that applications based on Article 9 ECHR were almost always declared inadmissible, very often as manifestly ill-founded.[14] The situation has changed remarkably in the last few years. Since 1993 the ECtHR has decided more than twenty cases related to freedom of religion.

---

[10] Article 9: '1. Everyone has the right to freedom of thought, conscience and religion; this right includes freedom to change his religion or belief and freedom, either alone or in community with others and in public or private, to manifest his religion or belief, in worship, teaching, practice and observance. 2. Freedom to manifest one's religion or beliefs shall be subject only to such limitations as are prescribed by law and are necessary in a democratic society in the interests of public safety, for the protection of public order, health or morals, or for the protection of the rights and freedoms of others.'

[11] Article 14: 'The enjoyment of the rights and freedoms set forth in this Convention shall be secured without discrimination on any ground such as sex, race, colour, language, religion, political or other opinion, national or social origin, association with a national minority, property, birth or other status.'

[12] Article 2 of the Protocol: 'No person shall be denied the right to education. In the exercise of any functions which it assumes in relation to education and to teaching, the State shall respect the right of parents to ensure such education and teaching in conformity with their own religious and philosophical convictions.'

[13] Indeed, the first case decided in the light of Article 9 was *Kokkinakis v Greece*, 25 May 1993. Until then only one case had raised a religious or conscience issue (and the decision was taken with reference to Article 2 of the First Protocol): *Kjeldsen, Busk Madsen and Pedersen v Denmark*, 7 December 1976. For an analysis of the case law of the European Court and Commission of Human Rights see the works by M. D. Evans (262–362) and Martínez-Torrón cited in note 1, where further bibliographical references can be found.

[14] The European Commission, not the Court, was then competent to decide when an application should be declared inadmissible (see above, nn. 6–7).

The reasons for this change are not entirely clear, but they may be connected with the recent expansion of the Council of Europe throughout Eastern Europe. For several decades, most member states protected religious freedom according to high standards, so that the ECtHR could maintain its 'margin of appreciation' approach in this field. However, beginning in the 1990s, there has been a generalized incorporation of post-communist countries into the system of the Convention. These countries do not have a recent democratic tradition; in particular, religious freedom was seriously restricted for a long time. They want to reconstruct a legal system based on respect for human rights, but in most of them there are strong long-established churches – often national churches belonging to the Orthodox tradition – that are not particularly friendly to more recent religious groups who develop an intense proselytizing activity. These circumstances may have moved the Court to define more carefully the content and limits of the right to freedom of thought, conscience and religion.

The case law of the ECtHR on religious freedom is a positive reality in itself, for it has shed a new light on some principles of the Convention which had remained in the shade for a long time and which are bound to develop a significant role in the future, especially as far as Eastern European countries are concerned. In my view, the Court could and should have adopted a more extensive interpretation of freedom of religion and belief. In this chapter I will analyse the main strengths and deficiencies of the case law of the ECtHR with regard to the individual as well as to the institutional aspects of religious freedom,[15] pointing out some aspects of the ECtHR's jurisprudence that ought to be modified to provide a more complete protection of religious liberty.[16]

[15] This analysis must be necessarily brief and include also the doctrine developed by the European Commission of Human Rights, eliminated in 1998 (see above, n. 6). By and large, the understanding of religious freedom proposed in the Commission's case law has been adopted by the jurisprudence of the Court after 1993.

[16] In this chapter, I will use the term 'religious freedom', 'religious liberty' or 'freedom of religion and belief', with essentially the same meaning as 'freedom of thought, conscience and religion' (the latter is the literal expression utilized by the ECHR and by most international documents). The reason is that, in my opinion, the reference to thought, conscience and religion does not intend to separate three different rights but merely indicate diverse profiles of the same fundamental right. On the other hand, as religion seems to be – historically as well as conceptually – the centre around which this right has been construed, the wording 'religious freedom' may be considered sufficiently expressive. For a more extensive explanation of this idea, see Martínez-Torrón, *La protección internacional*, 186–93.

Church and State Relations

As with every human right, freedom of thought, conscience and religion is primarily an individual right, but it has a very significant institutional or 'collective' dimension as well. Since the late 1970s the Strasbourg jurisdiction has firmly held that every religious confession is entitled to religious freedom, no matter whether it is a traditional major church or a recent and atypical group – it would be artificial to differentiate between the religious freedom of a church and that of its followers.[17] A religious organization may, as such, exercise on behalf of its members the rights guaranteed by Article 9 ECHR, and it is therefore fully entitled to file the corresponding application before the ECtHR.[18]

Accordingly, all religious denominations must have freedom to act in any country, without being the object of an unjustified restriction or persecution. This principle applies also to minority groups that defend moral values conflicting with the values widely accepted by a certain society, and constitutes one of the main criteria by which to judge the legitimacy of the European systems of church–state relations within the framework of the ECHR.

In this regard, the Strasbourg jurisprudence has been generally respectful of the systems in which, for historical or socio-political reasons, the state collaborates with religious groups, even when there is a privileged collaboration with a traditional major church. The Court has implicitly recognized that there is a certain margin of appreciation with respect to the ways that states structure their relations with religious communities. In particular, various forms of cooperation between the state and religious confessions can exist, even when the state does not cooperate in a strictly equal fashion with all religions. Equality (Article 14 ECHR) must be applied rigorously in many contexts to preserve religious freedom, but some flexibility is permissible in structuring cooperation with religious communities, particularly where failure to do so would disrupt long-established patterns and expectations. Thus, not even

---

[17] See the European Commission's decision in Dec. Adm. 7805/77, 16 *Decisions and Reports* 70 (application filed by the Church of Scientology against Sweden).

[18] See *The Jewish Liturgical Association Cha'are Shalom Ve Tsedek v France*, 27 June 2000, n. 72; *Metropolitan Church of Bessarabia v Moldova*, 13 December 2001, n. 101.

systems of a hidden confessionality of the state (as in Greece),[19] or an established church (as in England or in some Scandinavian countries) have been considered contrary to the Convention, so long as membership of the official church is not mandatory.[20] The important thing, in the Court's view, is that the relationships of privileged collaboration do not produce, as a side effect, significant discriminatory impact on individuals or unjustified harm to the freedom to act that the rest of the groups and individuals must enjoy in religious and ideological matters.

Other expressions of state cooperation with religious bodies have been also accepted as compatible with the Convention, although they did not correspond with the principle of equality. For instance, to grant financial aid to some churches (in the form of tax exemptions,[21] or in the form of assigning some of the taxes collected by the state to sustain the official church[22] or the church to which the tax payer belongs[23]); to grant to the churches standing to sue their followers before the state courts in order to enforce the payment of religious taxes;[24] and to collaborate with the teaching

[19] Thus, in the *Kokkinakis* case, after a careful scrutiny of the legal restrictions on religious proselytism in Greece – and notwithstanding the fact that the judgment was in favour of the applicant – the Court did not question that the close connection between the Greek Orthodox Church and the state was a legitimate political choice (*Kokkinakis v Greece*, 25 May 1993). The same conclusion can be drawn from the Commission's report in the case of *The Holy Monasteries v Greece*, a dispute on ecclesiastical property, which ended with a friendly settlement (see Rep. Com. 13092/87 and 13984/88, 14 January 1993; the decision of the Court, accepting the terms of the agreement, was delivered on 1 September 1997).

[20] This was the European Commission's reasoning in the *Darby* case; see Rep. Com. 11581/85, n. 45. The Commission had also admitted that in a system of an established church as in Sweden the government can dismiss a minister for intentionally neglecting the civil duties attached to his religious office (see Dec. Adm. 11045/84, 42 *Decisions and Reports* 247).

[21] Dec. Adm. 17522/90 (the 'El Salvador' Baptist Church argued that it suffered a discriminatory treatment because its places of worship were not exempted from the real property taxes in Spain, as Catholic premises were).

[22] Rep. Com. 11581/85 (*Darby* case, concerning the payment of local taxes aimed at supporting financially the Swedish Lutheran Church).

[23] Dec. Adm. 10616/83, 40 *Decisions and Reports* 284ff. (concerning the ecclesiastical tax in a Swiss town, aimed at supporting financially the churches which were legally recognized; the tax had to be paid by the people registered as members of the respective church in the civil registry).

[24] Dec. Adm. 9781/82, 37 *Decisions and Reports* 42ff. (the Catholic Church in Austria sued a Catholic married couple before the civil courts to claim the payment of the ecclesiastical tax that Catholics must pay in every Austrian diocese).

of the Christian doctrine by the official church in public schools, provided that this teaching is done in an objective and pluralist manner, and assuming that the collaboration of the state cannot be considered indoctrination.[25]

The status of the traditional major churches has been so profoundly respected that sometimes it has been given preference even over freedom of expression. Thus, the ECtHR has held that, when free expression of ideas is characterized as blasphemy, the protection of the religious feelings of citizens must prevail. In the cases of *Otto-Preminger-Institut* and *Wingrove*, the Court upheld the ban on the commercial distribution of some films that had been considered offensive to the feelings of Christian people by the Austrian and British authorities respectively.[26]

In summary, the attitude of the Court is that Article 9 ECHR is aimed at providing an adequate guarantee of freedom of religion and belief, but not at establishing certain uniform criteria for church–state relations in the Council of Europe member states. Underlying this approach is the idea that the state's attitude towards religion is primarily a political issue, and is the result, to a large extent, of the historical tradition and the social circumstances of each country (although the natural evolution of European democracies might lead to a common model of church– state relations, or at least to some common patterns). On the other hand, Article 9 has not been construed by the ECtHR as imposing a compulsory official secularism (*laïcité*). The references of ECtHR to state neutrality must not be interpreted as demanding a separation between church and state; neutrality has been understood by the Court as impartiality, that is, the obligation to respect the religious choices of citizens, whether or not they adapt to the widespread

---

[25] Dec. Adm. 4733/71, 14 *Yearbook of the European Convention* 664ff., and Dec. Adm. 10491/83, 51 *Decisions and Reports* 41ff. (concerning religious education in Swedish public schools).

[26] The case of *Otto-Preminger-Institut v Austria*, 20 September 1994, related to a satirical film entitled *Council in Heaven*, in which God was presented as a senile man prostrated before the Devil and Jesus Christ as a mentally retarded person; an erotic relationship between the Devil and the Virgin was also insinuated. The case of *Wingrove v United Kingdom*, 25 November 1996, referred to a video of eighteen minutes' duration containing a peculiar interpretation of St Teresa of Avila's ecstasy, in a pornographic setting with homosexual connotations.

religious beliefs in the country, and whether such beliefs are popular or unpopular. In the words of the Court, 'the State's duty of neutrality and impartiality . . . is incompatible with any power on the State's part to assess the legitimacy of religious beliefs'.[27]

Minority Religious Groups

Within the foregoing context, in recent years the Strasbourg Court has paid increasing attention to the rights of minority religious groups under Article 9 ECHR. Its approach is that such groups are entitled to a genuine freedom to act, and not merely to toleration. This broad principle may be illustrated by reference to the case law of the Court.

Interpretation of the Equality Principle

Under Article 14, discrimination on religious grounds is forbidden.[28] Therefore, individuals have the right not to suffer discriminatory treatment on account of their membership of a minority religion, even if their belief and behaviour contrast sharply with commonly accepted social customs. Thus, in *Hoffmann* the ECtHR held that differential treatment on the sole ground of religion is unacceptable when a national court decides on the custody of

---

[27] *Metropolitan Church of Bessarabia v Moldova*, 13 December 2001, n. 123.

[28] More precisely, what Article 14 prohibits is discrimination in regard to 'the rights and freedoms set forth in this Convention', but not in regard to other provisions of national laws. This latter aspect, which certainly enlarges the scope of the equality principle, is the object of Protocol 12 to the Convention. Article 1 of Protocol 12 (*General prohibition of discrimination*) provides: 'The enjoyment of any right set forth by law shall be secured without discrimination on any ground such as sex, race, colour, language, religion, political or other opinion, national or social origin, association with a national minority, property, birth or other status.' Protocol 12 was open for signature on 4 November 2000, but is not yet in force (ten ratifications are necessary for its entry into force; twenty-six countries have signed the new Protocol but to date only one – Georgia – has ratified it).

children in a case of divorce.[29] Similarly, even though the doctrine of the Court is not conclusive on this point, members of minority religious groups may not be kept under surveillance in the absence of a compelling justification other than mere religious affiliation.[30] The same rule must be applied to the confinement of people in order to subject them to a process of deprogramming from their membership in a group characterized as a sect: this is something that cannot be done against a person's will.[31]

The prohibition of discrimination embodied in Article 14 ECHR, in principle, is applicable not only to discrimination against individuals but also to discrimination against religious groups as such. However, the ECtHR does not seem to have interpreted this

---

[29] *Hoffmann v Austria*, 23 June 1993. The case was decided in the light of Article 14 in conjunction with Article 8 ECHR (right to respect for private and family life). A housewife had converted to the Jehovah's Witnesses and taken her children with her when divorce proceedings were still pending. The Court reversed the decisions of Austrian national courts, which had granted the children's custody to the father. In my opinion, although the principles stated by the ECtHR are right, the decision was wrong: the wife had unilaterally broken the marital agreement, according to which children had to be educated in the common religion of the parents (they were both Roman Catholics at the time). It is very significant that the decision was adopted by five votes to four. See the dissenting opinion of Judge Mifsud Bonnici. In another recent case concerning custody of children after their parents' divorce (*Ignaccolo-Zenide v Rumania*, 25 January 2001), the father alleged – at a certain stage of the proceedings before Romanian courts – that the mother belonged to a sect not recognized in Romania (cf. n. 45 of the decision). This assertion, however, does not seem to have had any important effect either on the decisions of the national courts or on that of the ECtHR.

[30] *Tsavachidis v Greece*, 21 January 1999. The case related to the surveillance of Jehovah's Witnesses by the National Intelligence Service. It ended in a friendly settlement in which the Greek government agreed to pay a sum of money by way of costs and submitted a formal statement declaring that 'the Jehovah's Witnesses are not, and will not in the future be, subject to any surveillance on account of their religious beliefs'. By then the European Commission had already elaborated its report on the merits of the case, and expressed the opinion that there had been a violation of Article 8 (13 votes to 4) but there had been no violation of Article 9 (9 votes to 8).

[31] *Riera Blume and others v Spain*, 14 October 1999. The case referred to some members of the so-called 'Centro Esotérico de Investigaciones' (Esoteric Research Centre). The applicants' homes were searched following a judicial order, and the applicants were subsequently confined in a nearby hotel against their will for deprogramming; the confinement did not follow any judicial order, and was carried out by a private 'anti-sects' association with some participation by the Catalan police. The Court avoided pronouncing any opinion under Article 9, and decided in favour of the applicants in the light of Article 5(1) (right to liberty and security).

principle in like fashion. An extensive interpretation of the principle of equality was adopted in the case of *Canea Catholic Church*. There the Court held that every religious denomination has not only the right to be accepted as existing *de facto*, but also the right to be granted legal personality under conditions that are fair and similar to those applied to other denominations. National governments cannot unreasonably discriminate between religious confessions with regard to the requirements that they – or their institutions – must fulfil in order to be acknowledged as legal persons in the secular sphere. This is particularly the case when legal personality is indispensable for claiming rights before the state courts. Otherwise, in addition to the implications for the right of religious freedom, there would be a violation of the right to a hearing by a tribunal, which is an integral part of the right to a fair trial (Article 6 ECHR).[32] In the recent decision *Metropolitan Church of Bessarabia*, the ECtHR has reaffirmed, unanimously, that Article 9 ECHR includes the right of new religious denominations to obtain legal personality in conditions equal to recognized churches, especially when the refusal to register a group causes an unjustified restriction on the exercise of religious freedom in its collective dimension (for example, with regard to internal autonomy, religious meetings, public worship, ownership of real property, commercialization of religious objects).[33]

[32] *Canea Catholic Church v Greece*, 16 December 1997. The case related to the Roman Catholic Church of the Virgin Mary in Canea, built in the thirteenth century, which is the cathedral of the Roman Catholic diocese of Crete. Two people living next to the church had demolished one of the surrounding walls, and opened a window looking onto the church in the wall of their own building. The Greek courts denied legal standing to the church, as it had not complied with the formal requirements generally stated by the Civil Code to acquire legal personality. This denial contradicted an abundant administrative and judicial practice in Greece in relation to the Roman Catholic Church. Furthermore, it constituted discrimination with regard to the Greek Orthodox Church and to the Jewish communities, which were granted legal personality and standing to sue without having to follow the civil formalities common to all associations. It is worth noting that the case was decided in the light of Article 6 (right to a fair trial), taken alone and together with Article 14. As a violation of Article 6 had been found, the Court declined to decide on the alleged violation of Article 9.

[33] See *Metropolitan Church of Bessarabia v Moldova*, 13 December 2001, especially nn. 105, 118 and 129. The case related to the creation, in 1992, of a new autonomous local Orthodox Church that claimed to be the successor, in the canonical order, of the old Metropolitan Church of Bessarabia, which existed until 1944. The new church comprised approximately one million members among Moldavian people, with 160 clergy, 117 communities in Moldavian territory, and some communities in other Eastern European countries. The Moldavian government had repeatedly refused to recognize the church.

By contrast, an example of a restrictive interpretation of the equality principle is the decision *Cha'are Shalom Ve Tsedek*, a complex case regarding the ritual slaughter of animals.[34] A strongly divided court – ten votes against seven – considered that national authorities enjoy a margin of appreciation to give different legal advantages to religious denominations, as far as it is not proved that an individual's freedom to practise his or her religion has been impaired. More precisely, it was held that neither the right to religious freedom nor the equality principle had been violated by the fact that French authorities granted an administrative permit for ritual slaughter exclusively to the Jewish Consistorial Association of Paris, while denying that permit to a minority Jewish association of ultra-orthodox orientation.[35] According to the Court, religious freedom was respected since members of the applicant association could actually obtain meat that satisfied their religious practices – they could buy that sort of food from a number of butchers or import it from Belgium. The principle of equality was not infringed either; French authorities had a margin of free appreciation and were allowed to grant permits only to a single institution representing Jewish communities, by reasons of public health (to ensure due hygienic conditions) and public order (to foster reciprocal toleration between different religious options).[36]

[34] *The Jewish Liturgical Association Cha'are Shalom Ve Tsedek v France*, 27 June 2000.
[35] The Consistorial Association is an institution representing most of the main denominations within Judaism in France. The applicant association, Cha'are Shalom Ve Tsedek, is not included among them, and considered that the examination performed by the inspectors of the Consistorial Association was not meticulous enough to guarantee the religious purity of food. According to the French legislation and the European Union directives, ritual slaughter constitutes an exception to the general rules aimed to guarantee the due hygienic conditions and to avoid unnecessary suffering to animals. This exception is granted in order to respect the ritual laws of some religions, especially Judaism and Islam. Ritual slaughter may be performed only by those persons who have been authorized by the religious bodies specifically approved by the French administration.
[36] On the contrary, seven justices affirmed, in a joint dissenting opinion, that the ECtHR had interpreted the equality principle in an unacceptably restrictive way. In their view, the Court had failed to emphasize that the state is obliged to provide analogous legal treatment as a means to guarantee pluralism, which is an indispensable condition to the exercise of freedom. The dissenting justices considered that the Court had omitted to analyse whether the applicant minority Jewish association was in a situation analogous to the Jewish Consistorial Association of

In another recent case, *Thlimmenos*, the ECtHR has added a new interesting nuance to the interpretation of the principle of equality. According to the Court, Article 14 ECHR is violated not only when states treat differently persons in analogous situations without providing an objective and reasonable justification. 'The right not to be discriminated against in the enjoyment of the rights guaranteed under the Convention is also violated when States without an objective and reasonable justification fail to treat differently persons whose situations are significantly different.'[37] In this regard, the Court held that behaviour inspired by personal beliefs constitutes a relevant differentiating factor when determining the consequences deriving from a criminal conviction. In particular, when a person has been convicted of felony for refusing to perform military service on account of his religious beliefs, he can legitimately claim to be exempted from the general rule that disqualifies people convicted of a felony from entering the civil service.[38]

Worship, Proselytism and Internal Autonomy

The ECtHR has recognized the right of religious groups to possess and manage their own places of worship and meeting. To deny this right without due justification is incompatible with the

Paris, as far as the legislation on religious bodies was concerned: that is, whether it was a body of a religious nature, and whether it pursued religious aims and utilized equivalent means. If that was the case, as it seemed to be, the right approach would have been to examine whether the French administration had an 'objective and reasonable justification' to grant the requested administrative permit for ritual slaughter to one Jewish association, and to deny the same permit to the other. Apparently that justification did not exist, and consequently, the dissenting opinion concluded, the association Cha'are Shalom Ve Tsedek had been a victim of discrimination.

[37] *Thlimmenos v Greece*, 6 April 2000, n. 44.

[38] The applicant in the *Thlimmenos* case was a Jehovah's Witness who had been convicted of insubordination in 1983 for refusing to perform unarmed military service on account of his religious beliefs, at a time of general mobilization. He was sentenced to four years' imprisonment, and was released on parole after two years. In 1988, he passed a public examination to become a chartered accountant, a liberal profession which, until 1993, could be exercised only by those who became members of the Greek Institute of Chartered Accountants. In spite of his successful examination – he came second among sixty candidates – the Executive Board of the Institute refused to appoint him because, according to the law, a person who did not qualify for the civil service could not be appointed a chartered accountant, and a conviction for a felony constituted a disqualification for the civil service.

Convention, according to the decisions of the Court in *Manoussakis* and *Pentidis*. Both cases were the result of applications submitted by Jehovah's Witnesses, who claimed that the Greek law on places of worship had been applied to them in a discriminatory and hostile manner. The Greek legislation pre-scribes that opening a public place of worship requires prior explicit permission to be granted by the civil authorities.[39] After analysing the relevant legislation, the ECtHR concluded that it granted an excessive discretion to the Greek authorities and that there were not sufficient guarantees to ensure an objective decision on the permit, among other reasons because representatives of the Greek Orthodox Church intervened in the decision-making process.[40]

Proselytism by religious minorities was the focus of the ECtHR's attention in another two cases against Greece. In the *Kokkinakis* case, the Court held that Article 9 ECHR includes the right of individuals and religious groups to disseminate their doctrines and to gain new followers through proselytism, provided that they do not use abusive, fraudulent or violent means.[41] An elderly man, a follower of the Jehovah's Witnesses, had been arrested and sub-sequently sentenced by the Greek courts under the law that declares proselytism a crime. This law, enacted in 1938, followed the constitutional ban on proselytism, dating from 1844 and maintained in the 1975 Constitution. Both provisions are aimed at

[39] The alleged aim of this provision is to guarantee that the place is not run by secret sects, that there is no danger to public order or morals and that the place of worship will not be used as a cover for acts of proselytism, which is explicitly forbidden by the Greek Constitution.

[40] *Manoussakis and others v Greece*, 26 September 1996; *Pentidis and others v Greece*, 9 June 1997. The latter case ended with a friendly settlement. After the condemnatory judgment received in *Manoussakis*, the Greek government granted the administrative authorization required by the Jehovah's Witnesses.

[41] *Kokkinakis v Greece*, 25 May 1993. As indicated above, this was the first case decided by the ECtHR in the light of Article 9 ECHR. For a detailed comment on this decision see J. Martínez-Torrón, 'Libertad de proselitismo en Europa: A propósito de una reciente sentencia del Tribunal europeo de derechos humanos', *Quaderni di diritto e politica ecclesiastica* 59–71 (1994/1); J. Gunn, 'Adjudicating Rights of Conscience under the European Convention on Human Rights', in J. D. van der Vyver and J. Witte (eds), *Religious Human Rights in Global Perspective* (The Hague, Martinus Nijhoff, 1996), 305–30. On the problems involved in determining a concept of proselytism in international law, see N. Lerner, 'Proselytism, Change of Religion, and International Human Rights', 12 *Emory International Law Review* 477–561 (1998).

protecting the social status of the Greek Orthodox Church. The Court did not declare the Greek law incompatible with the European Convention, for it was possible to construe that law as a means to protect the rights and freedom of others. However, it held that the right of individuals and groups to disseminate their beliefs was part of the right to religious freedom enshrined in Article 9 ECHR. Consequently, the prohibition of Greek law was legitimate only as applied to 'improper proselytism', for instance, proselytism that entailed the use of violence, fraud or brainwashing.

More recently, in the *Larissis* case, the Court has added new interesting nuances to this doctrine, when proselytism is carried out in certain special environments, such as the armed forces. More precisely, it was held that restrictions on proselytism are legitimate when applied in a superior/subordinate relationship; that is, when a superior tries to convert a subordinate, even if it has been done merely through respectful conversations on religious topics. Such restrictions are justified by the need to avoid the risk that the relationship can degenerate, causing subordinates to act under improper pressure from their superiors. However, restrictions on proselytism are not justified when the same kind of religious conversation takes place between an officer and a civilian, even if the latter lives within a military environment, because they are not linked by any superior/subordinate relationship.[42]

Turning to the rights of religious groups, it seems natural that Article 9 ECHR should be construed to include the rights of religious groups to be recognized and to have internal autonomy and control of their own affairs. This interpretation has been recently supported by some decisions of the ECtHR. In the *Serif* case,[43] the Court held that, unless there is a 'pressing social need', the state is not entitled to interfere in a purely religious question decided by a religious community, even when that community is sharply divided over the issue. The possible social tension derived from that religious division is one of the unavoidable effects of pluralism, which is in turn inseparable from democracy.[44] In particular, 'the Court does not consider that, in democratic

---

[42] *Larissis and others v Greece*, 24 February 1998. The case involved three officers of the Greek Air Force who belonged to the Pentecostal Church.

[43] *Serif v Greece*, 14 December 1999, n. 52.

[44] See also recently, with regard to freedom of association, *Freedom and Democracy Party (ÖZDEP) v Turkey*, 8 December 1999, n. 37.

societies, the State needs to take measures to ensure that religious communities remain or are brought under a unified leadership'.[45] The case regarded the appointment of a religious Islamic leader (mufti) in a region of Greece (Thrace) with a significant Muslim population of Turkish origin. He had been elected by the Muslim community without the intervention of the state authorities as prescribed by Greek law governing the election and appointment of muftis.[46]

A similar doctrine has been expressed by the ECtHR in the subsequent decision *Hasan and Chaush*, which also concerned the intervention of state authorities in the election and appointment of a Muslim religious leader and the religious disputes between two different factions of the Bulgarian Muslim community, following the process of democratization commenced at the end of 1989.[47] The Court reiterated that national authorities interfere in the exercise of religious freedom when they fail to remain neutral with regard to changes in the leadership of a religious community, or when they try to force the community to come together under a single leadership against its own wishes.[48] In the recent case of *Metropolitan Church of Bessarabia*, the ECtHR has confirmed that doctrine for the third time in two years.[49]

---

[45] *Serif v Greece*, n. 52.

[46] It must be noted that the law had been changed a few days before the election took place and after it had been organized. The Greek government justified the intervention by the state by reference to the administrative and judicial functions exercised by muftis. The case also involved some interesting issues concerning certain international treaties signed by Greece in the 1910s and 1920s, but the Court decided not to express any opinion on the subject.

[47] *Hasan and Chaush v Bulgaria*, 26 October 2000. The Bulgarian government supported one of the rival religious leaders, after the inability, over some years, to reach any agreement. The Council of Ministers even disobeyed an order of the Bulgarian Supreme Court urging it to register Mr Hasan (the applicant) as the Chief Mufti in Bulgaria. The government did not provide any specific ground for its decision. It should be noted that, according to Bulgarian law, only the Muslim leadership registered by the Directorate of Religious Denominations enjoys the legal representation of the religious Islamic community and has the right to use its property and assets.

[48] In the present case, the Court concluded that governmental interference could not be considered legitimate under Article 9(2) ECHR, because national legislation gave a virtually unlimited power to public authorities to decide which religious leadership was the legitimate one and consequently had the right to be registered.

[49] See *Metropolitan Church of Bessarabia v Moldova*, 13 December 2001, especially n. 117. See above, n. 33.

The interpretation of Article 9 ECHR afforded by the foregoing religion cases is reinforced by other ECtHR decisions involving freedom of expression and freedom of association, in particular those concerning the dissolution of political parties for allegedly opposing principles of the Turkish Constitution.[50] In those cases, the Court declared that there is a close connection between freedom of association (Article 11 ECHR) and freedom of expression (Article 10 ECHR). In a democratic society, protection of the freedom to express an opinion, even when such opinion may 'offend, shock or disturb', is one of the objectives of freedom of assembly and association. In such a sensitive area, restrictions on freedom of association must be construed strictly and can be justified only by convincing and compelling reasons.

Naturally, this reasoning is also applicable to the freedom of thought, conscience and religion. It follows that, in this regard, religious freedom must be construed as broadly as the ECtHR has construed the freedom of association. The same is probably true with regard to the connection between freedom of religion and freedom of expression, because these provisions of the Convention are all aimed at protecting pluralism, without which – as the Court has repeatedly emphasized – democracy cannot exist. By implication, any limitations on freedom of religion must be construed at least as narrowly as constraints on expression and association values. Indeed, in *Kokkinakis* the Court affirmed that:

> freedom of thought, conscience and religion is one of the foundations of a 'democratic society' within the meaning of the Convention. It is, in its religious dimension, one of the most vital elements that go to make up the identity of believers and their conception of life, but it is also a precious asset for atheists, agnostics, sceptics and the unconcerned. The

---

[50] See *United Communist Party of Turkey v Turkey*, 30 January 1998, especially nn. 42–3; *Socialist Party v Turkey*, 25 May 1998, n. 41; *Freedom and Democracy Party (ÖZDEP) v Turkey*, 8 December 1999, n. 37. The three cases were decided in favour of the applicants under Article 11 ECHR (freedom of association). See also *Sidiropoulos and others v Greece*, 10 July 1998, n. 40. *Sidiropoulos* involved the refusal to register a cultural and political association aimed at promoting Macedonian autochthonous values.

pluralism indissociable from a democratic society, which has been dearly won over the centuries, depends on it.[51]

The Individual Exercise of Freedom of Conscience

The ECHR, like all international documents on human rights, considers the freedom of thought, conscience and religion as a right that belongs primarily to individuals. On a conceptual level, the right of religious groups appears to be derivative from that of its members. Yet ironically, the strictly individual dimension of this freedom has been disregarded more often and has arguably received less protection from the Strasbourg jurisdiction than the corporate dimension of the right.

[51] *Kokkinakis v Greece*, n. 31. See also *Serif v Greece*, n. 49. The foregoing analysis seems unaffected by the Court's controversial decision in the recent case of *Refah Partisi (The Welfare Party) v Turkey*, 31 July 2001, although this decision raises some questions concerning the future interpretation of freedom of association and freedom of religion. The Refah Partisi was a political party with a specific Islamic orientation. In fact, although accepting the constitutional principle of secularism (*laïcité*), which has been considered essential to keep a peaceful political life in Turkey since the establishment of the republic, the party proposed a reinterpretation of that principle. Such reinterpretation of *laïcité* included a project to promote a 'multi-legal system' in the country, i.e. the notion that each group would be governed by its specific religious laws. Based on diverse declarations and activities of members of the Welfare Party, the Turkish Constitutional Court inferred that there was a hidden agenda of the party itself, which aimed at setting up a political system incompatible not only with the principle of *laïcité* but also with the very notion of democracy – namely, the establishment of a theocratic system based on the *Sharia* or Islamic law, through recourse, if necessary, to the *jihad* or holy war. The ECtHR substantially accepted the Turkish Court's assumption and affirmed that the dissolution of the Welfare Party was justified on the basis of 'pressing social need'. The ruling was therefore legitimate from the Convention's perspective. The consequences that the *Refah Partisi* decision will produce in the case law are still uncertain. The principles governing the interpretation of freedom of association do not seem to be very much affected, but some aspects of the *Welfare Party* case suggest that this decision may acquire a special relevance. On the one hand, the Welfare Party, created in 1983, was a very significant party in the political spectrum of Turkey. On the other hand, some of the statements of the Court might have a deep future influence on the conception of the state's power to limit the manifestations of freedom of religion and belief, especially where Islam is concerned. In particular, the ECtHR declared that the establishment of *Sharia* or Islamic law as a political regime is 'difficult to reconcile with the fundamental principles of democracy, as conceived in the Convention taken as a whole' (n. 72).

The Meaning of 'Practice' in the European Convention

The problem arises from the terminology utilized by the ECHR, as well as by most other international texts that describe the content of the freedom of religion and belief. Among the aspects of this freedom that deserve protection, Article 9(1) ECHR mentions the right to manifest one's religion or belief in worship, teaching, practice and observance. If we direct our attention to the term 'practice', the most obvious interpretation seems to be that Article 9 guarantees the right of individuals to behave according to the dictates of their own conscience.[52] This guarantee should be granted whether or not the individual judgments of conscience correspond to the tenets of an institutionalized religion or derive from strictly personal beliefs. Also, it should be irrelevant whether the individual's conscience is grounded on religious or on non-religious beliefs. Of course this guarantee is necessarily limited (Article 9(2) ECHR), since the freedom to act is never absolute.

This broad construction of freedom of conscience has been proposed by the General Comment of the Committee of Human Rights on Article 18 of the 1966 UN International Covenant on Human Rights.[53] However, the attitude of the European Court and Commission has been rather different with regard to Article 9 ECHR. What follows is an attempt to summarize their approach to this issue.[54]

The case law of Strasbourg has stressed that it is necessary to distinguish between the internal and external aspects of religious liberty. The former is the freedom to believe, which embraces the freedom to choose one's beliefs (religious or non-religious) and the freedom to change one's religion. The latter consists of the freedom to manifest one's religion or belief. The internal dimension of religious freedom is *absolute* and may not be restricted, while the

---

[52] It does not seem accurate or appropriate to interpret the term *practice* as the mere practice of rites, since the ritual dimension of religious freedom is alluded to in other words used in Article 9, particularly the terms *worship* and *observance*.

[53] The General Comment on Article 18 was adopted by the Committee on 20 July 1993. For an analysis of the text, see Tahzib, *Freedom of Religion*, 307–75.

[54] See also, on this subject, M. D. Evans, *Religious Liberty*, 293–314.

freedom to act is by its very nature *relative* and may be subjected to the restrictions specified in Article 9(2).[55]

All this seems indisputable. It is obvious that public authorities cannot take or permit a direct action to impel the citizens to believe or not to believe in something. For this reason, the ECtHR held in 1976, in the *Kjeldsen* case, that the State, when organizing the educational system, is not allowed to develop any activities that amount to the indoctrination of students with a particular religious or moral view of life contrary to the convictions of their parents.[56] In a similar manner, much more recently, the Court affirmed, in the *Buscarini* case, that a citizen cannot be compelled by the law to express a religious belief against his will as a requirement to hold a public office voluntarily assumed. More specifically, the Court stated that it was incompatible with the Convention to deprive two elected members of Parliament of their office if they did not take their oath on the gospel; it would be tantamount to requiring them 'to swear allegiance to a particular religion'.[57]

However, the crucial question is how to understand the relative character of the freedom of individuals to act according to the dictates of their own conscience, which is an issue closely con-

---

[55] Dec. Adm. 10358/83, 37 *Decisions and Reports* 147, in which the Commission utilizes the expression '*forum internum*'. The same doctrine is reiterated in Dec. Adm. 10678/83, 39 *Decisions and Reports* 268, and Dec. Adm. 14049/88. See also Rep. Com. 11581/85 (*Darby* case), n. 44. The Court, following the Commission's approach, has subsequently alluded to this double aspect of religious freedom, and has emphasized that the limits stated in Article 9(2) are applicable only to the freedom to *manifest* one's religion or belief, not to the freedom to *choose* one's religion or belief (*Kokkinakis v Greece*, nn. 31 and 33).

[56] *Kjeldsen, Busk Madsen and Pedersen v Denmark*, 7 December 1976. The case related to the implementation of a new system of sex education in public schools, with the purpose of preventing unwanted pregnancies among teenagers. Some parents alleged conscientious objection to this teaching, as they considered that sex education was the exclusive domain of parents. *Kjeldsen* was the first case decided by the Court concerning religious beliefs, and the only one until *Kokkinakis* in 1993. The decision focused on the interpretation of Article 2 of the First Protocol (right to education, and the right of parents to ensure their children's education in conformity with their own religious and philosophical convictions).

[57] *Buscarini and others v San Marino*, 18 February 1999. The San Marino law requiring newly elected members of Parliament (General Grand Council) to swear on the gospel was changed shortly after the facts alleged in the application took place. A statute of 1993, following the practice of many European countries, introduced a choice between the traditional oath and one in which the reference to the gospel was replaced by the words 'on my honour'.

nected with the problem of conflicts between law and conscience, and between legal and moral duties. In my opinion, the framework proposed by the European jurisdiction is not the most desirable. The Commission's approach consisted traditionally in drawing a line of separation between the concepts of *manifestation* and of *motivation*. From this perspective, it would not necessarily guarantee the right to practise any particular external behaviour adapted to one's belief. In other words, the term *practice* does not include each and every act motivated or influenced by religion or belief.[58]

Neutral Laws and Moral Obligations: The Indirect Restriction of Religious Freedom

The foregoing approach seems reasonable in the abstract, for behaviour *obliged* by conscience (which seems to be the behaviour protected by Article 9) is different from behaviour simply *permitted* by conscience. Nevertheless, the truth is that the case law of the Commission reveals that it has traditionally adopted a rather restrictive attitude. Namely, it has tended to consider that the protective umbrella of Article 9 ECHR does not necessarily extend to an individual's behaviour imposed by his or her own conscience.[59] This is especially true when an individual attempts to adapt his conduct to his moral obligations in ordinary life but his

[58] This doctrine has been repeatedly stated by the Commission. See Rep. Com. 7050/75, 19 *Decisions and Reports* 19–20 (the *Arrowsmith* case, concerning a British pacifist sentenced to a term of imprisonment for having distributed illegal leaflets among English soldiers in Northern Ireland); Dec. Adm. 10358/83, 37 *Decisions and Reports* 147 (conscientious objection to paying taxes, in the percentage of the state budget aimed at military costs); Dec. Adm. 10678/83, 39 *Decisions and Reports* 268 (conscientious objection to contributing to the public system of pensions); Dec. Adm. 11579/85, 48 *Decisions and Reports* 255 (conflict between the laws governing religious and civil marriages); Dec. Adm. 14049/88 (conscientious objection to paying taxes, in the percentage of the state budget aimed at financing legal abortions in France).

[59] For further details on this approach of the Commission, see J. Martínez-Torrón, 'La giurisprudenza degli organi di Strasburgo sulla libertà religiosa', *Rivista internazionale di diritti dell'uomo* 335–79 (1993).

behaviour does not strictly constitute religious teaching or correspond to specific ceremonial practices.[60]

In this regard, the ECtHR has often implicitly drawn a distinction between a state's actions that have a direct and an indirect impact on religious freedom. In the Court's view, the state interferes with the exercise of freedom of religion or belief when an individual's behaviour is prevented or punished by a law or by other state activity *directly* aimed at restricting the manifestation, the worship or the expansion of certain or of all religions. In these cases, the ECHR requires that the state justifies the interference with the individual's freedom according to Article 9(2), especially proving that the restrictive measures are necessary in a democratic society.

This was indeed the approach of the Court when it decided in favour of the applicant in the *Kokkinakis* case[61] because the Greek courts, based on the laws against religious proselytism, had sentenced a Jehovah's Witness without enough evidence that he had been engaged in improper proselytism, that is, trying to convert people through abusive or deceitful means. To apply the law indiscriminately against proselytism was equivalent to restricting, without due justification, the freedom to manifest one's religion or beliefs in teaching. The same occurred in the *Buscarini* case,[62] where the Court held that Article 9 ECHR 'entails, *inter alia*, freedom to hold or not to hold religious beliefs and to practise or not to practise a religion'; the religious oath requirement could not be considered 'necessary in a democratic society', for it amounted to imposing on the applicants an obligation to declare their belief in a religion that was not their own.

Similar reasoning was adopted by the Court when it declared inadmissible the application of a Swiss teacher in a public primary

---

[60] Moreover, the Court has stated that certain professional situations voluntarily assumed may entail additional specific restrictions on religious freedom; this occurs particularly within 'a system of military discipline that by its very nature implie[s] the possibility of placing on certain of the rights and freedoms of members of the armed forces limitations incapable of being imposed on civilians' (*Kalaç v Turkey*, 1 July 1997, n. 28). The case involved the compulsory retirement of an officer of the Turkish army, required by the Supreme Military Council, for his membership of an Islamic fundamentalist movement supporting ideas contrary to the constitutional principle of secularism.

[61] See n. 41 and accompanying text.

[62] *Buscarini v San Marino*, nn. 34, 39. See n. 57 (above) and accompanying text.

school, who converted to Islam and who, in application of a cantonal law aimed at preserving the secular character of public schools, had been prohibited from wearing the traditional prescriptive veil on her head when teaching her students.[63] Although the Court here reached a final conclusion contrary to that in *Kokkinakis* and in *Buscarini*, its analysis also began by recognizing that imposing upon teachers the prohibition from carrying strong religious symbols constituted an interference with the applicant's religious freedom and the state had to provide a sound justification under Article 9(2) ECHR.[64]

The Commission and the Court's approach has been very different with regard to 'neutral' laws, that is, laws that pursue legitimate secular goals. When the legal duties imposed by a neutral law collide with the moral obligations of individuals, these persons see their right to practise their religion or belief as being *indirectly* but nonetheless unavoidably restricted by that law – this is the case with the different types of conscientious objection.[65]

---

[63] *Dahlab v Switzerland,* a decision on the admissibility of App. No. 42393/98, 15 February 2001.

[64] In this case, the ECtHR shared the opinion of the Swiss Federal Court on the consequences of the neutrality principle (*laïcité*); namely, that this principle entailed some restrictions on the civil servants' right to manifest their religion or belief, especially in the educational environment, where students may be more easily influenced and 'religious peace' must be protected with extreme care. In my opinion, the Court showed too much respect for the state's margin of appreciation in the *Dahlab* case. First, the 'religious peace' of the school does not seem to have suffered any serious threat, for the applicant had worn the Islamic *foulard* for approximately five years until she was prohibited from doing so by the (female) general director of primary schools of Geneva's canton. Secondly, I do not fully understand why the principle of *laïcité* (neutrality, secularism) should require, in a country enjoying religious peace such as Switzerland, that no religious personal symbols are discernible in the teachers' dress, instead of allowing students to see in their own school evidence of the religious pluralism existing in Swiss society.

[65] The phenomenon of conscientious objection goes far beyond the most well-known type, that is, conscientious objection to military service. An extensive analysis of conscientious objection in international and comparative law, with numerous bibliographical and case law references, can be found in R. Navarro-Valls and J. Martínez-Torrón, *Las objeciones de conciencia en el derecho español y comparado* (Madrid, McGraw-Hill, 1997); there is also an Italian version: *Le obiezioni di coscienza: Profili di diritto comparato* (Turin, Giappichelli, 1995). The case law of the United States is especially rich in dealing with these situations. For an interesting and comprehensive study, see R. Palomino, *Las objeciones de conciencia: Conflictos entre conciencia y ley en el derecho norteamericano* (Madrid, Montecorvo, 1994).

The immediate consequence is that a moral burden is placed upon the shoulders of these people, as they must choose between disobedience to the law and disobedience to their conscience – one results in a worldly punishment, the other entails a spiritual sanction. In those cases, the European jurisdiction, and especially the Commission, has apparently tended to deny that Article 9 ECHR offers any protection, for it could not be demonstrated that there has been state interference with religious freedom. In short, its analysis can be summarized as follows: it is not necessary to consider whether the state can provide a legitimate justification for the legislation under attack (according to Article 9(2)) because the right to freedom of thought, conscience and religion (according to the description of its content in Article 9(1)) has not actually been directly violated.

It would be inaccurate to assert that there is a conclusive doctrine of the ECtHR on the issue of conflicts between neutral laws and an individual's freedom of conscience, but in three cases it is possible to observe some traces of this mode of reasoning. Significantly, all three cases referred to problems arising in the field of education, which might lead one to consider them as correct for education cases rather than those of freedom of religion.

The first of them is *Kjeldsen, Busk Madsen and Pedersen*, in 1976.[66] It concerned the opposition of some students' parents to compulsory sex education for teenagers in Danish public schools. They claimed, unsuccessfully, an exemption from those classes for their children, arguing that Article 2 of the First Protocol protected the right of parents to ensure that the education provided by the state was 'in conformity with their own religious and philosophical convictions'.[67] The Court, however, proposed a very restrictive interpretation of that article, holding that the state was free to organize the educational system, and particularly the curricula of public schools, even if the religious or philosophical convictions of parents were disregarded. The fact that some parents objected, upon grounds of conscience, to certain contents of the school curriculum did not grant them any right to require of the state a

---

[66] See n. 56 and accompanying text. For a more detailed analysis of the *Kjeldsen* decision, see Navarro-Valls and Martínez-Torrón, *Las objeciones de conciencia*, 199–203.

[67] See above, n. 12.

special exemption for their children. Consequently, the state was not obliged either to grant such exemption or to justify its refusal. The state's power to control the educational environment, as previously noted, was only limited by the prohibition of indoctrination.

Twenty years later, the twin decisions in *Efstratiou* and *Valsamis*[68] dealt with a relatively similar problem. The respective applications had been filed by two secondary school students who had refused, on religious grounds, to take part in a national celebration organized by their schools and had consequently received an academic punishment. The ECtHR decided the case in the light both of Article 9 ECHR and of Article 2 of the First Protocol (as interpreted in *Kjeldsen*). The decision upheld the Greek government's position, giving particular regard to two facts. One was the moderate punishment imposed to the students, which could not amount to a deprivation of the right to education. The other was that the Court could 'discern nothing, either in the purpose of the parade or in the arrangements for it, which could offend the applicants' pacifist convictions'.[69] The Court noted additionally that the Commission had considered, in its report on the case, that 'article 9 did not confer a right to exemption from disciplinary rules which applied generally and in a neutral manner and that in the instant case there had been no interference with the applicant's right to freedom to manifest her religion or belief'.[70]

In my opinion, this interpretation of Article 9 ECHR inverts the logical order of concepts in this matter. It is universally accepted that human rights must be construed broadly. Therefore, in order to understand the exact meaning of the freedom to manifest one's religion or belief in practice, it seems that we should approach the

---

[68] *Efstratiou v Greece*, 18 December 1996; *Valsamis v Greece*, 18 December 1996. The texts of both decisions are almost identical, as indeed were the facts in issue. Two Greek secondary school students, both followers of the Jehovah's Witnesses, had refused, for religious reasons, to participate in the school parades organized during the national festival to commemorate the outbreak of war between Greece and fascist Italy in 1940. They argued that their conscience prohibited them from being present in a civic celebration in which a war was remembered and in which military and ecclesiastical authorities took part. The two students were denied permission to be absent from the parade, and their failure to attend was punished by one day's suspension from school.

[69] *Efstratiou v Greece*, n. 32; *Valsamis v Greece*, n. 31.

[70] *Efstratiou v Greece*, n. 37; *Valsamis v Greece*, n. 36.

question in the following sequence: freedom to practise one's religion or belief must be understood as protecting, in principle, every act of the individual when he obeys the dictates of his own conscience; however, paragraph 2 of Article 9 (the limits on religious liberty) will be utilized, when necessary, as a corrective element for a freedom which, by its own nature, tends to be exercised in an undefined and unpredictable way. Thus, we manage to reconcile two paramount interests that are inclined to conflict with each other: the maximum degree of initial protection of the freedom of belief and the security that the legal order demands. Furthermore, we introduce an important assumption: the state has the burden of proof with regard to the necessity of a restrictive measure, that is, it must affirmatively prove that, in a particular case of conflict, it is necessary in a democratic society to restrict the exercise of religious freedom. Following this approach would obstruct the development of policies that ignore the needs of religious freedom and that are especially harmful to minority groups.

In any event, the Court neither subscribed to nor rejected explicitly the Commission's interpretation of Article 9 ECHR in *Efstratiou* and *Valsamis*. The Commission's view might be expressive of a certain state of mind in the Strasbourg jurisdiction, along the lines of *Kjeldsen*. However, we might well assume also that the Court is hesitating about which path it should follow beyond the strict borders of the educational environment. In this regard, we should note that the Commission's restrictive interpretation of freedom of conscience seems at variance with the Court's own words in the recent *Hasan* case: 'but for very exceptional cases, the right to freedom of religion as guaranteed under the Convention excludes any discretion on the part of the State to determine whether religious beliefs or the means used to express such beliefs are legitimate.'[71]

Behaviour in accordance with the dictates of one's own conscience in daily life is an evident and most important expression of freedom of religion and belief. However, it is not clear yet whether these words of the *Hasan* decision will constitute a twist in the former doctrine of the Commission, or whether they will rather be understood as applicable only to the typical expressions of

[71] *Hasan and Chaush v Bulgaria*, 26 October 2000, n. 79.

religious liberty and particularly to those directly related to the internal affairs of religious communities.

Concluding Remarks: Freedom of Conscience and Protection of Minorities

One of the aforementioned aspects of the ECtHR's reasoning in *Efstratiou* and *Valsamis* is particularly problematic. When the ECtHR examined the arguments of the applicants, it declared that the parades that the Jehovah's Witnesses morally disapproved of were merely civic acts without any particular political or ideological connotation, and, consequently, they could not offend the pacifist convictions of the students.[72] Thus, the Court in effect substituted its own judgment for the conscience of the persons involved, defining what was reasonable for them to believe with regard to their participation in a national commemorative ceremony.

In my opinion, this is a dangerous mistake. This could set the Court on a path to determining which beliefs are reasonable and which are not. Naturally, it is necessary to verify – as far as possible – that parties are not deceitfully alleging moral convictions they do not actually or sincerely hold in order to avoid fulfilling a legal duty. But this does not mean that a secular court is competent to elucidate when the beliefs of a person are sufficiently consistent from an objective point of view. This is a slippery slope. The conviction that public authorities, in a neutral secular society, must refrain from pronouncing on the truth or falsehood of a religious dogma or a moral belief is deeply rooted in Western legal culture.[73]

In the above-mentioned decisions, the ECtHR seemed to let fall into oblivion the fundamental philosophy underlying the protection of religious liberty in our civilization. The reason why the freedom of each individual conscience must be respected is not that it is objectively correct – the courts would then have to judge the truth of the alleged beliefs, as a sort of new Inquisition. Rather, freedom of conscience must be respected because it is considered a

---

[72] See *Valsamis v Greece*, nn. 31, 37; *Efstratiou v Greece*, nn. 32, 38.

[73] See, in this regard, the statement of the ECtHR in *Metropolitan Church of Bessarabia*, above, n. 27 and accompanying text.

fundamental area of the individual's autonomy in democratic societies, and, consequently, the legal system has determined that nobody may interfere with the individual's conscience as long as other prevailing juridical interests are not endangered. What freedom of religion or belief protects is the right to choose the truths which one is willing to believe. Hence, Article 9(2) ECHR provides that the state may restrict the exercise of that freedom only when it is necessary in a democratic society.

In other words, governments are not obliged to respect and protect religious freedom because they consider the convictions of their citizens to be correct, or even convenient. They are obliged to protect the freedom to believe and to act accordingly because this freedom constitutes an essential element of a democratic system. The protection of that freedom is a paramount *public* interest and not merely a *private* interest of individuals and groups. This is something that is easily understood with regard to other liberties (for instance, freedom of expression or of association) but is sometimes inexplicably ignored when dealing with religious liberty. This fact is even more shocking when we realize that the ECtHR itself has repeatedly emphasized that an adequate protection of these three freedoms (religion, expression, association) enshrined in Articles 9–11 ECHR is necessary to preserve pluralism, which is in turn indispensable for democracy.[74]

The prejudice about the exercise of religious freedom – when compared with other fundamental liberties – might have some relationship with the former concept of religion as a private matter, typical of the first liberalism, especially in its French interpretation. To maintain, implicitly or explicitly, that position today may amount to 'secular indoctrination', and we should bear in mind that the aim of indoctrination is one of the clear limits that the state cannot exceed according to the ECtHR's interpretation of freedom of religion or belief. In effect, a state's failure to facilitate actual religious pluralism in society, and the corresponding external expressions of that pluralism, would be equivalent to

---

[74] With regard to freedom of expression and freedom of association, see *United Communist Party of Turkey v Turkey*, 30 January 1998, nn. 42–3; *Socialist Party v Turkey*, 25 May 1998, n. 41; and *Freedom and Democracy Party (ÖZDEP) v Turkey*, 8 December 1999, n. 37. With respect to freedom of thought, conscience and religion see *Kokkinakis v Greece*, 25 May 1993, n. 31; and *Serif v Greece*, 14 December 1999, n. 49.

supporting a certain belief (secularism, that is, no-religion) over the others (religions). This is what occurs when a radical interpretation of the neutrality principle is held, without proving that the consequent restrictions on external manifestations of citizens' religion or beliefs are necessary in a democratic society by reason of a pressing social need. In my view, a too strict conception of state neutrality could easily lead to a sort of secular fundamentalism.

It is therefore important that the ECtHR open its mind to all the consequences inherent in a global notion of pluralism, which demands a wider protection of the individual aspects of freedom of religion and belief. The outcome of the Court's approach in this area is bound to transcend the individual sphere. As already stated, the ECtHR had positively impelled the acknowledgement of the rights of minority groups.[75] Nonetheless, it should be added that, if the Court followed the Commission's previous restrictive doctrine on individuals' right to manifest their religion or belief in practice, it would produce negative effects for some religious minorities, particularly for those minorities that defend ideas openly contrary to the ethical choices assumed by the majority of people in a certain society.

In effect, the laws considered neutral usually conform – as does any law – to the ethical values that are dominant in a determined social environment at a certain moment. Neutral laws will rarely conflict with the morals or life practices of the major churches, but they can more often cause conflicts with minority religious groups that engage in conduct that is socially atypical. To hold that a neutral law must automatically prevail and that the state is under no obligation to justify denial of exemptions from the general application of the law as being necessary in a democratic society would constitute a significant risk for the rights of minorities.

---

[75] See the discussion above.

6

Freedom of Religion: Public/Private, Rights/Wrongs

IAN LEIGH*

Introduction

Human rights have been hailed by Francesca Klug as a source of values for a godless age.[1] Others have gone further and argued that human rights ideology has many of the trappings of a proselytizing religion, bent on subordinating other thought systems to its own.[2] Many orthodox believers from the major religions are understandably suspicious. Human rights claims are often presented in a one-sided way, both in emphasizing apparently unbridled individual autonomy without responsibility, and in the specific uses to which they are put. Part of my purpose is to show that, in the field of religious liberty, many of these claims are over-ambitious and, under the Human Rights Act 1998, legally unsustainable. In the process I hope to demonstrate also that some of the key articles of the European Convention on Human Rights present a much more balanced and restrained approach to individual autonomy than is often claimed.

Before we enter this debate, however, it is first appropriate briefly to outline the main Convention rights at stake. There is a variety of ways in which the ECHR might apply to religious bodies across a range of areas. Of primary relevance is Article 9, guaranteeing

*I acknowledge gratefully the support of the Arts and Humanities Research Board under its Research Leave Scheme.

[1] F. Klug, *Values for a Godless Age: The Story of the UK's New Bill of Rights* (London, Penguin, 2000).

[2] M. Evans, 'Human Rights, Law and Religion: Locating the Debate', in P. Edge and G. Harvey (eds), *Law and Religion in Contemporary Society: Communities, Individualism and the State* (Aldershot, Ashgate, 2000), 183.

freedom of thought, conscience and religion and the limited right to manifest one's religion or belief.[3]

The Convention also contains in Article 14 a wide-ranging non-discrimination principle:

> The enjoyment of the rights and freedoms set forth in this Convention shall be secured without discrimination on any grounds such as sex, race, colour, language, religion, political or other opinion, national or social origin, association with a national minority, property, birth or other status.

Nevertheless, this only applies where another Convention right can be invoked. Outright state discrimination on religious grounds is (royal marriage prohibitions notwithstanding) uncommon in the UK.[4] Article 14 has been supplemented recently by the Twelfth Protocol – a free-standing discrimination provision which includes religion among its prohibited grounds – which would apply to all actions of public authorities. The UK government has, however, stated that it does not intend to sign the Protocol, due, no doubt, to uncertainty over how it might be used (mainly in the UK's case anyway) with regard to the other prohibited grounds of discrimination.[5] It seems likely that another European measure – the new framework employment directive, from the EU's Council of

---

[3] On the scope of Article 9 see: C. Evans, *Freedom of Religion under the European Convention on Human Rights* (Oxford, Oxford University Press, 2001); D. Harris, M. O'Boyle and C. Warbrick, *The Law of the European Convention on Human Rights* (London, Butterworths, 1995), ch.10; P. Van Dijk and G. Van Hoof, *The Theory and Practice of the European Convention on Human Rights*, 3rd edn (The Hague, Kluwer, 1998), 547–56; T. Gunn, 'Adjudicating Rights of Conscience under the European Convention on Human Rights', in J. Van de Vyer and J. Witte (eds), *Religious Human Rights in Global Perspective: Legal Perspectives* (The Hague, Kluwer, 1996); M. Evans, *Religious Liberty and International Law in Europe* (Cambridge, Cambridge University Press, 1997).

[4] See, though, Broadcasting Act 1990 (sched. 2, Part 2, para. 2) which disbars religious groups from holding certain broadcasting licences. In May 2002 the government published a draft Communications Bill, signalling an intention to relax these provisions.

[5] HL Debs. 11 October 2000, WA 37; HL Debs. 23 October 2000, WA 14.

Ministers – will be of greater importance.[6] This requires the UK to introduce legislation against religious discrimination in the fields of employment and training by December 2003.

Finally, in the sphere of education Article 2 of the First Protocol provides a right for parents to have their children educated in accordance with their religious and philosophical convictions.

Churches: Public Authorities or Private Associations?

There is contrast between the way in which many human rights advocates and devout people in the UK perceive religious bodies. The former tend to be most exercised by the position of minority religions within what they perceive as a Christian-dominated country. From this perspective the introduction of protection against religious discrimination is necessary to strengthen the position of Muslims especially. The establishment of the Church of England is seen as an outmoded symbol of Christian dominance no longer appropriate in a pluralist society.[7] In contrast, many religious people, not just Christians but also orthodox Muslims and Jews, perceive contemporary Britain to be an overwhelmingly secular state, increasingly intolerant of religious belief and practice. From this viewpoint the remaining trappings of the establishment may be valued as denoting recognition (albeit weakly) of the importance of a spiritual sphere to life.[8] Debates over religious liberty reflect these two contrasting positions.

[6] *Council Directive 2000/78/EC* of 27 November 2000, establishing a general framework for equal treatment in employment and occupation. For analysis see I. Leigh, 'Clashing Rights, Exemptions and Opt-Outs: Religious Liberty and "Homophobia"', in R. O'Dair and A. Lewis (eds), *Law and Religion*, Current Legal Issues 4, 2001 (Oxford, Oxford University Press, 2001). On implementation see: B. Hepple QC and T. Choudhury, *Tackling Religious Discrimination: Practical Implications for Policy-Makers and Legislators* (Home Office Research Study 221, Home Office, London, 2001) and *Towards Equality and Diversity: Implementing the Employment and Race Directives* (London, Cabinet Office, December 2001). See also D. McClean, 'Letter from Brussels' (2002) 6 *Ecc.LJ* 375.

[7] For example, P. Weller, 'Equity, Inclusivity and Participation in a Plural Society: Challenging the Establishment of the Church of England', in P. Edge and G. Harvey (eds), *Law and Religion in Contemporary Society: Communities, Individualism and the State* (Aldershot, Ashgate, 2000).

[8] T. Modood, 'Establishment, Multiculturalism and British Citizenship', (1994) 65 (1) *Pol Q* 53; J. Sacks, *The Persistence of Faith: Religion, Morality and Society in a Secular Age* (London, Weidenfield and Nicholson, 1991), 97.

Naturally, human rights advocates believe in the fundamental importance of individual freedom of thought, belief and conscience – in Britain this emerged (after long conflict) as the first civil liberty, from which all others have followed. However, religious *organizations* are less valued and may even be seen as potential violators of human rights.

The Lord Chancellor, perhaps unwittingly, illustrated the point when, during the parliamentary debates on the Human Rights Act 1998 he suggested several ways in which the Act might bind such bodies:

> If a court were to hold that a religious organisation, denomination or church, in celebrating marriage, was exercising a public function, what on earth would be wrong with that? If a court were to hold that a hospice, because it provided a medical service was exercising a public function, what on earth would be wrong with that? Is it not also perfectly true that schools, although underpinned by a religious foundation or trust deed, may well be carrying out public functions? If we take, for example, a charity whose charitable aims include the advancement of religion, the answer must depend on the nature of the function of the charity.[9]

It is clear from his rhetorical questions that he expected that the function of the body concerned would determine whether the Human Rights Act applied, rather than whether it was established for a religious purpose. The danger this poses to such bodies, however, is that the application of human rights norms to their functions may dilute their purposes. Critics asked, for example, whether under the Human Rights Act clergy would be required to perform same-sex 'marriages', whether the consecration of female bishops would be required, whether abortion clinics could require Catholic newspapers to carry their advertising and whether religious hospices would be required to employ staff who were in favour of euthanasia.

In fact, as I hope to show, many of these fears are misplaced. I shall argue that it is a misapplication of the ECHR to suggest that most religious bodies can be liable for violations of an individual's Convention rights. Arguably, to impose liability upon them (if this

[9] HL Deb., vol. 583, col. 800, 24 November 1997.

is what the Human Rights Act does) is itself a violation of other Convention rights, namely freedom of thought, conscience and religion, which in guaranteed under Article 9, to people 'either alone or in community'.

Moreover, the right of freedom of association (guaranteed by Article 11) is an important recognition that the state should not interfere too closely with the affairs of private associations, whether religious or otherwise. In his classic *Democracy in America*, De Tocqueville remarked that freedom of association is 'by nature almost as inalienable as individual liberty'.[10] As a note in *Harvard Law Review* puts it, private associations allow citizen participation, act as a counterweight to the power of the state and are 'one of the principal building blocks of social diversity and pluralism'.[11] It continues: 'The essence of freedom to form a voluntary association is the freedom to select some members and exclude others. Thus, freedom of association also implies a right not to associate.' Interestingly, the High Court has recently reached the same position in holding that Article 11 included the right of the RSPCA to refuse membership to potential applicants who the society thought might damage its objectives (including those seeking to reverse its stance against hunting with dogs) and that such applicants had no countervailing right of freedom of expression which demanded admittance.[12]

Neglect of the importance of freedom of association is the primary cause of confusion in the debate over whether the HRA applies to churches and other religious bodies. The attempt in the parliamentary debates to exclude religious bodies from the scope of the Act was seen by critics as special pleading. Religious groups, on the other hand, were puzzled at the inability to see that they were no more public bodies than are private clubs (or political parties) and that freedom of religion has a delicate collective dimension which is easily damaged by state regulation.

---

[10] A. de Tocqueville, *Democracy in America*, ed. J. Mayer and M. Lerner (1966), 178.

[11] Note, 'State Power and Discrimination by Private Clubs: First Amendment Protection for Nonexpressive Associations', (1991) 104 *Harvard LR* 103, 1838–9.

[12] *RSPCA v A-G and others*, [2001] All ER (D) 188, Lightman J. However for other reasons relating to the arbitrary nature of the process, the proposed change in membership rules was not permitted to be implemented.

The issue is not a new one. The early twentieth century saw a vigorous academic debate[13] on the nature of legal personality enjoyed by associations such as churches. This was fuelled in part by the continental anti-clericalism in France and Prussia. In Britain, however, interest in the status of the churches was by analogy with that of the trade unions. On the one side were inheritors of the Hobbesian distrust of 'partial associations' – that is, apart from the state. Hobbes had argued that there were no associations in the 'state of nature' and that their existence was derived from Leviathan.[14] The constitutionalist Dicey develops a variant on this perspective in characteristic Edwardian prose: 'If X or Y or Z may each of them lawfully, as is certainly the case, cut A because of his hateful religious or political opinions, they may all it would seem, agree together to cut him.'[15] For Dicey, then, religious associations are a communal expression of the negative liberty of individuals. However, he acknowledges that, since they are created by a surrender of liberty, such bodies limit to some degree the freedom of each of their members.

For a second group of writers, the Pluralists, however, the state itself is an example of the principle of association at work. Thus, Laski argues that associations are real and do not all emanate from the state:

> Men belong to it [the state]; but, also, they belong to other groups, and a competition for allegiance is continuously possible . . . Whether we will or no, we are bundles of hyphens. When the centres of linkage conflict a choice must be made.[16]

Laski is not asserting that religious associations necessarily have a higher claim to allegiance in conflict, nor is this an argument for the primacy of individual conscience. Nevertheless, ecclesiastical

---

[13] For references to the literature see J. MacLean, 'Personality and Public Law Doctrine', (1999) 49 *U Tor. LJ* 123; J. MacLean, 'Intermediate Associations and the State', in M. Taggart (ed.), *The Province of Administrative Law* (Oxford, Oxford University Press, 1997), 160 ff.

[14] MacLean, 'Personality and Public Law Doctrine', 125.

[15] A. V. Dicey, 'The Combination Laws as Illustrating the Relation between Law and Opinion in England during the Nineteenth Century', (1904) 17 *Harvard LR* 511, 513.

[16] H. Laski, 'The Personality of Associations', (1915–16) 29 *Harvard LR* 404, 425.

lawyers at any rate will see the similarity to the division of allegiance between God and Caesar.[17]

This minor diversion into the history of legal and political theory has some contemporary relevance. Interest in the role of voluntary associations within civil society has been growing, not least as the direct role of the state recedes, both in the UK and elsewhere. Private (that is, non-governmental) associations may find themselves fulfilling functions or offering services to often quite large sections of the public.[18] Government policy increasingly looks for cooperation between state and voluntary bodies, including religious organizations, but this raises questions about the accountability and transparency of the voluntary sector.

Nor can it be assumed that the terms of cooperation will be as favourable as those which have allowed church schools to retain a distinctive ethos while drawing most of their funding from the state. The terms of cooperation are now less likely to be contained in some grand compact like Rab Butler's 1944 Education Act, than in a 'contract' with a government agency or local authority imposed as a condition of grant funding, which there are few opportunities for the voluntary body to challenge. In Australia, for example, where churches have become primary providers of welfare under such contractual arrangements with government, there is some concern at the invasiveness of grant conditions, which may tie the church too closely to a secular, liberal, agenda.

The controversy about the proper role and status of religious bodies was surprisingly revived in the parliamentary debates over whether or to what extent religious organizations are bound by the Human Rights Act. Are bodies such as churches to be treated legally merely as aggregations of rights-bearing individuals? If so, it makes sense to treat them (as does the European Convention) as collective recipients of the rights of freedom of belief, speech and property that their members possess.[19] Does this approach apply

---

[17] *Mark* 12: 17.

[18] See A. Dunn (ed.), *The Voluntary Sector, the State and the Law* (Oxford, Hart Publishing, 2000); J. Morison, 'The Government–Voluntary Sector Compacts: Governance, Governmentality and Civil Society', (2000) 27 *Journal of Law and Society* 98.

[19] After initially refusing standing to churches (*Church of X v UK*, Appl. No. 3798/68, 13 YB Eur. on Conv. 306) the European Commission accepted that it was artificial to distinguish between the rights of individual members and of the religious body itself (*X and the Church of Scientology v Sweden*, Appl. No.

equally to entities such as schools and charities with a religious foundation? Or should such bodies be treated as independent sources of power in their own right, with the potential to oppress their members, so that attempts should be made to legally constrain their actions? Do human rights apply horizontally to such non-state bodies and, if they do, does this detract from the collective enjoyment of rights by the bodies concerned?

I shall first consider the position in the Strasbourg jurisprudence before moving on to the effect of the Human Rights Act 1998.

Established Churches and the Convention

The argument that the establishment amounts to a form of impermissible state preference of one religion over others or none does not gain much support from the Convention. Freedom of religion in Europe does not require a state to adopt the equivalent to the non-establishment clause of the First Amendment to the United States Constitution. Although the ECHR forbids discrimination by member states in the enjoyment of Convention rights on various grounds, including religion or belief,[20] the Court has held that mild forms of state preference for one religion over another do not violate the Convention.[21] The Commission has held that the failure to criminalize publications offending non-Christians under the UK law of blasphemy did not of itself amount to a violation of freedom of religion.[22] Since there was no right to be protected in this way no question concerning discrimination in the enjoyment of a

7805/77, 16 Eur. Comm. HR. Decisions and Reports 68 (1979)). See C. Evans, *Freedom of Religion*, 12–14. More recent admissibility decisions appear, however, to show inconsistency of approach, with occasional denial of standing to collective bodies on the grounds that an individual is the true victim: J. Rivers, 'Religious Liberty as a Collective Right', in O'Dair and Lewis (eds), *Law and Religion*, 228–9.

[20] Article 14. See, for example, *Hoffman v Austria* (1994) 17 EHRR 293.

[21] *Otto-Preminger Institute v Austria*, Series A 295 (1994). The existence of a church established under national law has been held not to violate the Convention per se: *Darby v Sweden* (1991) 13 EHRR 774. The Court, however, determined the question (of the liability of a non-national to pay tax where a portion went to the Swedish Lutheran church to support its religious activities) as a matter of discrimination as regards the enjoyment of property (Swedish nationals were able to benefit from an exemption if they chose). By contrast the Commission had found a violation of Article 9.

[22] *Choudhury v UK*, No. 17439/90, 12 HRLJ (1991).

Convention right for the purpose of Article 14 arose. The degree of permitted state preference is controversial, however, as is clear from the range of judicial opinions expressed in the *Kokkanakis* case[23] in which the conviction of a Jehovah's Witness in Greece for 'improper proselytism' (an offence designed to 'protect' Greek Orthodox believers) was found to violate Article 9.

The risk of preference for the Church of England (or Christianity) being found to violate the Convention should be relatively minor, therefore. This is unsurprising in view of the fact that many European states give preference to Christianity or to specific churches in their constitutional arrangements.[24]

A greater risk perhaps arises from the possibility that the identification of the church with the state through establishment may lead to its institutions being treated as 'public authorities' under the Human Rights Act.[25] If the established church is held to be a governmental organization it appears that it may be debarred from complaining as a victim under Article 34 ECHR (and, consequently, as a matter of domestic law under section 7 of the HRA).[26] In fact, however, the position under the Strasbourg jurisprudence is not so straightforward.

What does the Convention tells us about the status of the churches? It should be acknowledged at the outset that the two (minor) Strasbourg cases involving complaints against the Church of England have both resulted in findings that the complaints were inadmissible without reaching an authoritative determination of whether the UK is liable under the Convention for the actions of church institutions.[27] Better guidance can be obtained from decisions of the Court concerning other national churches.

[23] *Kokkanakis v Greece* (1993) 17 EHRR 397.

[24] See K. Boyle and J. Sheen, *Freedom of Religion and Belief: A World Report* (London, Routledge, 1997).

[25] See the discussion below.

[26] Local authorities have been debarred from complaining in a number of instances: *Rothenturm Commune v Switzerland* (1988) 59 DR 251; *Ayuntamiento de M. v Spain* (1991) 68 DR 209; Van Dijk and Van Hoof, *Theory and Practice*, 46 (n. 143).

[27] See *Tyler v UK*, Appl. No. 00021283/93, 5 April 1994, reproduced in M. Hill, *Ecclesiastical Law*, 2nd edn (Oxford, Oxford University Press, 2001), 677–81 (no violation of Article 6(1) in consistory court and Court of Arches procedure and composition) and *Williamson v UK*, Appl. No. 00027008/95, 17 May 1995 (challenge to Ordination of Women Measure for violating individual priest's rights under Article 9 inadmissible). For decisions by UK courts under the Human Rights Act on the status of the Church of England see below.

When Greece passed legislation the effect of which was to transfer large parts of the estate of the monasteries of the Greek Orthodox Church to the state, it was found by the Strasbourg court to have violated the monasteries' right to peaceful enjoyment of their possessions under Article 1 of the First Protocol to the Convention.[28] The Greek government had argued by way of preliminary objection that the monasteries were governmental organizations because of the constitutional status of the Greek Orthodox Church and so were not entitled to complain as victims of a violation of the Convention, since they were not 'non-governmental' organizations under what is now Article 34. The Court's reasons for dismissing this argument[29] have considerable bearing on the status of the Church of England.

In Greece historical links between the Orthodox Church and its institutions were reflected in the 1975 constitution and in legislation.[30] The church and its institutions were treated in Greek law as public law entities ascribed with legal personality,[31] and some of their decisions were open to review by the Administrative Court. Although monasteries were technically separate they had strong links with the church and the state: the Minister for Education and Religion Affairs played a part in initiating proposals to found, merge or dissolve individual monasteries. However, the Court did not regard the legal classification of the monasteries as public law entities as decisive: it treated this as intended to confer protection from challenge by third parties equivalent to that enjoyed by state institutions. The crucial factor was that the objectives of the monasteries (whether ecclesiastical, spiritual, social or cultural) were not analogous to those of governmental organizations: their legal powers were confined to spiritual and internal

---

[28] *Holy Monasteries v Greece* (1995) 20 EHRR 1. Claims that Article 9 had been violated were dismissed since there was no interference with the objects intended for celebration of divine worship (para. 87).

[29] *Holy Monasteries*, paras 48 and 49.

[30] See Article 3 of the Greek Constitution of 1975, discussed in *Kokkinakis v Greece* (1993) 17 EHRR 397.

[31] The European Court of Human Rights has also held that the discriminatory denial of legal personality to some churches, so that they are unable to litigate unless registered with the state, violates Articles 6 and 14: *Canea Catholic Church v Greece* (1999) 27 EHRR 521. Absence of domestic legal personality is not fatal, however, to standing under Article 34: *Christian Association of Jehovah's Witnesses v Bulgaria* (1997) 24 EHRR CD 52; Appl. No. 8652/79 DR 26, 89.

questions and supervision was by the local archbishop, and not by the state. Accordingly, they were to be regarded as non-govern-mental organizations.

The *Holy Monasteries* decision is helpful in demonstrating that domestic constitutional classifications are not determinative of whether a religious organization is entitled to make a Convention complaint. As in Greece, the body may be a public authority in domestic law but nevertheless be treated for Convention purposes as 'non-governmental'. As we shall see, the distinction is particularly important when considering the Human Rights Act.

The Convention makes a clear distinction between state institutions which can be liable for human rights violations and non-state actors. That distinction can be seen in an admissibility decision of the European Commission in which it held to be manifestly ill-founded a complaint that a prohibition concerning the form of liturgy to be used in the Church of Sweden violated Article 9.[32] As in the earlier decision from Greece, the Commission found that the status of the Church of Sweden and its parishes as public law corporations did not preclude an individual parish from being treated as a 'non-governmental organization' for the purpose of making a complaint. This aspect is important in recognizing that Article 9 confers rights on religious organizations as well as on individuals.[33] However, it also followed from the 'non-govern-mental' status of the church that the state could not be liable for alleged violations of freedom of religion resulting from the decision of the Church Assembly about the form of liturgy.[34] This ruling that Article 9 does not have 'horizontal effect' means that the capacity for individual congregations to use the Convention against church episcopal or denominational authorities, or for individual church members against the congregation or clergy, in doctrinal, liturgical or disciplinary disputes would seem to be

[32] *Hauanemi v Sweden* (1996) 22 EHRR CD 155. The issue arose from the prohibition on use of the liturgy of the Finnish Evangelican-Lutheran Church (the parish was Finnish-speaking). On establishment in Sweden, see F. Cranmer, 'The Church of Sweden and the Unravelling of Establishment', (2000) 5 *Ecc. LJ* 417.

[33] See n. 19 above.

[34] In any event, the Commission would have concluded that there was no violation of Article 9 since there the parish had the option of leaving the church if it wished to continue using the prohibited liturgy, Finnish priests could conduct services elsewhere in the parish, nor did the decision otherwise limit the applicant's freedom of religion; cf. *Karlsson v Sweden*, Appl. No. 12356/86, 57 DR 172 (1988).

virtually non-existent.[35] The lesson is that freedom of association requires clear limits to the freedom of individuals.

How do these principles apply within the domestic sphere under the Human Rights Act 1998?

Religious Associations and the Human Rights Act[36]

In the UK the structure of the HRA causes some difficulty because, while it follows the Convention scheme as regards victims, it departs from it in the case of respondents. Under section 7, the Convention test which entitles a non-governmental organization to complain under Article 34 is mirrored in UK law. The status that individual religious organizations may have as public authorities should not, therefore, debar them from asserting Convention rights in the UK courts.

The potential for domestic confusion first becomes apparent when considering the question from the alternative direction – the *liability* of religious organizations under section 6 of the HRA. This provision can apply in one of two ways: to 'pure' public authorities (such as government departments), in respect of all their activities, and to 'hybrid' public authorities, in respect of their public functions only. Unfortunately, however, there is no restraint on UK courts to confine the ranks of public authorities to those that Strasbourg would treat as such. The clear distinction under the Convention between non-governmental bodies, which can be victims but not perpetrators of human rights violations, and governmental ones, which can be respondents but not victims, has been muddled. Ministers made parliamentary statements to the effect that they anticipated that wherever the UK would be liable for the actions of a public body at Strasbourg the courts would treat it

---

[35] See also *X v Denmark*, Appl. No. 7374/76 D and R 5, 157; No. 122242/86, Dec. 6.9.89, DR 62, p. 151.

[36] See also P. Cumper, 'Religious Organisations and the Human Rights Act', in P. Edge and G. Harvey (eds), *Law and Religion in Contemporary Society: Communities, Individualism and the State* (Aldershot, Ashgate, 2000); J. Rivers, 'From Toleration to Pluralism: Religious Liberty and Religious Establishment, the UK's Human Rights Act', in R. Ahdar (ed.), *Law and Religion* (Aldershot, Ashgate, 2000); J. Rivers, 'Religious Liberty as a Collective Right', in O'Dair and Lewis (eds), *Law and Religion.*

as a 'public authority' under section 6.[37] That is not the problem
here. The difficulty is that the legislation fails to exclude the
converse situation – UK courts are not *precluded* from treating as
public authorities under section 6 religious organizations that
Strasbourg would treat as non-governmental bodies under Article
34. This potential liability opens a possible form of horizontal
application of human rights, since its true effect is to make what are
in Strasbourg terms private (or at least 'non-governmental') associations subject to HRA duties owed to other private individuals.[38]

In a recent article[39] Professor Dawn Oliver paints an apocalyptic
picture of the consequences for a number of private bodies,
including sporting associations, educational institutions, privatized
utilities and (presumably, on the same basis) religious bodies, if
they were found to be public authorities. She argues that they
would be deprived of Convention rights, with nothing to prevent
appropriation of their property without compensation, denial of
their right to associate and discrimination against them.[40] This
brings home vividly the dangers of upside-down application of
human rights standards to non-state bodies.

The crucial step in this argument is the equation of a 'public
authority' under section 6 HRA with a 'governmental organization' under Article 34 (and, hence, section 7 HRA).[41] It is noteworthy, however, that the government refused to accept a
parliamentary amendment to harmonize the two tests in the same
way as with the victim test for the purpose of standing.[42] Nevertheless, this does not prevent the UK courts from using the Article
34 jurisprudence as an aid to determining the boundaries of what
constitutes a 'public authority'.[43] If the domestic courts fail to do

[37] For example, Jack Straw, HC Deb. vol. 314, col. 406 (17 June 1998).

[38] Elsewhere I have described this effect as 'public liability horizontality':
I. Leigh, 'Horizontal Rights, The Human Rights Act and Privacy: Lessons from the
Commonwealth?' (1999) 48 *ICLQ* 57.

[39] D. Oliver, 'The Frontiers of the State: Public Authorities and Public Functions
under the Human Rights Act', (2000) *Public Law* 476.

[40] Ibid., 491.

[41] ' "Public authority" seems to be the domestic rendering of "governmental
organisation" ', ibid., 491.

[42] An amendment designed to replicate the Convention jurisprudence under Cl.
6 was unsuccessfully moved in the Committee stage: HC Deb., vol. 314, cols. 419ff.
(17 June 1998).

[43] UK courts are required under section 2 of the Human Rights Act to 'take into
account' the Strasbourg jurisprudence, whenever decided, in interpreting the

so, in the light of the dangers highlighted by Professor Oliver, there are good reasons to insist on differentiating the two concepts: otherwise an expansive domestic reading of section 6 will undercut rights that religious organizations enjoy under the Strasbourg case law. It is to be hoped, then, that Strasbourg continues to exercise an external restraint by applying an independent test of whether religious organizations are 'non-governmental', regardless of whether the UK courts treat them as 'public authorities', through the application of judicial review. As we shall see, the problem is far from a hypothetical one, due to a recent judgment of the Court of Appeal.

The situation is more complex still once we take account of the Convention rights of the religious organizations themselves. In the case of an organization treated as a 'hybrid' public authority it is easy to see how, in respect of 'private' functions, the organization may appear as a victim in claiming violation of its Convention rights, although for some purposes ('public functions') it might be a respondent. However, if the UK courts give an expansive reading to section 6 beyond what Strasbourg would consider to be 'governmental organizations', it is possible to envisage even 'pure' public authorities enjoying Convention rights. There is also the possibility that horizontal human rights claims might be made against some religious organizations that are clearly private associations for all purposes. In all three situations a court would be bound, by virtue of section 6 of the HRA (and, if legislation was involved, under section 3), to consider the implications for the religious organization or association's own Article 9 and other rights of any ruling that it had violated the Convention rights of another person. The outcome would then depend on which rights each side invoked and their relative priority.

I will return to the issue of churches as 'pure' public authorities. First, however, I will consider the issue of 'public functions' (relevant to 'hybrid' public authorities), horizontal rights and, finally, the attempt to placate religious critics by inserting a protective clause (section 13) into the Act.

Convention rights. However, Article 34 is not among the 'Convention rights' specified under the HRA, sched. 1. Nevertheless, *R v Secretary of State for the Home Department, ex parte Brind* [1991] 1 AC 696 (HL) requires that statutory ambiguity (here, concerning the meaning of 'public authority' in section 6 HRA) should be resolved in a Convention-friendly manner.

The Public Functions of Churches

Traditionally the judiciary has been reluctant to involve itself in
ıı liᵤiᴵᴵᴵ ılᴵᴵᴵᴵᴵᴵᴵ ᴵᴵᴵᴵᴵᴵᴵᴵᴵ ᴵᴵᴵᴵᴵᴵᴵᴵ, ᴵᴵᴵᴵᴵᴵᴵ ᴵᴵ ᴵ ᴵᴵᴵᴵᴵᴵᴵᴵᴵᴵᴵ ᴵ ᴵᴵᴵᴵᴵᴵᴵ
disputes, in the criminal sphere or, more recently, in public law.
Thus, for the purpose of judicial review, religious bodies and
officials have generally not been treated as exercising public
functions.[44] In the well-known case of *ex p. Wachmann*, the Chief
Rabbi, as the highest source of spiritual guidance to a Jewish
congregation, was held not to be subject to judicial review in a case
in which he accepted the report of a commission of inquiry into
the misconduct of a rabbi, who was then dismissed.[45] Simon Brown
J. argued that the Chief Rabbi's functions were intimate, spiritual
and religious in character: in the absence of such a role Parliament
would not legislate for these functions, nor would the government
seek to discharge them. Interestingly (and of potential importance
with regard to the Church of England and the Church of
Scotland[46]) he argued that the mere recognition of the Chief Rabbi
in legislation and the conferral on him of certain statutory powers
did not render his other, non-statutory, roles subject to judicial
review.[47] Similarly, in a second case the refusal of an Imam (the
spiritual leader of a mosque) to admit certain people on to the roll
of voters at the mosque was held not to be subject to judicial
review.[48] The court found that the case did not have a public law
element since it concerned only a small religious community in
Luton, there was no statutory underpinning for the Imam's functions and this was not an area in which Parliament would intervene

[44] The principle of a self-governing ecclesiastical sphere is weaker, however, in
the case of the established church. See generally M. Hill, 'Judicial Approaches to
Religious Disputes', in R. O'Dair and A. Lewis (eds), *Law and Religion*, esp. at
411.

[45] *R v Chief Rabbi of the United Congregations of Great Britain and the
Commonwealth, ex p. Wachmann* [1993] 2 All ER 249; and see *R v London Beth
Din, ex p. Bloom* [1988] COD 131.

[46] For the position in the (non-established) Church in Wales: see *R v Provincial
Court of the Church in Wales, ex p. Williams* (1999) 5 Ecc LJ 217 and *R v Dean and
Chapter of St Paul's Cathedral and the Church in Wales, ex p. Williamson* (1998) 5
Ecc LJ 129.

[47] As to statutory functions, see, however, *R v Rabbinnical Commission, ex p.
Cohen* (1987, unreported) where it was held that a licensing decision of the
Commission under the Slaughterhouses Act 1974 was subject to review.

[48] *R v Imam of Bury Park Lane Jame Masji Luton, ex p. Sulaiman Ali* [1992]
COD 132.

if the internal affairs of the mosque were not properly regulated. Moreover, the court felt incompetent to undertake an examination of religious law and customs and the traditions of the local religious community which would be fundamental to determining the issue.[49]

The validity of a self-governing ecclesiastical sphere was recognized also by the government during parliamentary discussion of the HRA, although as a consequence of the 'private functions' test under section 6, rather than because the Church was not a public authority *per se*. According to the Home Secretary: 'the regulation of divine worship, the administration of the sacrament, admission to church membership or to the priesthood and decisions of parochial church councils about the running of the parish church are, in our judgment, all private matters.'[50] This assumes that in at least some areas churches may exercise public functions and so, by virtue of section 6, fall to be treated as 'hybrid' public authorities. In the parliamentary debates education was offered as an example.[51] Church schools would probably be regarded as public authorities[52] because of the underpinning of a specific statutory regime and the state origin of the majority of their funding.[53] However, the impact as regards freedom of religion of this line of reasoning is likely to be minimal because detailed and clear primary legislation already applies to matters such as collective worship,[54] religious education,[55] admission of pupils to church

---

[49] Cf. *R v Chancellor of St Edmundsbury and Ipswich Diocese, ex p. White* [1948] 1 KB 195. See also M. Hill, 'Judicial Review of Ecclesiastical Courts', in N. Doe, M. Hill and R. Ombres (eds), *English Canon Law* (Cardiff, University of Wales Press, 1998).

[50] HC Deb., 20 May 1998, col. 1015.

[51] Ibid. Professor Oliver points out that to treat education as a public function (whether or not provided by a public authority) would be consistent with the developing EC law of 'service of general interest': 'Frontiers of the State' (n. 39 above).

[52] In *National Union of Teachers and others v Governing Body of St Mary's Church of England Junior School* [1997] 3 CMLR 630, the Court of Appeal decided that the Church of England school was an emanation of the state and therefore bound by the vertical direct effect of a European Community Directive.

[53] In a case involving the University of Cambridge the ECJ has held that where more than 50% of funding comes from the state it is to be treated as a contracting authority under EC public procurement law: *R v HM Treasury ex p. University of Cambridge, Case C–380/98*, [2000] 1 WLR 514, ECJ.

[54] Schools Standards and Framework Act 1998 (hereafter, SSFA), s. 70 and sched. 20.

[55] SSFA, s. 69 and sched. 19.

schools[56] and religious discrimination in the employment of teachers.[57] Consequently, there is little opportunity to use Convention rights under sections 3 or 6 of the HRA.

Another area in which some religious organizations act as state substitutes is in the formalities of marriage, particularly in the cases of the Church of England,[58] and Jewish and Quaker marriages.[59] In these cases the religious ceremony suffices and, unlike other Christian denominations or religions,[60] there is no need for a civil ceremony. It can thus be argued that in these specially recognized cases the religious organization or minister of religion is acting as a public authority under the HRA. The differential treatment between religious groups might perhaps itself found a claim in Strasbourg that there is discrimination on grounds of religion contrary to Article 14 in the enjoyment of the Convention right to marry guaranteed by Article 12, although the restriction affects the formalities rather than the right as such. Once again, however, domestic challenge on these grounds would have little prospect of success in view of the clarity of the relevant provision and the lack of interpretive space. Concerns that the Act might require clergy to conduct marriages against their consciences were rebutted by the government.[61]

Horizontal Rights

The question of the possible 'horizontal effect' of the Human Rights Act has already attracted a burgeoning academic literature,[62] due mainly to the complex variety of routes by which the

---

[56] SSFA, ss. 86(3)(b) and 91; and see *Choudhury v Governors of Bishop Challoner Roman Catholic Comprehensive School* [1992] 3 All ER 277, HL; *R v Lancashire CC, ex p. F* [1995] ELR 3.

[57] SSFA, ss. 58–60.

[58] Marriage Act 1949, ss. 21 and 25.

[59] Marriage Act 1949, ss. 26 and 47.

[60] Where a marriage takes place in a registered place of worship (Marriage Act 1949, ss. 41, 42 and 44, as amended) the minister of religion can take the place of the registrar or other authorized person in conducting the civil ceremony. Legally, the religious service is of no effect in itself.

[61] See further HL Deb., 5 Feb. 1998, cols. 757–8; HL Deb., 19 Jan. 1998, cols. 1344 and 1346.

[62] For example, Hunt, [1998] PL 423; Leigh, (1999) 48 ICLQ 57; Markensinis, (1999) 115 LQR 47; Phillipson, (1999) 62(6) MLR 824; Phillipson and Fenwick, (2000) 63(5) MLR 660; Buxton (2000) 116 LQR; Wade (2000) 116 LQR 217; Lester and Pannick (2000) 116 LQR 380; N. Bamforth [2001] *Public Law* 34.

Act can apply in civil litigation and some enigmatic comments by ministers in the course of the parliamentary debates.[63] This is not the place to re-enter the controversy. A broad measure of agreement has emerged among commentators that there are differing degrees of horizontal effect. The Act certainly applies to all legislation (including Ecclesiastical Measures) and to all courts and tribunals (including the consistory courts, the provincial courts and the Court of Ecclesiastical Causes Reserved), whatever type of litigation they are hearing. Moreover, the indirect effect of the Convention is widely acknowledged in private law.[64] The major remaining controversy concerns 'full horizontal effect' – whether the Act is a source of new legal rights and obligations between individuals. It is hard, however, to see what practical effect this issue could have for freedom of religion or for religious institutions. The underdeveloped nature of the Article 9 jurisprudence at Strasbourg makes it an unlikely source of new domestic causes of action.

That said, there are isolated pronouncements from the European Court of Human Rights suggesting that Article 9 may require positive protection as well as simply acting as a restriction on the state itself. In *Otto-Preminger-Institut v Austria* the Court declared that the state has a responsibility 'to ensure the peaceful enjoyment of the right guaranteed under Article 9 to the holders of those beliefs and doctrines'.[65] There has been no further elucidation of what this positive duty may entail, but, clearly, civil remedies would be one possibility where the threat is from other individuals. Against that tantalizing possibility one must, however, count the failure to rule that Article 9 applies in contractual situations.

If the Strasbourg jurisprudence is followed, there would seem to be little room for the horizontal application of Article 9 against religious organizations because of the restricted view taken of the scope of the protection under that provision. Thus, in *Stedman v UK*[66] the applicant's claim that dismissal for refusal to work on Sundays constituted a denial of her rights under Article 9 was declared to be manifestly ill-founded by the Commission. Her

---

[63] HL Debs., 3 Nov. 1997, col. 1231; HL Deb., 24 Nov. 1997, col. 783; HC Deb., vol. 315, col. 561 (2 July 1998).

[64] For example, re Articles 9 and 14: *Blaythwayt v Baron Cawley* [1976] AC 397.

[65] (1995) 19 EHRR 34, para. 47.

[66] (1997) 23 EHRR CD 168.

employer was a private sector company so the state's liability could only be said to be engaged indirectly.[67] The result would have been identical, however, even had she been a state employee.[68] The Commission found that the cause of dismissal was not her religious convictions but rather a refusal to respect contractual working hours. Since she retained the right to resign (which she exercised, claiming constructive dismissal), the Commission argued that there could be no question of restriction of her right to manifest her religion.[69]

This is consistent also with the approach of the European Court of Human Rights in a case from Turkey in which the dismissal of a senior legal adviser in the Turkish air force was held not to violate Article 9. He had been dismissed for having adopted 'unlawful fundamentalist views'.[70] The Court held that the complainant had voluntarily accepted limitations on manifestation of his beliefs in embracing a system of military discipline.[71] Within these limitations he was permitted to pray five times daily, to observe Ramadan and to attend Friday prayers. The dismissal was found to be based on his conduct and attitude, rather than the way in which he manifested his religion. The Turkish government argued that the complainant had manifested a lack of commitment to the secularist foundation of the Turkish state which the army was supposed to guarantee. In the words of the Court, 'Art. 9 does not protect every act motivated or inspired by a religion. Moreover, in exercising his freedom to manifest his religion, an individual may need to take his specific situation into account'.[72] The limitations here on his rights were self-chosen.

---

[67] Cf. *Young, James and Webster v UK* (1982) 4 EHRR 38, para. 49.

[69] For a similar conclusion as regards a state employee see Appl. No. 24949/94, Dec. 3.12.96.

[69] Similarly, her claim that her right to family life under Article 8 had been violated was manifestly ill-founded given the almost inevitable compromise between family life and work where both partners work (the Sunday working was in any event part of a five-day week rota).

[70] *Kalac v Turkey* (1999) 27 EHRR 552.

[71] Ibid., paras 27 and 28. See also *Larissis v Greece* (1999) 27 EHRR 329 where the ECtHR found that convictions of Jehovah's Witness servicemen for proselytism of other (subordinate) airmen were not contrary to Article 9. Proselytism of civilians was treated differently: paras 58–61.

[72] Para. 27

Section 13[73]

In anticipation of the risk that litigation under the Human Rights Act might be used to undermine their distinctive ethos and rights of self-government, a coalition of religious organizations successfully lobbied for the inclusion of safeguards. The result is section 13 of the HRA.

> If a court's determination of any question arising under this Act might affect the exercise by a religious organisation (itself or its members collectively) of the Convention right of freedom of thought, conscience and religion, it must have particular regard to the importance of that right.[74]

The specific reference to a 'religious organization' was intended to embrace not just churches, but also religious charities and other religious non-charitable bodies and to acknowledge the collective exercise of these rights. This was intended to meet concerns that Article 9 might be interpreted in an unduly individualistic way by the courts and so impede doctrinal decisions.

Section 13 falls short, however, of giving automatic primacy to freedom of belief over other rights, such as privacy or freedom of expression. The Home Secretary argued, when commending it, that to do so would itself contravene the Convention. Instead, the requirement to 'have particular regard to the importance of the right' steers the courts in that direction, without giving (as had earlier amendments)[75] either an exemption for religious organizations from the Act or a statutory defence for religiously motivated conduct.

Commentators tend to support the government's earlier contention that special protection is unnecessary[76] and so regard section 13 as largely symbolic in its effect.[77] Certainly, comparing the

---

[73] See also I. Leigh, 'Towards a Christian Approach to Religious Liberty', in P. Beaumont (ed.), *Christian Perspectives on Human Rights and Legal Philosophy* (Carlisle, Paternoster, 1998); P. Cumper, 'The Protection of Religious Rights under Section 13 of the Human Rights Act 1998', [2000] *Public Law* 254.

[74] New Cl. 9. HC Deb., 20 May 1998, cols. 1013ff.

[75] See Leigh, 'Christian Approach'.

[76] Lord Lester of Herne Hill and D. Pannick, *Human Rights Law and Practice* (London, Butterworths, 1998), paras 2.13 and 2.13.1. Note also the comments of Lord Justice Sedley in the Preface to this volume.

[77] Cumper, 'Religious Rights'.

judicial approach to the parallel provision drawing the attention of
the courts to the importance of freedom of expression (section 12),
then is little reason to be confident that section 13 will be of much
effect. The expression 'have particular regard' (in that instance, to
freedom of expression) has not prevented the courts from over-
riding the interest in the first major cases involving a clash of
rights.[78] Overall, then, section 13 is likely to be of less importance
than the Convention jurisprudence to which I have referred. This
opinion is confirmed by the earliest cases invoking Article 9 under
the Human Rights Act. It is noticeable that section 13 has had no
discernible effect in cases in which individuals have claimed (unsuccessfully) that their freedom of religion was violated by over-
inclusive legislation regulating drugs[79] and prohibiting corporal
punishment in schools,[80] respectively.

The Church of England and the Human Rights Act[81]

The discussion so far has suggested that, on the basis of the
Strasbourg approach, fears that the Church of England and
perhaps other churches might be held to be subject to the Human
Rights Act were not wholly fanciful, but that plausible counter-
arguments could be put. Government ministers, perhaps unduly
influenced by its domestic constitutional status, seem to have
assumed in the parliamentary debates that the Church of England,
at least, might be treated as a 'hybrid' public authority (meaning
that some but not all of its functions might attract HRA protection).

In two areas in particular – the interpretation of church
legislation and jurisdiction of church courts – it could be safely
predicted that the Human Rights Act would apply, because of the

---

[78] *Venables and another v News Group and others*, [2001] 1 All ER 908; *Douglas
and others v Hello! Ltd*, [2001] 2 WLR 992; *Ashdown v Telegraph Group Ltd.*,
[2001] 3 WLR 1368; *A v B plc and another* [2001] 1 WLR 2341.

[79] In *R v Taylor (Paul Simon)*, 23 October 2001, [2001] EWCA Crim 2263.

[80] In *Williamson v Secretary of State for Education and Employment*, 15
November 2001, [2001] EWHC Admin 960.

[81] See also M. Hill, 'The Impact for the Church of England of the Human
Rights Act 1998', (2000) 5 *Ecc LJ* 431; J. Rivers, 'From Toleration to Pluralism:
Religious Liberty and Religious Establishment, the UK's Human Rights Act', in
R. Ahdar (ed.), *Law and Religion* (Aldershot, Ashgate, 2000), 143–4.

legal status of Church of England institutions and the express terms of the Act. These are discussed below. First, however, it is necessary to discuss an altogether less predictable development, that the courts would find the Church of England to be a 'pure' public authority, that is, bound in all respects by the Convention rights under the HRA.

In *Aston Cantlow and Wilmcote with Billesley Parochial Church Council v Wallbank*[82] the Court of Appeal held that a Parochial Church Council of the Church of England (a 'PCC') is a 'public authority' under section 6 HRA. The case involved a challenge to the liability of a 'lay rector' at common law to pay for repairs to the chancel of the parish church – an obscure duty under the law of real property arising from the status of glebe lands. The Court of Appeal found that the enforcement by the PCC of the common law liability to repair the chancel would infringe the defendants' right to the peaceful enjoyment of their possessions. This would breach Article 1 of the First Protocol to the ECHR because it took the form of an arbitrary tax and, moreover, in singling out for liability the owners of what was once glebe land, the common law was discriminatory and violated Article 14 of the Convention. It is the conclusion that the PCC was bound by the Human Rights Act which is of most interest here.

The Court's conclusion that the PCC was a public authority[83] was premised on the 'unique status'[84] of the Church of England in law, and the special position within it of the PCC. The Court

---

[82] [2001] 3 WLR 1323. Note however that this decision is subject to an appeal waiting to be heard in the House of Lords. See also D. Oliver, 'Chancel Repairs and the Human Rights Act', (2001) *Public Law* 651.

[83] Several indicators were given, although none was conclusive in itself, of the approach to be taken to identifying a public authority. First, the test of a public authority was not purely 'functions-based' in all instances (although this is the test under s. 6(3)(b) for 'hybrid' authorities): p. 1332, (para. 33). Secondly, the case law on amenability to judicial review, while relevant, is not determinative (p. 1333 (para. 34)) either in the cases of 'pure' or 'hybrid' authorities since section 6 reflects the Convention's underlying distinction between 'the state' and persons, groups and non-governmental organizations (p. 1332 (para. 33)). Thirdly, however, the judicial review case law did yield a useful distinction between functions of 'public governance' (in *R v Panel on Takeovers and Mergers, ex parte Datafin plc* [1987] QB 815) and functions of 'mutual governance' (in *R v Disciplinary Committee of the Jockey Club, ex parte Aga Khan* [1993] 1 WLR 909), although neither was precisely defined. Finally, the presence or absence of statutory power could be a useful indicator.

[84] See p. 1331 (para. 31); and see *Marshall v Graham Bell* [1907] 2 KB 112, 226.

emphasized that, since the Reformation, both spiritual and temporal courts were the King's courts, although enforcement of chancel repairs fell to the latter. The PCC was a body corporate under statutory powers, exercised by the Church of England: 'That a Measure of its National Assembly can make every PCC a statutory corporation is an index both of the public character of the Church of England and (to some extent) of that of a PCC.'[85]

The PCC's functions under section 2 of the Parochial Church Councils (Powers) Measure 1956 included those of former vestries and – importantly in this context – recovery of the cost of chancel repairs from 'lay rectors'. In the historical development of real property law any elements of mutuality which had once existed between the church and the person liable for chancel repairs had long ago been lost:

> The relationship in which the function arises is created by a rule of law and a state of fact which are independent of the volition of either of them. In our judgment it is inescapable, in these circumstances, that a PCC is a public authority. It is an authority in the sense that it possesses powers which private individuals do not possess to determine how others should act. Thus, in particular, its notice to repair has statutory force. It is public in the sense that it is created and empowered by law; that it forms part of the church by law established; and that its functions include the enforcement through the courts of a common law liability to maintain its chancels resting upon persons who need not be members of the church. If this were to be incorrect, the PCC would nevertheless, and for the same reasons, be a legal person certain of whose functions, chancel repairs among them, are functions of a public nature. It follows on either basis by virtue of section 6 that its acts, to be lawful, must be compatible with the rights set out in Schedule 1 to the Human Rights Act 1998.[86]

The emphasis on distinctive legal powers mirrors the test of an 'emanation of the state' for the purposes of identifying which bodies are bound by European directives.[87]

---

[85] See pp. 1331–2 (para. 32), referring to the Parochial Church Councils (Powers) Measure 1956 (as amended), s. 3, made under the Church of England Assembly (Powers) Act 1919.

[86] See p. 1333, paras 34 and 35.

[87] *Foster v British Gas* [1990] 3 All ER 897, ECJ. Applied by the Court of Appeal in *National Union of Teachers and others v Governing Body of St Mary's Church*

The judgment also raises the possibility that, if the PCC were not to be treated as a 'pure' public authority, it would nevertheless, be liable as a 'hybrid' public authority. From a purely pragmatic viewpoint the latter approach (though still questionable) would be preferable since this would allow some discrimination over which situations the HRA is to apply to.[88] This was apparently also the government's expectation. The Church of England did not feature among the illustrations given by ministers of 'pure' public authorities[89] and, to the contrary, they seem to have assumed that it would be treated as a 'hybrid' body, some of whose functions (for example, education) would be regarded as public and others as private. It is noteworthy that Jack Straw, the then Home Secretary, included among the functions that he anticipated would be regarded as 'private' under the HRA: 'the regulation of divine worship, the administration of the sacrament, admission to church membership or to the priesthood and *decisions of parochial church councils about the running of the parish church*'.[90]

Had the court been prepared to look at the parliamentary material some of the difficulties of treating the Church of England as a 'pure' public authority might have become clearer to it.[91] This failure to engage with the wider implications is unfortunate in view of the extensive concerns expressed in Parliament about whether or how section 6 would apply to religious bodies and the attempts at reassurance given by ministers, such as the one quoted above. One unintended consequence of the Court of Appeal's ruling is that the areas listed by the Home Secretary enjoy no special immunity and will only be protected to the extent that a limitation can be found within the Convention right in question.

of England Junior School [1997] 3 CMLR 630, to rule that a Church of England school which had voluntary aided status was an emanation of the state.

[88] On 'hybrid' authorities see *Poplar Housing v Donoghue* [2001] 3 WLR 183 (housing association was a public authority in so far as it provided homelessness accommodation on behalf of a local authority in view of the close connection between them); *R (on the application of Heather) v Leonard Cheshire Foundation*, QBD (Admin. Court), 15 June 2001, *Daily Telegraph*, 26 June 2001 (registered nursing home not a public authority despite being in receipt of public funding and state regulation).

[89] For example, HL Deb., 24 Nov. 1997, cols. 809–11.

[90] HC Deb., 20 May 1998, col. 1015; emphasis added.

[91] The Court of Appeal refused to consider the parliamentary debates under the rule in *Pepper v Hart*, claiming that the expression 'public authority' was not ambiguous or obscure: p. 1331 (para. 29).

The judgment will also lead to anomalies. Identical situations will be treated differently in the Church of England and other denominations. First, individuals will be able to claim Convention rights against the Church of England that they would be unable to claim against other churches, and, secondly, those churches will themselves have Convention rights where Anglican parishes may be deprived of them.

The second point follows because the UK courts will be required to apply the Convention under section 6 in situations where the European Court of Human Rights would regard a complaint as inadmissible *ratione personae*. Although the Court of Appeal professed to be aware of the issue – this was a reason for not treating the judicial review case law as determinative – it failed to engage in a detailed analysis of the Strasbourg jurisprudence cited earlier. In effect the judgment has extended in the domestic sphere the Strasbourg jurisprudence on the applicability of Convention, since, as we have seen, the Convention organs have declined to rule that the Church of England is a 'governmental organization'.[92] It was strictly unnecessary to hold that the PCC was a 'pure' public authority – the same outcome could have been reached by treating chancel repairs to be a 'public function' under section 6(3). However, in doing so the court has brought the nightmare scenario of some religious critics of the HRA a stage closer. For, if PCCs are 'public authorities' for all purposes this leaves little or no space for them to complain as 'victims' under section 7 of a Human Rights Act violation, unless a future court is prepared to address the question of the discrepancy between what constitutes a 'public authority' under section 6 HRA and a 'governmental organisation' under Article 34.[93]

I turn now to the less contentious areas of church legislation and the church courts.

Church Legislation

As in other spheres, Measures of the General Synod are treated under the Human Rights Act as primary legislation,[94] with the

---

[92] See n. 27 above.

[93] Cf. *Holy Monasteries v Greece* (text at n. 28 above) and *Hauanemi v Sweden* (text at n. 32 above).

[94] See Church of England Assembly (Powers) Act 1919, s. 4; *R v Archbishops of Canterbury and York, ex p. Williamson, The Times*, 9 March 1994, CA,

consequence that they cannot be set aside by the courts, although a declaration of incompatibility can be given by the High Court, Court of Appeal, House of Lords or Privy Council.[95] It is worth observing that ecclesiastical Measures therefore have a higher constitutional status than Acts of the Scottish Parliament. This is more likely a sign of respect for the place of Westminster within the process than out of deference to the General Synod. Like all legislation, the duty under section 3 on all courts and tribunals to interpret the provision 'so far as is possible to do so' in conformity with a person's Convention rights applies to church legislation. The practical effect may be limited, however, since the Convention organs have recognized the right of churches to self-government by consistently dismissing Convention claims brought against them by their members.

In this respect the outcome of the challenge brought before the European Commission on Human Rights in relation to the Measure permitting the ordination of women to the priesthood is instructive.[96] The Commission found the complaint that the Measure violated the Reverend Paul Williamson's Article 9 rights to be manifestly ill-founded. It stressed that he had the option of leaving the ministry or the church and that nothing had been done, strictly, to punish or coerce him. In any event rights under Article 9 were not absolute and in this instance the church's legislation was plainly 'prescribed by law' and could be said either to be for the 'protection of the rights and freedoms of others' (namely women within the church) or for the 'protection of morals' (in following its view of scripture). The church's action was consistent with the elimination of discrimination under Article 14 of the Convention.

Church Courts

Church courts, like any other court, will be treated as 'public authorities' by virtue of section 6(3). The HRA has already had some impact in consistory court judgments, via the court's duty to apply the Convention as a public authority. Hence, in *In Re*

---

reproduced in M. Hill, *Ecclesiastical Law*, 2nd edn (Oxford, Oxford University Press, 2001) 672–6; N. Doe, *The Legal Framework of the Church of England* (Oxford, Oxford University Press, 1996), ch. 3.

[95] HRA, ss. 4 and 21(1).

[96] *Williamson v UK*, Application No. 00027008/95, 17 May 1995.

Durrington Cemetery,[97] the court considered a request for a faculty to disinter the body of a Jewish man from a municipal cemetery where the ground was consecrated according to the rites of the Church of England so that the deceased could be re-interred in a Jewish cemetery. Although there had been a delay of eighteen years from the time of death, Hill Ch. accepted that there were exceptional circumstances for agreeing to the request. He considered the Human Rights Act as though it were already in force and concluded that:

> this court would be seriously at risk of acting unlawfully . . . were it to deny the freedom of orthodox Jewish relatives of the late Mr Saunders to manifest their religion in practice and observance by securing re-interment of his cremated remains in a Jewish cemetery in accordance with Jewish law.[98]

Some aspects of the composition and procedure of church courts may, perhaps, be open to challenge under Article 6 of the ECHR: for instance, the requirement that appellate judges determining matters in the Judicial Committee of the Privy Council or the Court of Ecclesiastical Causes Reserved should be communicant members of the Church of England.[99] Bearing in mind that *any person* resident in a parish has a right to object to the granting of a faculty, the same issue may arise in relation to a consistory court, where the chancellor is appointed by the diocesan bishop. In all cases, however, any defect is inherent in the governing measures and cannot be interpreted away. Change could only arise following challenge at Strasbourg or the making of a declaration of incompatibility.

An unsuccessful challenge was made to the composition of the consistory court and the Court of Arches in *Tyler v UK*,[100] an

---

[97] [2001] Fam 33, [2000] 3 WLR 1322. Applied in *In re Crawley Green Road Cemetery*, Luton [2001] 2 WLR 1175, in which a faculty was granted to allow the re-interment of a humanist by his widow. This was held to be manifestation of her rights under Article 9. However, Bursell Ch. stated (ibid., at 1179) that the rights of others (for example, religious convictions about burial in consecrated ground) would have had to have been considered under Article 9(2) if the widow had wanted to scatter the ashes instead of re-interring the body.

[98] Ibid., 1326.

[99] Ecclesiastical Jurisdiction Measure 1963, s. 10.

[100] Appl. No. 00021283/83, 5 April 1994, reproduced in M. Hill, *Ecclesiastical Law*, 677–81.

admissibility decision of the Commission arising from 'criminal proceedings' leading to a finding of conduct unbecoming against the applicant clergyman which was upheld on appeal. The Commission found to be manifestly unfounded the applicant's claim that determination of 'civil rights and obligations' had not been before 'an independent and impartial tribunal' in violation of Article 6(1). In dismissing the applicant's attack on the composition of the consistory court, the Commission stressed that the chancellor's appointment was permanent and was subject only to removal in exceptional circumstances and there was a requirement that he or she be a qualified lawyer and swear a judicial oath. There was no reason to assume that the four assessors (two clergy and two lay) were not independent and, in view of the disciplinary character of the proceedings, it was appropriate that members of the church should participate. For similar reasons, the Commission rejected challenges to the Dean and other members of the Court of Arches.

It should be noted, however, that the Convention approach to impartiality in judicial appointments might be said to have hardened somewhat since *Tyler* in more recent cases.[101] The domestic climate has changed too. In view of the findings of the Scottish courts in the 'temporary sheriffs' case[102] (not to mention *Pinochet*),[103] one cannot dismiss the possibility that the domestic courts might now find that the composition of these church courts is not in accordance with Article 6(1) and issue a declaration of incompatibility under section 4 HRA.

Conclusion

I began by referring to the distrust of human rights among many orthodox believers. The issues that I have discussed raise common concerns about how far it is appropriate to apply secular legal norms to religious bodies. There is a delicate balance to be struck within an essentially secular society between, on the one hand, the

[101]Notably *Bryan v UK*, (1995) Series A- No. 335-A and *McGonnell v UK*, (2000) 30 EHRR 289.

[102]*Starrs v Ruxton* (2000) SLT 42.

[103]*Ex parte Pinochet (No. 2)* [1999] 1 All ER 577, HL; *Locabail (UK) Ltd. v Bayfield Properties Ltd.* [2000] 2 WLR 870, CA.

imposition of a liberal standard on people and groups who have fundamentally different values and, on the other, creating indefensible exemptions from community standards. In conclusion let me make clear where I think the line should be drawn.

In his well-known book *The Culture of Disbelief*,[104] the Yale law professor Stephen Carter argues that the churches play an important part as 'mediating institutions' between citizens and the state and that the autonomy of religious institutions should be respected. For him autonomy entails that religious groups 'should not be beholden to the secular world, that they should exist neither by the forbearance of, nor do the bidding of the society outside of themselves'.[105] Again, 'to be truly free [they] must be able to engage in practices that the larger society condemns'.[106] In the current climate it is no accident that Carter gives the illustration of discrimination on grounds of sexual orientation.[107] Stressing that autonomy requires more than the freedom of *individual* believers, Carter argues:

> Religions are . . . independent centers of power with bona fide claims on the allegiance of their members, claims that exist alongside, are not identical to, and will sometimes trump the claims to obedience that the state makes. A religion speaks to its members in a different voice from that of the state, and when the voice moves the faithful to action, a religion may act as a counterweight to the authority of the state.[108]

> To try to make the religions, in their internal organisation, conform to the state's vision of a properly ordered society is not simply a corruption of the constitutional tradition of religious freedom, it is also an assault on the autonomy of religions as bulwarks against state authority.[109]

As we have seen, it is not just in the United States that the autonomous nature of religion is in danger. There is a fear that in Britain also the Human Rights Act may pose a threat to the ability of religious bodies to maintain a distinctive ethos.

[104] Stephen L. Carter, *The Culture of Disbelief: How American Law and Politics Trivialize Religious Devotion* (New York, Anchor Books, 1993).
[105] Ibid., 34–5.
[106] Ibid., 34.
[107] Ibid., 41.
[108] Ibid., 35.
[109] Ibid., 38–9.

Although real, we can conclude that the danger is exaggerated – provided, that is, the UK courts remain true to the principles governing the application of Convention rights to individuals and associations such as churches. The Convention jurisprudence establishes three important points. First, that mild state preference for one religion over another, as in the position of the Church of England, does not generally violate the Convention. Second, the Convention cannot generally be invoked by religious dissidents or minorities against religious bodies. Third, that churches are generally seen as 'non-governmental' bodies that are entitled to complain as victims under the Convention machinery of violation of their collective rights.

As we have seen, section 6 of the HRA does not follow the pattern that the Convention assumes. If the UK courts were to adopt an excessively wide reading of what constitutes a public authority or an overly narrow approach to private functions under section 6 of the HRA there would be a risk that the respect that the Convention shows for the ability of religious bodies to govern themselves would be undermined domestically. However, if judges continue to exercise the restraint shown before the HRA in relation to judicial review of spiritual matters this should not arise.

These sanguine conclusions are thrown into some doubt by early experience of the application of the HRA.[110] The Court of Appeal's ruling in the *Aston Cantlow* case goes considerably wider than necessary in holding a PCC to be a 'pure' public authority under the HRA. The implications may threaten church autonomy and religious liberty if they foreshadow a new willingness on the part of the judiciary to intervene in church affairs. In contrast, there could be no objection to holding church legislation and church courts to be subject to the HRA, where the application of the ECHR is clearly mandated by sections 3 and 6 of the HRA. Some aspects, especially procedural, of ecclesiastical law may be found wanting.

The Church of England is clearly in a special category of its own, however, and even in these cases it should be borne in mind that the Convention rights are shot through with limitations for the rights and freedoms of others and with recognition of community

---

[110]Individuals' claims under Article 9 against the state are outside the scope of the discussion here but these have not fared well either under the Human Rights Act: see nn. 79 and 80 above.

values. Notwithstanding isolated and obscure historical curiosities, like chancel repairs, it can hardly be argued that any religious body in contemporary Britain poses a threat to individual freedom, so that the judiciary should favour the individual human rights claimant over it. There may be a case to be argued for using the Human Rights Act against non-state bodies, for example, to protect individuals from the overbearing behaviour of multi-national companies, but voluntary religious bodies are in an entirely different category. We are not dealing here with either 'Jaws or Leviathan' (to use Lord Justice Sedley's phrase).[111]

Overall, there is ample space to recognize the distinctive collective or associational attributes of religious bodies within the Convention framework. It is crucial that domestic judges faithfully reflect the Strasbourg jurisprudence and are sensitive to this aspect of religious liberty. It is all too easily overlooked in an individualistic emphasis on human rights. We neglect it at our peril: not just our religious liberties but also the diversity of society as a whole depends upon it.

[111] Stephen Sedley, *Freedom, Law and Justice* (London, Sweet and Maxwell, 1999), 31–2.

7

The Development of the Law of Employment and Education

DAVID HARTE

Introduction

Since the Human Rights Act 1998 came into force it has already begun to colour the general law in England. However its long-term effects will depend upon governmental priorities in introducing new legislation and on the vagaries of litigation. There are probably few who would have guessed two of the earliest topics relating specifically to the Church of England where Convention rights have already been considered, namely chancel repairs and exhumations.

In *Aston Cantlow v Wallbank* Mr and Mrs Wallbank were called on to meet the bill for repairs to the chancel of Aston Cantlow church as owners of a farm in the parish which carried with it the obligations of lay rectors. Even though they had acquired the farm in the knowledge of this liability, the Court of Appeal held that they were not bound by the obligation since it constituted a tax which did not apply to similar property owners and was therefore contrary to the right to the 'peaceful enjoyment of [their] possessions' under Article 1 of the First Protocol to the Convention.[1] At a stroke, the Court of Appeal deprived parish churches of a major source of finance for the upkeep of the important historic buildings for which they are the public custodians.[2]

---

[1] [2001] 3 All ER 393. Leave to appeal to the House of Lords was granted by the appeal committee on 11 February 2002.

[2] A major issue in this case was the extent to which the Church of England is subject to Convention rights under the Human Rights Act generally as a public body within s. 6 and where it is carrying out particular functions of a public nature such as caring for heritage buildings.

The *Wallbank* case illustrated the new vulnerability in the general courts of settled principles of church property law. *Re Crawley Green Road Cemetery, Luton* illustrated the importance of Convention rights in the church courts.[3] There, Chancellor Bursell granted a faculty for the exhumation from consecrated ground of the remains of a man who had had no Christian allegiance and whose wife had not realized that the burial site was consecrated. Established legal principle would have led the chancellor to refuse a faculty but he granted one on the basis of the widow's Article 9 Convention rights to freedom of conscience.[4]

Both the *Wallbank* case and *Re Crawley Green* illustrate the subjection of the church to Convention rights as a result of the Human Rights Act. Discussion of the Act in church circles often tends to concentrate on the possible use of the Act by individuals to challenge the church and to oppose its stance where these conflict with the wishes of secularists, members of other faiths or its own disaffected members. However, both Article 9 rights which specifically include religious liberty and a number of other Convention rights may be used either in ways which challenge the church and religious associations of various faiths or in ways which support them. Disputes where Convention rights are invoked will frequently involve balancing the demands of conflicting belief systems and the church must therefore be prepared to take part in litigation so that the law is developed in a manner which is consistent with religious faith rather than allowing it to be moulded increasingly by secular agendas. This will require an alertness to the long-term influence of cases which may in themselves appear to deal with peripheral points and may not at first sight affect the church. It could require a readiness to intervene in litigation, or in providing expert evidence on ethical and other implications raised by a case.[5]

---

[3] [2001] Fam 308.

[4] There the deceased was of Jewish origin and he and his wife followed a non-Christian humanist philosophy. See too the decision of Hill Ch. in *Re Durrington Cemetery* [2001] Fam 33 where a faculty was granted for the removal of the remains of a Jewish man to a Jewish cemetery. This was at the instance of his family some years after a burial which had been arranged by a non-Jewish widow.

[5] Note here, for example, the readiness of the Court of Appeal to take serious account of the submissions provided by the Cardinal Archbishop of Westminster in respect of the very difficult issues posed in the case of *Re A (Separation of Conjoined Twins)* [2001] Fam 147, CA where permission was eventually given to

Two areas where the Human Rights Act is likely to have a significant effect are the laws of employment and of education. The right to freedom of thought, conscience and religion under Article 9 of the Convention raises many questions as to the future development of the law in these areas. A number of these questions will involve balancing Article 9 rights against other Convention rights, notably the right to respect for private and family life under Article 8, the right to freedom of expression under Article 10 and the right to education as framed in Article 2 of the First Protocol to the Convention. Both employment law and education law pose problems as to how these various rights may be enjoyed without discrimination, as provided for by Article 14. The purpose of this chapter is to identify some of the likely points which may arise in the context of the existing law on employment and education.

The Framework of Employment Law

The European Convention on Human Rights does not contain specific rights with regard to employment. It does not, for example, set out an explicit right to work. The prohibition of discrimination under Article 14 of the Convention only applies to discrimination in the enjoyment of other Convention rights and therefore does not specifically apply to discrimination in employment law on grounds such as religious belief. Nevertheless Convention rights such as the right to respect for private life and the rights to freedom of belief and freedom to manifest one's beliefs have important implications with regard to employment and where these are raised the prohibition against discrimination may be called in aid. Take the example of a Muslim employer who allowed his Muslim employees to leave work at midday on a Friday so as to attend worship in the mosque but required Jewish workers and Jehovah's Witnesses to continue working after dark so that they were working on the sabbath. There, the Jewish and Jehovah's Witness workers would have been discriminated against in that

separate Siamese twins so that one would survive although the other would die immediately, rather than both lingering for a very short shared life. Note also the role of the advocate to the court (formerly styled *amicus curiae*). See *Memorandum: Requests for the Appointment of an Advocate to the Court* issued by the Attorney General and the Lord Chief Justice on 19 December 2001.

they were not allowed to manifest their faith in a manner which was allowed to their Muslim colleagues.[6]

In the example above, of discrimination against non-Muslim employees over Friday prayers, the breach of Articles 9 and 14 of the Convention could be invoked directly under the Human Rights Act if the employer were a public authority, for example, a local council in an area with a significant Muslim population.[7] Generally, there is considerable uncertainty over the circumstances where bodies such as a church or a religious charity carrying out functions of a public nature are doing acts of a public nature which will make them subject to the Act and where they are doing acts of a private nature, in which case the Act does not directly apply.[8] The national institutions of the Church of England, such as the Archbishops' Council,[9] the Church Commissioners,[10] the Central Board of Finance,[11] the Pensions Board,[12] the Council for the Care of Churches and the Churches Conservation Trust[13] might seem to be public bodies for the purposes of the Act. Diocesan, cathedral and parochial institutions also might seem to be public bodies.[14] They certainly carry out certain public functions which would make them subject to the Act when fulfilling those functions. Thus a verger or church organist employed by a Church of England cathedral or a Parochial Church Council would seem to be

[6] By his treatment of Muslim employees, the employer in this example demonstrated that it was practicable to allow workers to finish early on a Friday. He would therefore not be able to claim that it was impracticable or unfair to other workers to release Jewish employees early; cf. *Ahmad v Inner London Education Authority* [1978] QB 36, [1978] 1 All ER 574 (CA). *Ahmad*'s case shows that the example of discrimination against a Jewish worker could equally be replaced by one of discrimination against a Muslim worker. There, however, the allegation of discrimination was unsuccessful because there was no disproportionate denial of rights to a Muslim by contrast with members of other faiths.

[7] Under the Human Rights Act 1989 s. 6(1) 'It is unlawful for a public authority to act in a way which is incompatible with a Convention right'.

[8] Ibid. s. 6(3)(b) public authority includes 'any person certain of whose functions are functions of a public nature' and by s. 6(5) 'in relation to a particular act, a person is not a public authority by virtue only of subsection 3(b) if the nature of the act is private'.

[9] Set up under the National Institutions Measure 1998.

[10] Church Commissioners Measure 1947.

[11] Church Funds Investment Measure 1958.

[12] Clergy Pensions Measures 1961–1997.

[13] Pastoral Measure 1983, s. 44, as amended by Pastoral (Amendment) Measure 1994, s. 13.

[14] See here *Aston Cantlow v Wallbank* [2001] 3 All ER 393.

employed to carry out work which would be public according to any relevant criteria. The work would be carried out in public, for the benefit at least in part of the public attending worship or visiting the church, and it would be work required and regulated under provisions of public ecclesiastical law.

There is wider uncertainty over how Convention rights may be applied indirectly to non-public bodies. These could include local church organizations when they are not fulfilling public functions. For example, a large parish church could make use of a company set up to run a Christian bookstall and cafeteria on the church premises. Employees of such a company would not be able to invoke the Human Rights Act directly against the company. Similarly, neither would an employee of a non-Christian religious association or of a Christian denomination other than the Church of England, such as a caretaker at a mosque or a Methodist church. Nevertheless, the Act is likely to have an impact in such cases.

First, the spirit of the Act is likely to prompt new legislation which will apply to private as well as to public employers. Thus the array of UK legislation which applies to discrimination on the grounds of race and sex and to some extent disability does not at present apply to discrimination on the grounds of religion except in Northern Ireland or where discrimination against a particular religion also amounts to racial discrimination. That would include discrimination against Jews or Sikhs, whose religion is identified with their race.[15] It would also include indirect discrimination where discriminating against members of a particular religion makes it more likely that members of certain races will be at a disadvantage in comparison with others.[16] As a result of the Human Rights Act the legislation against discrimination in employment is likely to be extended to cover religious discrimination generally.

Second, the Act requires courts and tribunals, as themselves public authorities, not to act in a way which is incompatible with a Convention right.[17] Therefore courts and tribunals are bound to interpret new and existing law so as to conform with Convention

[15] *Seide v Gillette Industries Ltd* [1980] IRLR 427; *Simon v Brimham Associates* [1987] IRLR 307 and *Mandla v Dowell Lee* [1983] 2 AC 548.

[16] Sex Discrimination Act 1975; Race Relation Act 1976. Cf. *Board of Governors of St Matthias Church of England School v Crizzle* [1993] ICR 401.

[17] Human Rights Act 1998, s. 6(3)(a).

rights. This will not empower a court to create a completely new right between private citizens. For example, if a private employer dismissed an employee for converting from one religion to another the courts could not extend the remedies which would apply under the existing law where an applicant was dismissed because he or she was of a particular sex[18] or race.[19] New legislation would be required. On the other hand, existing rights are likely to be interpreted more expansively. Under the wide-ranging concept of unfair dismissal,[20] it would have been unlawful in most circumstances to dismiss an employee for changing from one faith to another even before the Human Rights Act came into force. However, in future, a tribunal or court reviewing a dismissal case will need to take express account of whether such a dismissal constituted discrimination conflicting with the employee's right to freedom of religion.

A further dimension to the application of Convention rights in employment law is the interrelation between the Human Rights Act and European Union legislation. In particular, the Framework Directive of 2000 establishing a general framework for equal treatment in employment and occupation has introduced an obligation on member states to ban discrimination in employment, including discrimination on the grounds of religion or belief.[21] Article 4 allows member states to provide for different treatment between individuals where 'by reason of the nature of the particular occupational activities concerned or of the context in which they are carried out, such a characteristic constitutes a genuine and determining occupational requirement, provided that the objective is legitimate and the requirement is proportionate'.

This exception would clearly allow for the requirement that ministers of religion should be trained in and committed to the faith in which they were appointed to work. Similarly, it would allow for the requirement that teachers of religious education in faith schools should practise the relevant faith.

Significantly, because of pressure from churches and other religious associations, particularly through the British government,

---

[18] Sex Discrimination Act 1975.
[19] Race Relations Act 1976.
[20] Employment Rights Act 1996, s. 94.
[21] Council Directive 2000/78/EC of 27 November 2000, Article 1.

Article 4, paragraph 2, now provides much more extensive safeguards for religious associations:[22]

> Member States may maintain national legislation in force at the date of adoption of this Directive or provide for future legislation incorporating national practices existing at the date of adoption of this Directive pursuant to which, in the case of occupational activities within churches and other public or private organisations the ethos of which is based on religion or belief, a difference of treatment based on a person's religion or belief shall not constitute discrimination where, by reason of the nature of these activities or of the context in which they are carried out, a person's religion or belief constitute a genuine, legitimate and justified occupational requirement, having regard to the organisation's ethos. This difference of treatment shall be implemented taking account of Member States' constitutional provisions and principles, as well as the general principles of Community law, and should not justify discrimination on another ground. Provided that its provisions are otherwise complied with, this Directive shall thus not prejudice the right of churches and other public or private organisations, the ethos of which is based on religion or belief, acting in conformity with national constitutions and laws, to require individuals working for them to act in good faith and with loyalty to the organisation's ethos.

So far as European Union law is concerned, considerable allowance is therefore made for churches or diverse religious associations such as a Muslim or a Christian legal practice or a Jewish medical practice to operate on a faith basis. On the other hand, the Directive precludes religious bodies discriminating on 'other grounds' than religion and belief. Thus discrimination on the basis of sexual orientation is itself prohibited by the Directive and there could be difficulty for a church which excluded employees who were homosexual or lesbian but who otherwise were fully

---

[22] This contrasts with the position of small businesses with fewer than five employees and private households. The Equal Treatment Directive 76/207/EEC was interpreted by the European Court of Justice to apply to these. Therefore their exclusion in UK anti-discrimination legislation was unlawful; *Commission of the European Communities v United Kingdom* [1984] IRLR 29; *Johnston v Chief Constable of the Royal Ulster Constabulary* [1986] IRLR 263. European Community legislation may therefore seemingly affect the freedom of families to choose employees according to a preferred race or sex. This is difficult to reconcile with the Article 8 Convention right to respect for private and family life.

committed to the beliefs and practices of that church. It may be
that individuals who are actively homosexual could properly be
excluded on the basis that their behaviour demonstrated that they
did not share a belief required by the church. On the other hand it
could be argued that protection from discrimination on the
grounds of sexual orientation is a specific right on its own account
which cannot easily be overridden.[23] Certainly if an employer took
steps to discover whether an individual was homosexual by prying
into his or her private life that would be likely to constitute a
breach of the Article 8 Convention right to respect for private and
family life.[24]

Such issues under European Union law will have to be resolved in
parallel with the working out of Convention rights under the
Human Rights Act and there the separate jurisdictions of the
different courts concerned could give rise to differing interpretations. In the case of rights asserted by European Union law, the
British courts are obliged to refer contentious issues to the Court of
Justice of the European Union in Luxembourg and to submit to its
rulings.[25] The Luxembourg court is required to comply with
human rights principles including those set out in the European
Convention on Human Rights.[26] The interpretation of the Human
Rights Act is conferred on the UK courts. They must 'take account'
of decisions of the European Court of Human Rights but they are
not bound by those decisions.[27] However, where a Convention right
is in issue in a case covered by European Union law it would seem
that the UK court will be required to refer the point to
Luxembourg. There could in theory be an impasse if the case were
then brought before the European Court of Human Rights in
Strasbourg and the Luxembourg interpretation were held to be
wrong.

In the context of employment law there are a number of points
where freedom of religion or other religious considerations raised

[23] In respect of Convention rights under Article 8 the issue would involve a
secular judge assessing the reasonableness of a restriction in terms of its necessity
for the protection of morals and the rights and freedoms of others. See further here
Dudgeon v UK, Judgement of 22 Oct. 1981, series A, No. 45; (1982) 4 EHRR 149.

[24] *Smith and Grady v UK* [1999] IRLR 734, ECtHR.

[25] Treaty of the European Union as substituted by the Treaty of Amsterdam,
1996, Article 234 (formerly Article 177).

[26] This is specifically set out in the Preamble to Council Directive 2000/78/EC.

[27] Human Rights Act 1998, s. 2.

by the Human Rights Act are particularly likely to arise. These include the stages of hiring and firing and various circumstances which may arise during the course of employment. Different issues may crop up depending on who is the employer and the circumstances where a matter of religious import is raised.

Selection of Employees

A major concern for the church and for many religious associations is that the Human Rights Act may make it more difficult to choose prospective employees who will maintain the ethos of their institutions. The Act does not impose a direct restriction here. Even the Church of England may not specifically be affected despite its character as a public body. Nevertheless, the Human Rights Act could have a chilling effect which would militate against an institution such as a major Christian church protecting its ethos by including in its internal law a requirement that key personnel should be Christians. The freedom of religious bodies to make appointments on their own criteria may not strictly be impaired but this chilling effect could reduce transparency and openness and lead to frustration for candidates. On the other hand, proper consideration of the Act may lead to religious bodies scrutinizing their decision-making more carefully. If a more expansive view is taken of the effect of the Act, the jurisprudence which it inspires could be invoked indirectly against religious bodies which are not open about their appointments.

Even if the Human Rights Act does not directly require that discrimination should be avoided in employment, it is likely to prompt legislation which will treat discrimination with regard to employment as unlawful when it is on the grounds of religion, as it already is on grounds of sex or race. On the other hand, the Article 9 Convention right to freedom of religion allows for such limitations to be imposed on its operation as are prescribed by law and are necessary for reasons appropriate in a democratic society, including the protection of the rights and freedoms of others. Similar riders allow for limitations to the Article 8 right to respect for private and family life, the Article 10 right to freedom of expression and the Article 11 right to freedom of assembly and association. An example of how legitimate limitations could be prescribed by the law of a member state would seem to be the principle contained in Article 4 of the European Union Equal Treatment Directive.[28] Thus English legislation designed to apply the Directive in respect of religious discrimination may be expected to permit churches and religious associations of all sorts to restrict employment to co-religionists for such work as the church or association consider necessary as a genuine, legitimate and justified occupational requirement, having regard to the organization's ethos.

Despite this reassuring conclusion an example of the possible chilling effect of the Act has already risen in respect of cathedral appointments. Each of the cathedrals of the Church of England was required to set up a transitional council to produce a new constitution and statutes to comply with the Cathedrals Measure 1999. These generally provide, among other things, for offices which are central to the work and ministry of the cathedral but whose occupants will not normally be ordained, such as vergers and directors of music. Some transitional councils wished to make clear that these posts were to be occupied by Christians, for example by limiting them to actual communicants of the Church of England or of other churches in communion with the Church of England, or, more ecumenically, widening access as far as members of other denominations who are in good standing in their own churches and who are therefore eligible to take communion in the Church of England.[29] However, in the event, such drafting was avoided on the basis that problems could arise both under existing anti-discrimination legislation and as a result of the Human Rights Act.

In practice a religious body is likely to want to select candidates for its posts from co-religionists. The ecclesiastical law of the Church of England restricts key ministerial posts to ordained clergy. Here it is significant that existing anti-discrimination legislation permits discrimination where it is justified as an occupational requirement.[30] The freedom to appoint ministers of

[28] Council Directive 2000/78/EC.
[29] Canon B 15A.
[30] Sex Discrimination Act 1975, s. 7, Race Relations Act 1976, s. 55. It is also significant that the state has tolerated the exclusion of women from ministry in certain Church of England parishes even since the ordination of women was approved.

religion is unlikely to be any more hampered by the Human Rights Act. The Convention right to freedom of thought, conscience and religion allows for limitations which are prescribed by law and which are necessary for the protection of the rights and freedoms of others. The position is more difficult where a religious body wishes to fill a post which is not so clearly identified with religious activities. Even though they will not normally be ordained, a verger or director of music is intimately involved in worship. However, some posts, such as that of a caretaker, bookshop manager or canteen supervisor, may not have such obvious religious content. Even so such employees too could be expected to take an active role in the pastoral work and the ministry of a church.

A restriction in internal law, such as a cathedral constitution or statute, could be used to make clear that key posts in the institution require Christian commitment. This could be valuable in underlining the nature of both the institution and the post. It could serve to reassure church members who fear creeping secularization and it could help to avoid misunderstanding on the part of secular applicants. These could easily see a verger's job as the equivalent to that of caretaker in a secular museum or the post of director of music as equivalent to a post with a similar name in a secular school or local authority department.

Before a provision was included restricting a post to Christians, the drafting body would need to consider specifically whether it was desirable to impose such a restriction or whether it would be better to leave open the possibility of appropriate individuals being appointed who were well qualified and sympathetic to the aims of the Church even if they were not practising Christians.

The decision whether or not to ring-fence posts in a cathedral constitution or statutes so as to protect their Christian nature should reflect a careful balancing of the consequences of such a provision. The omission of such restrictions may be deliberate and considered or it might simply suggest an unawareness of any potential problem. It could, however, provide an illustration of a chilling effect of the Human Rights Act on the freedom of action by the church. The chill would be the more striking since it would not be a response to the direct effect of the Act but to fear of further legislation to which the Act could lead. If such safeguards have been excluded to avoid a risk of future conflict with the secular authorities there is a real cause for concern. If it is afraid to make a requirement of religious commitment in key employees clear in its public documents, the church may be inhibited in ensuring that such employees are indeed committed Christians or if it does apply such a policy the danger is that it may prove less than frank in its advertisements and appointment procedures.

The scheme of existing anti-discrimination legislation under English law restricts discrimination in the selection of employees, first by prohibiting advertisements and other arrangements for recruitment which are discriminatory and then by requiring that the various stages of the selection process avoid discrimination. Where an advertisement, for example, is discriminatory, complaint may be made to an Employment Tribunal by the Equal Opportunities Commission.[31] Where a candidate is rejected on the basis of unlawful discrimination he or she may be able to bring a direct complaint.[32] However, it is notoriously difficult to prove discrimination in the eventual selection if reasons are not given for choosing one candidate rather than another, and even if reasons are given it may often be possible for those making the selection to find another plausible reason even though their selection is really based on unlawful discrimination.

Employment depends upon the framework of contract law and the regulation of discrimination within employment may be seen as a statutory intervention in the contractual relationship. By contrast, a right to protection from discrimination where a person has not yet been appointed may be seen as a distinctive free-standing right in public law. However, discrimination at this stage may also be analysed in terms of contract. An advertisement or interview could be seen as importing a contractual obligation to applicants who reply to the advertisement or at least to those who attend interview. It would seem possible to imply into such a contract a term that applicants should be considered fairly and equally. The Human Rights Act could influence the development of such implied terms and their interpretation to protect the religious sensitivities of candidates. If such an approach were developed aggressively by the courts, a prospective employer could be prevented from asking questions of a candidate for a job which was not specifically religious as to his or her religious beliefs or about

---

[31] Sex Discrimination Act 1975, s. 38.
[32] Ibid. s. 6(1).

other matters which could be morally significant, for example, personal sexual relations.[33]

In the case of an appointment to a Church of England post where the church authorities had failed to make clear in advance their view that religious commitment and adherence to Christian standards of morality were a necessary requirement of the job, it could be difficult to justify such questions. The relevant church body could be liable to proceedings under section 7 of the Human Rights Act. If appointing panels carefully avoided such questions, it would be difficult to challenge the appointment of a candidate who was in fact chosen specifically because of his or her religious commitment, unless there were new legislation prohibiting religious discrimination. However, it would seem to be highly regrettable if the religious requirement were not made explicit at an early stage, not least to save the wasted time and resentment of disappointed candidates.

Termination of Employment

If the Human Rights Act affects appointments of candidates for posts in religious organizations, it may be expected to have at least as much impact on the termination of employment. Again, this will be particularly true for the Church of England, because of its public character. Whatever the position with appointments, termination of employment is clearly a subject of contract law. The right of an employer to terminate the contract of an employee is circumscribed both at common law and by anti-discrimination legislation which at present relates to discrimination on the grounds of race or sex. The Act is likely to stimulate the extension of this legislation to religion.

Here, the sort of issues which might have avoided a person being appointed, if they had been openly faced at the appointment stage, may pose more difficulty if they later lead to dismissal. For example, it might become apparent that a church caretaker was not a committed church member as those appointing him or her had thought. The appointee might subsequently turn out to be an

---

[33] Such probing could be seen as inconsistent with the Article 8 right to respect for private and family life.

atheist; or a person who had been a church-goer when appointed
might subsequently be converted to another religion or become an
atheist.

Prior to the Human Rights Act, courts were generally reluctant
to intervene in matters of belief on behalf of dissenting individuals
who called the general courts or the state employment tribunal
system in aid.[34] They allowed the relevant church authorities to
determine their own doctrine and to discipline those who
challenged them.[35] With the advent of the Act it will be more difficult for the courts to avoid investigating the weight to be attached
to religious doctrinal positions where these are used by a religious
association to justify what an individual claims is a breach of a
Convention right.[36] Disputes may certainly be expected in employment law.

Potential conflict between the sensitivities of churches and other
religious associations on the one hand and the religious demands
of individuals on the other are likely to be particularly difficult to
resolve where an individual challenges the church on a matter of
principle. Dissent may arise simply in respect of belief or it may be
manifested in behaviour. If individuals insist on the freedom to
practise behaviour which the religious associations employing
them consider unacceptable, the rights of other members of the
associations may be severely affronted. On the other hand, a
dissenting individual may claim that his or her behaviour is
specifically underwritten by another Convention right. An obvious
area for potential conflict is over the rights of practising homo-
sexuals and lesbians who may insist on remaining in a church
which classifies their behaviour as inherently immoral. More

---

[34] There have been striking examples when individuals have mounted a challenge
against changes in doctrine, as with the introduction of women to the ordained
ministry (*R v Archbishops of Canterbury and York, ex parte Williamson*,
unreported, 1 March 1994, CA; see M. Hill, *Ecclesiastical Law*, 2nd edn (Oxford,
Oxford University Press, 2001), 672. Note also M. Hill, 'Judicial Approaches to
Religious Disputes', in R. O'Dair and A. Lewis (eds), *Law and Religion*, Current
Legal Issues 4 (Oxford, Oxford University Press, 2001), 409.

[35] *Gill v Davies*, 19 December 1997, reproduced in Hill, *Ecclesiastical Law*, 707.

[36] The courts have already demonstrated a new readiness to question the basis
for administrative decisions which previously would have satisfied the non-
interventionist *Wednesbury* test; cf. *Associated Provincial Picture Houses Ltd v
Wednesbury Corpn* [1948] 1 KB 223, CA and *R (Daly) v Secretary of State for the
Home Department*, House of Lords, [2001] UKHL 26, [2001] 3 All ER 433.

widely, the very idea of heterodoxy is difficult to relate to the Act. A person's views may change after they have been appointed to a post. Honesty may require them to state their new beliefs openly or the church authorities, sensing a decline in commitment, may challenge them and obtain an admission that they now have beliefs incompatible with the faith of the church or association. However, both the investigation and any subsequent disciplining could be subject to challenge under the Act.

Apart from Article 9 rights to freedom of religious and other belief, other Convention rights may be called in aid against a church in such situations. Thus, the Convention right under Article 8 to respect for private and family life could be put in issue where a person working for an organization with a religious ethos entered into a private relationship which was at odds with the beliefs of the organization but which did not directly disrupt working arrangements. A typical case, such as the popular media continually crave for, would be that of the clergyman leaving his wife for the wife of a colleague, or an organist entering into sexually illicit relations with members of the church choir. The tension between how secular and religious values will be applied under the Act could be particularly striking here. Church authorities which pried into the private lives of individuals to ensure orthodox behaviour could be challenged for interfering with privacy. Ironically, if steps were taken to restrict publicity of the affair by the popular media, the media would doubtless rely on the Article 10 right to freedom of expression.[37]

The outcome of such disputes is difficult to foresee. However, it does seem likely that the Act will make the decisions of religious associations more subject to scrutiny than in the past and in certain circumstances the state, particularly through the courts, may be impelled to assess the acceptability of doctrinal positions. If this leads to a clearer and more reasoned articulation of religious positions and to their accommodation within common standards of behaviour the Act may positively benefit religious life. However, if the courts begin to protect employees and indeed office holders

---

[37] It is significant that the right to freedom of expression is specifically emphasized in s. 12 of the Act. This key liberty for the media is therefore singled out in a similar manner to the key liberty for religious people under s. 13. 'Particular regard' is to be had by courts to the importance of each of these rights.

and members of religious associations against removal and other disciplinary proceedings for heterodoxy the Act may undermine the coherence of religious traditions. It could pose a real threat of the state imposing secular interpretations of the Act on churches.

Issues Arising during the Course of Employment

During the course of employment, tensions could arise over issues which have already been mentioned as possible causes for rejecting a candidate for employment or for dismissal. These could lead to a church employer issuing an ultimatum which the employee could treat as constructive dismissal.[38] More thick-skinned employees could ignore the ultimatum but claim compensation against the employer. In practice an employer may be indifferent to employees' religious beliefs unless they interfere with work. There the Act may be significant, for example, where employees claim time off work for worship or where they claim the right to wear distinguishing religious insignia.

In a British context, a major area for potential conflict is the religious demand for freedom to participate in worship and religious festivals. Here, the Act may prove of particular benefit to the church as well as to individuals of all faiths. The traditional Christian English Sunday was set aside from work and kept free for common worship. Although this could be oppressive and the legal bans on most secular activities on Sundays have been abolished,[39] part of a compromise with the churches was a continuing ban on the opening of large shops except for a single period of no more than six hours between 10.00 a.m. and 6.00 p.m.[40] Even this restriction is subject to continuing sniping from commercial interests which want unfettered trading on Sundays and promote shopping as a leisure pursuit in competition with religious worship. The Sunday Trading Act 1994 which contains the restrictions on shop opening also provides rights for shop workers to opt out of

[38] Employment Rights Act 1996, s. 95.

[39] Notably the Sunday Observance Act 1780, which prohibited most forms of Sunday recreation, has for practical purposes been eliminated by a series of Acts including the Sunday Entertainment Act 1932 and the Theatres Act 1972.

[40] Sunday Trading Act 1994, s. 1 and sched. 1.

work on Sundays.[41] The Human Rights Act could make it more difficult to demolish this safeguard for Sunday worship. However, it may also lead to claims for similar rights for members of other religions to time off work on particular days or for special festivals.[42]

Where an employee has been openly chosen by a church or other religious association from another faith, tensions over the freedom of the employee to practise that faith may be unlikely to arise. The discussion above has emphasized the importance for religious people to be free to choose to work with co-religionists: for a mosque to insist that its caretakers are Muslim or a synagogue that its catering staff are Jewish, or a Christian medical or legal practice that its members are Christians. Often, however, Christians and other religious groups will be happy to choose employees or work partners who do not belong to their faith. They may positively prefer their work structures to be plural rather than faith-based, provided the decision is left to them and not enforced by the state even on the basis of the Human Rights Act. In such a setting, open religious employers may be particularly keen to ensure that employees have time off for their religion's festivals and feel comfortable to wear any distinguishing insignia of their faith, whether it is, for example, a Sikh turban or a Christian cross.

The question of insignia is, however, one which could cause problems if society becomes more aggressively secular or if members of minority faiths feel threatened by the insignia of other religions. In France and Northern America vociferous opposition to personal insignia and religious symbols in public places may seem to British observers depressing examples of secular intolerance but they certainly illustrate possible points of conflict under the Human Rights Act.[43] British case law before the Act suggests

---

[41] Ibid. s. 4 and sched. 4.

[42] Secular critics may find it more difficult to undermine laws which are designed to protect the Christian faith where members of other faiths call for them to be extended rather than abolished. Thus the offence of blasphemy has not been abolished and Muslim commentators have called for its protection to be extended to their faith; cf. *Whitehouse v Lemon* [1979] AC 617 and *R v Chief Metropolitan Magistrate, ex p Choudhury* [1991] QB 429.

[43] J. Bell, 'Religious Observance in Secular Schools: A French Solution' (1990) 2 *Education and the Law* 121 and S. Poulter, 'Muslim Headscarves in Schools: Contrasting Approaches in England and France' (1997) 17 *Oxford Journal of Legal Studies* 43.

that the rights of individuals to manifest their faith with distinctive religious jewellery or symbols may be upheld more vigorously in England than the Convention requires. In particular, in *Mandla v Dowell Lee*,[44] a private Christian school was held in breach of anti-discrimination legislation where it excluded a Sikh pupil unless he gave up his turban. The case was brought on the basis of racial discrimination because of the distinctive cultural and ethnic identity of the Sikh religion. However, as specifically religious discrimination comes to be controlled by the Act the principle seems likely to be extended to religious insignia. In France a secular ban on religious insignia has been held justified as preventing a potentially disturbing sense of difference amongst pupils, exactly the argument which was rejected in *Mandla*'s case.

Education and the Religious Rights of Employees

Public education law is an area where the Church of England, the Roman Catholic Church and a number of other faith bodies are partners with the state in the provision of a major public good. In the context of employment law, the Human Rights Act could be used by secularists to erode the autonomy of religious bodies. They could be hampered in choosing and regulating those who work within a church or at any rate within an organization which does not have a specifically religious purpose but which carries on commonplace activities, in a profession or business on the basis of a specific religious tradition. In respect of education, Article 2 to the First Protocol of the Convention offers definite support to churches and other religious associations against such trends. This is the more important because most schools are state schools clearly within the public sphere. School authorities are therefore directly subject to the Act in a way that private employers are not.[45]

From a faith perspective, schools are of immense importance, because they inevitably shape a child's understanding of the world and his or her attitude to religion. The importance of education for human rights is explicitly recognized in Article 2 to the First Protocol which guarantees a right to education and the right of

---

[44] [1983] 2 AC 548.
[45] Human Rights Act 1998, s. 6.

parents to determine the ideological ethos of their children's education:

> No person shall be denied the right to education. In the exercise of any functions which it assumes in relation to education and to teaching, the State shall respect the right of parents to ensure such education and teaching in conformity with their own religious and philosophical convictions.

English law already provides a sophisticated framework for religion in schools which would seem to comply with and go beyond this Article. The effect of the Act may largely be to reinforce the existing position which entrenches the role of Christianity against attack by secular forces but it may also encourage a more balanced recognition of the aspirations of other faiths and of humanist ideologies within the education system, a development which would seem likely to be welcomed by many Christians.

The basis of the modern English school system is schools 'maintained' by the state through local government districts. These provide primary education in relatively small local schools to the age of eleven, followed by secondary education in large comprehensive schools.[46] At each level there is a distinction between general state 'community schools' and 'foundation' and 'voluntary schools', which represent particular religious traditions. The distinction dates back to the nineteenth century when some schools were provided by the Church and others by local authorities. The two forms of school were integrated in a single state system under

---

[46] There are a number of variations on this basic pattern. Thus some local authorities operate a three-tier system with primary school to age nine, middle schools to thirteen and upper schools for the final phase prior to university. Also, some local authorities continue to separate children at eleven into more academic grammar schools and technical schools or general secondary modern schools. During the Conservative governments of the 1980s and 1990s there were attempts to give greater autonomy to schools and a tier of schools was set up which were maintained directly by central government. These have largely been reabsorbed under local authority supervision but local authority schools as a whole are now given a greater element of control over their own budgets. Current legislation does still allow for certain distinctive schools such as City Technology Colleges. Generally, however, all these schools either relate to the general state pattern for religion which is found in community schools described in the main text of this chapter or they may opt for their own specific faith ethos.

the Education Act 1944. Typically, faith schools will be voluntary schools originally set up by the Church of England or the Roman Catholic Church. The may be 'voluntary controlled' where the local education authority provides all the finance and exercises general control or they may be voluntary aided schools. For these the church provides the site and may recover it if the school is closed. The church must also provide up to 15 per cent of maintenance costs for the buildings but has a higher level of control over such key matters as the appointment of staff.[47]

The Human Rights Act reinforces the existing legal place of religion in schools. The law already strikes a careful balance between the religious rights of teachers and other employees and other rights within the education system, notably parental rights over the religious content of their children's education. The education system already includes clear safeguards for the beliefs of employees, with carefully framed exceptions which allow schools with a particular religious ethos to require teachers to practise the faith which the school represents. Thus, the School Standards and Framework Act 1998 guarantees wide-ranging freedom of religion for staff in state schools which do not have a particular religious character. Section 59 prohibits discrimination by reason of a person's religious opinions or of their omitting to attend religious worship, in respect of their being employed at the school as a teacher or otherwise. No teacher may be required to give religious education. A teacher's pay must not be reduced on religious grounds nor are they to be disqualified from promotion or any other advantage.

Section 58 of the 1998 Act makes significantly different provisions in voluntary faith schools. In voluntary controlled schools, a proportion of teachers may be 'selected for their fitness and competence' to give religious education. A reserved teacher for religious education in a voluntary controlled school or any teacher in a voluntary aided school may be dismissed if the governors consider that he or she failed to give religious education 'efficiently and suitably'. Such teachers may be given preference for appointments, remuneration or promotion on the basis of their religious opinions according with the tenets of the school. If employment is terminated, regard may be had to any conduct by the teacher

---

[47] Education Act 1996, ss. 32, 34, 41–8, 59–75.

'which is incompatible with the precepts, or with the upholding of the tenets' of the relevant religion or denomination.[48] In controlled schools regard may be had in appointing a head teacher 'to that person's ability and fitness to preserve and develop the religious character of the school'.[49] On the other hand, religious opinions and practice may not be taken into account in employing staff other than teachers, even in a voluntary aided school.[50]

In addition to state schools, there are a significant number of independent schools.[51] These are often religious foundations. Many are Anglican or other Christian 'public schools' which continue to offer a daily devotional framework throughout the school week. It is generally assumed that, even if the state school system were secularized and its faith schools phased out, independent religious schools would continue to meet the aspirations of religious parents who were prepared to pay for their preference. Certainly, any attempt by the state to abolish independent schools would be seen as a major breach of Article 2 of the First Protocol to the Convention. What is not so clear is how the Human Rights Act and any employment legislation which it may inspire could affect the freedom of such schools to appoint and regulate their own staff.

It may be argued that independent schools are public authorities directly subject to the Human Rights Act. There is a statutory obligation for parents to ensure that their children are satisfactorily educated and independent schools are a recognized means of complying with that duty. Thus they are fulfilling functions of a public nature as envisaged in section 6(3)(b) of the Act. Given the balance struck in state schools, it would certainly seem necessary that any legislation passed to restrict discrimination on religious grounds should include exceptions which would allow independent religious schools to require their teachers to be practising members of the faith embodied in the school. Unlike voluntary schools it is arguable that independent schools should be free to extend the requirement to other staff.

---

[48] School Standards and Framework Act 1998, s. 60.

[49] Ibid., s. 60(4).

[50] Ibid., s. 60(6).

[51] The successful setting up of a number of independent Islamic schools has helped pave the way to the introduction of Islamic voluntary schools within the state sector.

If it is treated as fulfilling a public function, an independent
school could be directly challenged under the Act by a member of
staff who had been prevented from manifesting his or her religious
beliefs. The school could well be allowed a margin of appreciation
in determining whether it needed to restrict staff to practising
members of the relevant faith so as to protect its ethos. However, if
such restrictions went much further than would be accepted in a
voluntary maintained state school they could be vulnerable. The
point could prove an important one if society continues to become
ever more diverse and there is a trend for faith groups to try to
insulate themselves and their children from its fragmented moral
ethos. In any event, although the Human Rights Act does not
normally directly affect employment law in the private sector it will
be very relevant to the framing of anti-discrimination law which
may affect the rights of parents to ensure education for their
children in accordance with their religious convictions and will
also affect the rights of employees and potential employees.

Education and the Rights of Parents and Children

The greatest significance of the Human Rights Act in the school
system may be in its effect on the development of a new relationship between church and state where the church and associations of
other faiths provide public goods as part of their religious
function. As with the balance between the rights of teachers and
other staff and the claims of a school to maintain its religious
character, there is a need to strike a balance between the religious
freedom represented by the school and the rights of pupils and
their parents. The existing law provides careful safeguards for
children at religious schools, as in all schools, which allow parents
to withdraw children from religious education and worship.[52] But
parents of a different religious or secular persuasion from a school
might use the Act to promote their opinions. For example, they
might challenge teaching as infringing their family rights and their
religious sentiments where they object to the treatment of religion
in a subject other than religious studies or in a primary school
integrated curriculum where they cannot withdraw their children.

[52] Education Act 1996, s. 389.

However, the courts may well be unwilling to upset the balance built into the existing legislation, particularly in view of the conscience clauses which it includes.[53]

A key issue is the extent to which distinctive faith schools will be allowed to develop in future within the state education system.[54] Although there is good provision of Church of England primary schools, at secondary level, unlike those of the Roman Catholic Church, there is a shortage of Church of England schools. The government has warmly endorsed the proposals of a report commissioned by the Archbishops' Council from Lord Dearing which has recommended a significant number of new Church of England secondary schools.[55] Proposed legislation is likely to make it easier for non-religious community schools to change to a particular faith status. It is significant that these proposals have drawn heated opposition, particularly from secular forces in the education system and in the media. In view of the margin of appreciation allowed to the government in the relevant Convention rights, it could hardly be argued that the Act would inherently require the provision of faith schools within the state system if they did not already exist. However, the government's support for specific faith schools certainly seems to be in accordance with the spirit of the Convention, particularly Article 9 and Article 2 to the First Protocol on respecting parents' religious and philosophical convictions in the provision of education.

The Human Rights Act does seem to support the protection of existing schools and could be used as a basis for challenging education authorities which tried to close them down or refused, unreasonably, to provide for new ones where a demand was objectively demonstrated from a significant number of parents. A practical difficulty with popular single-faith schools is the framing of admission policies. Debates in the media during early 2002 on a new government Education Bill prompted demands for single-faith schools to admit a proportion of children who did not belong to

---

[53] *R v Secretary of State for Education ex p R and D*, unreported, CO/2202/92, 26 February 1993.

[54] For a discussion of existing case law at Strasbourg in this area see C. Evans, *Freedom of Religion under the European Convention on Human Rights* (Oxford, Oxford University Press, 2001), 88–96, 'Freedom of religion and belief and the *forum internum* in education'.

[55] *The Way Ahead: Church of England Schools in the New Millennium* (London, Church House Publishing, 2001).

the relevant faith. As a matter of principle it may be important for a faith school or the religious association to which it belongs to operate its own admissions policy. However, so as to further social harmony, it is necessary for the state to agree on the policy, to lay down rules, in the syllabus and by other means, which ensure that pupils are part of the wider community, and to provide regular inspection. Significantly, opinion within the Church of England has emphasized that admissions policies for Church of England schools should take account of diocesan policies and those are likely to favour a significant proportion of places being made available to applicants from non-Christian homes where there is a demand.

The position of independent faith schools may also be strengthened by the Act. The state may increase supervision of standards but the Act would seem to support the claims of independent religious schools and the families whom they serve to be free to regulate their own affairs. Here, the introduction of rights relating specifically to religion could redress what might be considered any imbalance in existing anti-discrimination legislation. Such an imbalance may be discerned in *Mandla v Dowell Lee*,[56] where a Christian head teacher was held to be in breach of the Race Relations Act in refusing to allow a Sikh boy to wear a turban in the school, even though this policy was expressly intended to express equality between pupils through uniform dress as a matter of Christian principle. Many Christians might well consider the policy of the school to be misguided but might nevertheless feel uneasy that the state should impose its view of equality on that of a faith school which was not within the state sector.

Conclusion

The practical effect of the Human Rights Act for the church and for the very diverse religious associations found in modern plural England will only become clear as the Act is applied in future legislation and case law. How it affects employment and education in particular will demonstrate whether the Convention rights are used to further a secular agenda for privatizing and playing down

[56] [1983] 2 AC 548.

religious belief as merely a matter for personal preference or whether they will provide a framework for developing a partnership of mutual respect between diverse value systems in a genuinely plural society.[57]

Where individual rights seem to conflict, it may be easier to reach common ground if respect is given to shared spiritual values and aspirations rather than seeking a new secular uniformity or bowing to the dictates of materialism. Cases which predate the Human Rights Act, such as *Ahmad*[58] and *Mandla v Dowell Lee*,[59] demonstrate some of the potential difficulties and opportunities. *Ahmad* illustrates how the European Convention may allow individual religious rights to be subordinated to the convenience of the majority. However, English judges could now take the view that the spirit of the Act should enable a genuinely plural solution to be achieved in such cases. The fact that the requirements of the major faiths differ over time to worship could make it easier to accommodate those needs in a single system. The main Muslim prayer time on Friday, the Jewish sabbath and the Christian Sunday fit conveniently into the British weekend which is a shared recreational period equally appropriate for secular families and individuals. Generally, the needs of members of various faiths to attend special festivals may be accommodated by allowing employees adequate choice of holiday time. If the rights of those like Mr Ahmad to time off work for religious observance were upheld under the Act, the cause of religious liberty would be advanced and the existing protection afforded to workers on Sunday which represents a survival of the Christian legacy of the country would be reinforced.

Dowell Lee may be interpreted as the imposition of a secular concept of equality on a religious organization. This was specifically to protect religious sensitivities of an individual member of another faith. The case is worrying because it allowed the state to interfere with the ethos of a private religious foundation. However, had the school in question been a Christian state school the

---

[57] Central here is the extent to which rights are afforded in law to religious associations rather than just individuals: J. Rivers, 'Religious Liberty as a Collective Right', in R. O'Dair and A. Lewis (eds), *Law and Religion*, Current Legal Issues 4 (Oxford, Oxford University Press, 2001), 227–46.

[58] See n. 6.

[59] See n. 44.

balance struck would have been unimpeachable. To function as a partner with the state a religious association must be prepared to accept a higher level of restriction than if it is operating solely in the private sphere. A religious association in partnership with the state must be free to offer its service in a manner which safeguards its own essential identity and ethos. On the other hand, it must be prepared not to impose its own religious position on those whom it is in partnership with the state to serve. By contrast, a religious association which does not operate within a public framework, such as a free church, may justifiably demand much greater freedom from state interference, even under the Human Rights Act, over whom it employs and how it functions.

Religion is a notoriously difficult concept to define and belief systems differ greatly in their expectations for relating to wider society. Some, such as Judaism or Sikhism, which are focused on a particular ethnic or racial identity, require freedom for their members to live out a distinctive lifestyle but make no claim to mould society as a whole. Other religious traditions, notably Christianity and Islam and various expressions of secular humanism, pursue a mission to transform society. For these there is a temptation to impose their value system on all. In a genuinely plural society this is unacceptable.

The Human Rights Act 1998 may be claimed by those in the Judeo-Christian tradition as a natural development of insights which have been revealed through the great world religions. Secularists may treat it as a foundation text for a humanist vision superseding religion. As the new jurisprudence based on the Act emerges, this brief discussion of its possible impact on employment and education law suggests that two issues may emerge of particular importance for religious liberty. First is the question of the extent to which religious people will be allowed to determine how their beliefs and value systems relate to the individual rights of the members and the employees of the religious associations to which they belong. Second is the question of how far the Act will enable a common system of public values to be developed which expresses a consensus between the major belief systems represented in society.[60]

[60] As to the problematic interrelation between these two issues see M. Evans, 'Religion, Law and Human Rights: Locating the Debate', in P. Edge and G. Harvey (eds), *Law and Religion in Contemporary Society: Communities, Individualism and the State* (Aldershot, Ashgate, 2000), ch. 9.

8
Canonical Approaches to Human Rights in Anglican Churches

NORMAN DOE

The Anglican Communion is a community of *sui juris* or self-governing churches in communion with the See of Canterbury,[1] and with each other. On the conventional level, Anglican churches are assembled together under the moral authority of the so-called instruments of Anglicanism: the instruments of faith (holy scripture, tradition, reason, the sacraments of baptism and eucharist, the historic episcopate and common patterns of worship);[2] and the institutional instruments of Anglican unity (the Archbishop of Canterbury, the Primates Meeting, the Lambeth Conference and the Anglican Consultative Council), which play a leading role but exercise no legal authority over individual churches.[3] On the juridical level, each Anglican church is autonomous: 'the true constitution of the Catholic Church involves the principle of the autonomy of particular Churches based upon a common faith and order'; as such, the churches 'promote within each of their territories a national expression of Christian faith, life and worship'.[4] Accordingly, in the absence of a formal, globally binding

---

[1] Lambeth Conference 1930, Resolution 49: the Communion is 'a fellowship within the One Holy Catholic and Apostolic Church, of those duly constituted dioceses, provinces and regional Churches in communion with the See of Canterbury'. Hereafter, in the notes, the Lambeth Conference is cited as LC.

[2] LC 1998, Res. III. 1, 2, 5 and 8.

[3] LC 1930, Ress. 48, 49: churches are bound together 'not by a central legislative and executive authority, but by a mutual loyalty sustained through the common counsel of the bishops in conference'. For the instruments of the Anglican Communion, see also LC 1998, Res. III. 6.

[4] LC 1930, Ress. 48, 49.

corpus of canon law,[5] the communion having no central canonical authority,[6] each Anglican church has its own internal legal system, seeking to serve the church in its own particular local circumstances.[7]

In view of the worldwide Anglican contribution to the human rights debate, as well as recent studies on the effect of human rights legislation on particular Anglican churches,[8] it seems timely to explore, in a preliminary and descriptive fashion, the relationship between human rights and Anglican canon law: to what degree, if at all, do the legal systems of Anglican churches promote human rights in civil society, and recognize and protect human rights in ecclesial society, within the life of those churches? The primary legal sources examined, from individual churches, may conveniently be measured against the Anglican understanding of human rights.[9]

The Concept of Human Rights in Anglican Thought

Resolutions of the Lambeth Conference indicate well, at a global level,[10] Anglican concern for,[11] and approaches, to human rights.

[5] However, for the idea of an unwritten common law of the Anglican Communion, manifested in shared principles induced from the profound similarities of individual Anglican legal systems, a *ius commune* rooted in the canonical tradition, see N. Doe, 'Canon Law and Communion', (2001) 20 *The Anglican 5*, a paper delivered to the Meeting of the Primates of the Anglican Communion, Kanuga, NC, USA, 6 March 2001.

[6] *Anglican Handbook* (1994), 19: 'Since the Anglican Communion does not have a central body with canonical authority, the list [of Anglican churches] is authorised by the Archbishop of Canterbury and the Anglican Primates'.

[7] See, for example, W. Hankey, 'Canon law', in S. W. Sykes and J. Booty (eds), *The Study of Anglicanism* (London, SPCK, 1988) 200.

[8] See, for example, M. Hill, 'The Impact for the Church of England of the Human Rights Act 1998', (2000) 5 *Ecc.LJ* 431.

[9] Much of the evidence employed in this study is derived from N. Doe, *Canon Law in the Anglican Communion: A Worldwide Perspective* (Oxford, Clarendon Press, 1998): this book does not, however, address the particular issues raised by this study. Needless to say, some of the legal provisions discussed in the book, based on a study carried out in 1996 and 1997, may now be out of date.

[10] For the persuasive effect of Lambeth Conference resolutions, see Doe, *Canon Law*, 346ff.

[11] See, for example, LC 1988, Res. 64: the Conference calls on 'each province to reassess, in the light of . . . our concern for human rights, its care for and attitude towards persons of homosexual orientation'.

First, the Conference recognizes the existence of human rights,[12] regarding them as fundamental,[13] and as of 'capital and universal importance',[14] not least in the context of the effects of their abuse and attacks on human dignity.[15] The theological foundation of its understanding of human rights is based on the idea of equality:

> all men, irrespective of race or colour, are equally the objects of God's love and are called to love and serve him. All men are made in his image; for all Christ died; and to all there is made the offer of eternal life . . . [e]very individual . . . has certain rights . . . [which] should be declared by the Church.[16]

In turn, human rights involve freedom to enable humankind to develop its relationship with God: '[e]very individual is . . . bound by duties towards God and towards other men, and has certain rights without the enjoyment of which he cannot freely perform those duties'.[17] As such, human rights are conceived as necessary to ensure that 'the divine dignity of every human being is respected and . . . justice is pursued',[18] and for humankind to fulfil its divine destiny: 'no view of man can be satisfactory which confines his interests and hopes to this world and to this life alone; such views belittle man and blind him to the greatness of his destiny'.[19] Indeed, the responsibility of the individual to God, and the development of individual personality, are both imperilled by any claim made either by the State or by any group within it to control the

---

[12] See, for example, LC 1998, Res. 1. 1: the Conference affirmed and adopted the United Nations Universal Declaration of Human Rights, on the fiftieth anniversary of its proclamation (in December 1948). The Conference thereby adopted the notion of the inalienability of human rights, though this precise idea does not expressly appear in Conference pronouncements.

[13] LC 1968, Res. 16: 'the Conference calls upon all the Churches to press upon governments and communities their duty to promote fundamental human rights and freedoms among all their peoples'.

[14] LC 1978, Res. 3.

[15] *Called to Full Humanity*: Section I Report, LC 1998, *The Official Report of the Lambeth Conference 1998* (Harrisburg, PA, Morehouse Publishing, 1999) 77: 'Millions of people across the world are the victims of war and violence, sectarian and racist strife, the abuse of political and economic power and the intolerance of the different faces of religious fundamentalism and exclusions'.

[16] LC 1948, Res. 6.

[17] LC 1948, Res. 6.

[18] LC 1988, Res. 33. 3.

[19] LC 1948, Res. 4.

whole of human life; '[p]ersonality is developed in community, but the community must be one of free persons'.[20] The Conference sometimes attacks breaches of human rights on the basis that they are contrary to the teaching of Christ.[21]

Secondly, the Conference explicitly classifies human rights in terms of political rights,[22] which include 'a fair and just share' in government and personal advancement and attainment,[23] and economic rights,[24] the latter embraced in so far as '[h]uman rights must include economic fairness and equity, and enable local economies to gain greater control over their own affairs'.[25] For the Conference, among human rights are: security of life and person; the right to work, to bring up a family and to possess personal property; the right to freedom of speech, of discussion and association, and to accurate information; and to full freedom of religious life and practice: 'these rights belong to all men irrespective of race or colour'.[26] Religious freedom and tolerance are sometimes classified as 'absolute rights',[27] and sometimes as a 'fundamental human right, the denial of which threatens all other liberties',[28] and practical action is recommended to ensure respect for the right.[29] The condemnation of racial discrimination is presented as based on 'the

[20] LC 1948, Res. 5.

[21] LC 1978, Res. 3; see also Res. 5: 'war as a method of settling international disputes is incompatible with the teaching and example of our Lord Jesus Christ'.

[22] LC 1920, Res. 75: 'The Church cannot in its corporate capacity be an advocate or partisan, "a judge or a divider", in political or class disputes where moral issues are not at stake; nevertheless even in matters of economic and political controversy the Church is bound to give its positive and active corporate witness to the Christian principles of justice, brotherhood, and the equal and infinite value of every human personality.'

[23] LC 1958, Res. 110.

[24] LC 1920, Res. 78: the church must 'give its full support to those clauses in the League of Nations Covenant which aim at raising by international agreement the status of industrial workers in all countries'.

[25] *Called to Full Humanity*, LC 1998, *Official Report*, 79.

[26] LC 1948, Res. 7; Res. 8 endorsed the proposed Covenant on Human Rights then before the United Nations.

[27] LC 1998, Res. 1. 2(a): the Conference called upon 'all faith communities, especially the Christian Church, to acknowledge our responsibility to mobilise our spiritual, moral and material resources to promote and protect as absolute rights, each person's freedom of thought, conscience and religion'.

[28] LC 1988, Res. 23; see also Res. 61 on the 'violation of fundamental human rights, including the right of religious belief, practice and propagation'.

[29] LC 1998, Res. III. 11: 'This Conference challenges Anglicans, as servants of Jesus Christ . . . (a) to respect the rights and freedom of all faiths to worship and

natural dignity and value of every man, of whatever colour or race, as created in the image of God'; all races should be allowed to participate in government, in the control, development and rewards of the natural resources of their country, and to associate freely in education, industry, recreation, and 'all other departments of the common life'.[30] Human exploitation is treated as a particular breach of human rights,[31] as are abuses in the administration of justice, such as 'any denial of the principle that a person is innocent until proven guilty by due, fair and impartial procedures of law'.[32]

Thirdly, the Lambeth Conference has developed a series of practical principles applicable to the promotion of human rights in civil societies, since, for the Conference, '[t]he Christian must . . . judge every social system by its effect on human personality'.[33] From the ecclesiastical perspective, the responsibility to promote human rights falls on a number of ecclesial classes. The Conference proposes a range of responsibilities for member churches: 'to speak out' against breaches of human rights;[34] 'to support all who are working for [the] implementation' of human rights instruments;[35] and to 'urge compliance with the United Nations Universal Declaration of Human Rights by the nations in which our various member Churches are located, and [by] all others over whom we may exercise any influence'.[36] Sometimes the responsibility is cast as a duty, whether the human rights concerned

---

practise their ways of life; (b) to work with all people of good will to extend these freedoms of worship, religious practice and conversion throughout the world; (c) to stand by those who are being persecuted for their faith by our prayers, protests and practical support; (d) to enter into dialogue with members of other faiths, to increase our mutual respect and explore the truths we hold in common and those on which we differ; (e) to witness to our faith in the reconciling and saving action of God in our Lord Jesus Christ working in us now through the power of the Holy Spirit; and (f) to equip ourselves for our witness, dialogue and service by becoming better versed in the teaching and practice of our own faith, and of at least one other faith'.

[30] LC 1958, Res. 110; see also LC 1968, Res. 16.

[31] LC 1978, Res. 3: 'We deplore and condemn the evils of racism and tribalism, economic exploitation and social injustices, torture, detention without trial and taking of human lives, as contrary to the teaching and example of our Lord in the Gospel. Man is made in the image of God and must not be exploited'.

[32] LC 1988, Res. 33. 3(d).

[33] LC 1948, Res. 5. See also *Called to Full Humanity*, LC 1998, *Official Report*, 87: 'In obedience to the teachings of Christ, the Church is obliged to live and proclaim the gospel and to promote and protect human rights'.

[34] LC 1988, Res. 33. 3.

[35] LC 1988, Res. 33. 1.

[36] LC 1998, Res. 1. 1(a).

are political,[37] or economic.[38] Individual members of particular Anglican churches too have a duty to promote and protect human rights.[39] Indeed, the promotion of human rights by the church corporately or its members individually should be achieved in concert with other citizens and organizations in their own countries.[40] Special objects of ecclesial action are the weak.[41] While 'the Church is not to be identified with any particular political or social system', for the Conference the duty to promote human rights is not confined to Anglicans: 'all Christians [are] to encourage their governments to respect the dignity and freedom of people within their own nations and the right of people of other nations to govern themselves'.[42] A central justification for the ecclesial promotion of human rights is that of witness.[43]

From the secular perspective, the Conference also urges national governments and the international community to promote and protect human rights.[44] Human rights 'should be declared by the Church, recognized by the state, and safeguarded by international law'.[45] However, the Conference also considers that the enjoyment of human rights may be subject to qualification: it believes that human rights:

[37] LC 1920, Res. 75: 'in matters of economic and political controversy the Church is bound to give its positive and active corporate witness to the Christian principles of justice, brotherhood, and the equal and infinite value of every human personality'; see also LC 1978, Res. 2.

[38] LC 1920, Res. 78: 'The Church is bound to use its influence to remove inhuman or oppressive conditions of labour in all parts of the world'.

[39] LC 1920, Res. 77: 'Members of the Church are bound to take an active part, by public action and by personal service, in removing those abuses which depress and impoverish human life'.

[40] LC 1920, Res. 77: 'In company with other citizens and organisations [members of the Church] should work for reform, and particularly for such measures as will secure the better care of children, including real opportunity for an adequate education; protection of the workers against unemployment; and the provision of healthy homes.'

[41] LC 1920, Res. 78.

[42] LC 1958, Res. 104.

[43] LC 1920, Res. 75 (see above n. 37); see also LC 1978, Res. 3.

[44] For example, with respect to freedom of religion, see LC 1998, Res. 1.2(e): the Conference calls on 'governments of all the nations our Churches represent to strive for creation of just and free conditions for people of all religions to practise their beliefs "either alone or in community with others and in public or private, to manifest his (or her) religion or belief in teaching, practice, worship and observance." (UN Universal Declaration of Human Rights, Article 18)'.

[45] LC 1948, Res. 6.

should be subject only to such limitations as are internationally recognized as necessary to protect public order, morals, and the rights and freedoms of others. Any such limitations should be clearly defined by law, and there should be appeal concerning them before impartial courts of justice.[46]

Moreover, the Conference calls on 'all Christian people to recognize their duty of exercising to the full their responsibility as citizens in the national and international policies of their governments'.[47]

Finally, however, there is no obvious, direct treatment in Lambeth Conference resolutions of the applicability of human rights *within* the church. The Conference's recognition of a duty on all 'governments and *communities*' to promote human rights,[48] and on 'all others over whom [members of the Conference] may exercise any influence',[49] is, by implication, perhaps the closest that the Conference comes to suggesting that the advancement of human rights is applicable to ecclesial communities as well as to civil society. Nevertheless, one report to the Conference on human rights, treating 'The Church as a Model Community', understands that '[e]very Christian community should be a model of mutual love, acceptance and reconciliation', in which Christians 'should examine their lifestyles critically and seek to develop honest and affirming relations with one another'. As a result, '[i]n recognition that the Church is the Body of Christ, efforts should be made to encourage participation by all of distinctive gifts, ministries, cultures and other qualities'. To achieve this goal, 'the Church discerns and identifies all discriminatory practices in its structures, images and symbols, and commits itself to reform and renewal'.[50]

Extrovert Canon Law: The Canonical Promotion of Human Rights in Civil Society

To what degree do the legal systems of individual Anglican churches implement the ideas and principles appearing in Lambeth

---

[46] LC 1948, Res. 8.
[47] LC 1958, Res. 102; LC 1978, Res. 3.
[48] LC 1968, Res. 16.
[49] LC 1998, Res. 1. 1(a).
[50] *Called to Full Humanity*, LC 1998, *Official Report*, 86.

Conference resolutions about the duty of the church corporately
and its members individually to promote human rights in secular
society? First, one opportunity for canon law to express the
imperative to promote human rights is to include this in legal texts
which spell out the purposes for which the particular institutional
church exists. While most canonical lists of ecclesial activities
emphasize purely spiritual matters,[51] some require the church to
advance the spiritual and moral welfare of society,[52] and others
refer to what may be styled the temporal mission of the church.[53]
But promotion of human rights in civil society as a corporate
activity of the church is not explicitly found in canonical lists of
church purposes. For this reason, the constitution of the church in
New Zealand is exceptional; the mission of the church includes:
'proclaiming the Gospel' and 'seeking to transform unjust
structures of society, caring for God's creation, and establishing the
values of the Kingdom'.[54] Occasionally, through its own laws, a
church claims for itself the benefit of human rights: the church
'shall of right be free in all spiritual matters from the direction or
interposition of any civil government'; spiritual matters are listed
as including worship, membership, spiritual office, confession of
and instruction in the faith, and church polity.[55]

Secondly, the laws of Anglican churches might promote human
rights in civil society through the establishment and work of
institutions of the church. Such canonical institutions are rare.[56] At

---

[51] See, typically, for example, South East Asia, Const. Preamble: the church
exists, *inter alia*, '[t]o give glory to God through united and common witness and
proclamation of the Gospel of our Lord Jesus Christ'; 'to strengthen and further
the Church's fellowship'; and 'to make disciples of all nations'; Ireland, Const.,
Preamble, I. 3: 'to minister the doctrine and sacraments and discipline of Christ'.

[52] Venezuela, Const. II: the church is to contribute to the 'moral and spiritual'
welfare of society.

[53] See, for example, North India, Const. II. I. II: the church must proclaim the
gospel and undertake service 'which may include educational, medical, social,
agricultural and other service'; see also Chile, Statutes, Article 2.

[54] New Zealand, Const., Preamble.

[55] North India, Const. I. IV. 2.

[56] Moreover, I have found no obvious examples of the promotion of human
rights listed among the legal functions of central assemblies in national, regional
or provincial churches: see generally, Doe, *Canon Law*, 48ff. However, the laws of
churches allow the discussion of such matters; for example, one of the legal
functions of the General Synod of the Church of England is 'to consider and
express [its] opinion on any . . . matter of religious *or public interest*': Synodical
Government Measure 1969, s. 2.

the national, regional or provincial level, the laws of churches fall into two broad categories. On the one hand, only a very small number of churches have institutions with a specific human rights brief. This is the case in the Philippines, where the Episcopal Church has a National Commission on Social Justice and Human Rights.[57] Similarly, the law of the church in the Province of the West Indies requires the Provincial Synod to appoint a Standing Commission on Social Justice and Human Rights: it is

> the duty of the Commission to keep under constant review all matters relating to Social Justice and Human Rights in the constituent territories of the Province and to make recommendations to the Synod on the development of strategies which will assist the Church in furthering its work on these issues.[58]

On the other hand, in the vast majority of churches, there are no special canonical bodies charged specifically with human rights promotion. Instead, this would seem to be subsumed within the work of canonical or (more usually) extra-canonical commissions and boards for social responsibility, as in the Church of England,[59] for peace and justice, as in ECUSA,[60] or for church and society, as in the Church in Wales.[61] Similar institutions may also be found at

---

[57] See *Social Concerns Resolutions and Statements of the Philippine Episcopal Church* (1988); see also Philippines, Const. Art. 1. 1; Cans. I. 2. 2(d): one of the functions of the Provincial Synod's Commission on Social Concerns and Development is 'to study the nature and root causes of poverty and underdevelopment in the country and review the participation of the Church in the development process'.

[58] West Indies, Can. 33. 1. C.

[59] The Board for Social Responsibility is 'to promote and coordinate the thought and action of the church in matters affecting the lives of all in society': see N. Doe, *The Legal Framework of the Church of England* (Oxford, Clarendon Press, 1996), 93; the board is now part of the Church and World Division of the Archbishops' Council: see M. Hill, *Ecclesiastical Law*, 2nd edn (Oxford, Oxford University Press, 2001), 28.

[60] ECUSA, Cans. I. 1(2)(n)(7): the Standing Commission on Peace with Justice is under a duty 'to develop recommendations and strategies which will be of concrete assistance to this Church in furthering the work on issues of peace with justice'.

[61] See *The Church in Wales: Composition of Committees* (2001), 14: the Church and Society Team is responsible to the Council for Mission and Ministry which, in turn, is responsible to the Bench of Bishops. Its function is to 'provide an effective Christian witness in contemporary society'.

the diocesan level.[62] Again, a permissive regime seems to function
at the level of the most local ecclesiastical unit, the parish or
pastorate, the assembly of which is often charged with promotion
of the whole mission of the church, pastoral, evangelistic,
ecumenical and social, but no specific mention is made of human
rights.[63]

Thirdly, the Lambeth call to individual members of Anglican
churches to promote human rights finds no direct echo in the
actual laws of churches.[64] Instead, this is only obliquely con-
templated, and this is a rare occurrence, in laws which occasionally
recognize a duty on church members to 'strive to live according to
Christ's teachings, to preach the gospel and to realize God's justice
in society',[65] or to use and develop their talents for the edification
of the church and for the community.[66] The constitution of the
church in South India is exceptional; it requires 'members . . . [to]
contribute to the total ministry of the Church . . . by responsible
participation in secular organizations, legislative bodies, councils
and panchayats, and in other areas of public life', so that 'the
decisions which are made in these areas may be controlled by the
mind of Christ and the structures of society transformed according
to His will'.[67] More commonly, catechetical instruments indirectly
contemplate the possibility of individuals contributing to the
promotion of human rights in their work for 'justice and reconciliation' in civil society.[68]

In short, there is little legal evidence from around the Anglican
Communion that the exhortation of the Lambeth Conference, for
churches corporately and their members individually to promote
human rights in secular society, has found canonical expression.
This may be contrasted with the polities of other Christian
churches. In the United Kingdom, for example, developments in
the internal rules of churches seem to indicate a greater willingness

[62] See, for example, the Church in Wales, Diocese of Monmouth, *Year Book*
(2001), 12: the Council for Social Responsibility.

[63] See, for example, Korea, Const. Art. 92. 1; Wales, Const. VI. 22(3); North
India, Const. II. V.

[64] Indeed, Anglican laws do not generally contain compendia of the duties of
individual members: see Doe, *Canon Law*, 167, and below.

[65] Korea, Cans. 42–5.

[66] Chile, Cans. A. 2; for a similar approach see Mexico, Can. 10.

[67] South India, Const., VI. 2.

[68] See, for example, Southern Africa, *Prayer Book* (1989), 434.

and opportunity for the publication by churches of their expectations of the State in the field of social justice and human rights. For
instance, under its constitution, one of the functions of the British
Evangelical Council, a grouping of several churches, is 'to represent the evangelical viewpoint *to government and public bodies
regarding matters of common concern and interest at home and
abroad'*.[69] One of the functions of the Evangelical Alliance, which
includes several Pentecostal churches, is to communicate the voice
of the church to the government and 'to make a difference to the
political scene today'.[70] In the Church of Scotland, the Church and
Nation Committee is 'to watch over developments of the national
life in which moral and spiritual considerations specially arise, and
to consider what action the Church may from time to time be
advised to take to further the highest interests of the people'. The
committee's 1999 annual report to the General Assembly contains
recommendations for church action on such secular matters as
criminal justice, electoral reform, welfare reform and human
rights.[71] In the Roman Catholic Church, the episcopal conference
of England and Wales has a Department of Christian Responsibility which, in turn, has a Committee of Community Relations; its
concern is 'social and racial justice in British society with
particular regard for ethnic minority communities and poor and

---

[69] Constitution of the British Evangelical Council (1969, amended 1998), 2;
constituent members of the Council include the Evangelical Presbyterian Church
in England and Wales, the Evangelical Fellowship of Congregational Churches,
and the Free Church of Scotland.

[70] The Evangelical Alliance has a Public Affairs Department and a
parliamentary officer at Westminster: websites carry prayers for the support or
defeat of proposed parliamentary legislation. See also the Seventh-Day Adventist
Church, *Statements, Guidelines and Other Documents*, a compilation from the
Communications Department of the General Conference (Watford, Herts., 1996):
issued by the church's General Conference, by its Administrative Committee, and
by the Office of the President of the General Conference, this expresses the
church's opinion with regard to a host of subjects, including: the family, the
environment, health-care institutions, racism, homelessness and poverty.

[71] For the functions of the committee, see A. Herron, *The Law and Practice of
the Kirk* (Glasgow, Chapter House Ltd, 1995), 403; see generally J. L. Weather-
head, *The Constitution and Laws of the Church of Scotland* (Edinburgh, General
Assembly, 1997).

marginalised people in urban priority areas'.[72] Finally, Churches Together in Wales (CYTUN), an ecumenical association including Baptists, Methodists, Anglicans and Roman Catholics, has a Laws Committee 'to review the effect of legislation on faith communities in Wales' enacted by the National Assembly for Wales.[73]

Introvert Canon Law: Canonical Declarations of Human Rights within the Church

As has been seen, the Lambeth Conference has not dealt directly with the promotion of human rights *within* Anglican churches, though it received a report in 1998 proposing that churches themselves should be model communities in which discrimination plays no part.[74] To what extent, then, do the laws of Anglican churches contain equivalents to those declarations or other charters of human rights so familiar in secular international and municipal law? The laws of Anglican churches seem to fall into two broad categories: those which incorporate a system of fundamental rights, and those in which fundamental rights are dispersed amongst a variety of regulatory forms.[75] The latter group is the more common.

---

[72] For information on the conference, see Doe, *Legal Framework*, 90. See also *The Common Good and the Catholic Church's Social Teaching* (Episcopal Conference of England and Wales, 1996): 'Every public policy should be judged by the effect it has on human dignity and the common good'; 'Religion is always personal, but never just a private affair'; 'The Church has the right and duty to advocate and protect a social order in which the human dignity of all is fostered, and to protest when it is in any way threatened. Thus the Church opposes totalitarianism because it oppresses people and deprives them of their freedom'; 'The Church does not present a political programme, still less a party political one. The social teaching of the Church expounded in this document, provides a set of consistent and complementary principles, values and goals'.

[73] CYTUN was set up in 1990 and its Laws Committee in 1999, following the establishment of the National Assembly under the Government of Wales Act 1998.

[74] See above for *Called to Full Humanity*, LC 1998, *Official Report*, 86.

[75] While a discussion of the following is not within the scope of this essay, it is worth noting that the Roman Catholic Church, in its Code of Canon Law (1983) has a special title devoted to 'The Obligations and Rights of all the Christian Faithful' (Book II, Part I, Title I, cc. 208–33); c. 208 provides: 'In virtue of their rebirth in Christ there exists among all the Christian faithful a true equality with regard to dignity and the activity whereby all cooperate in the building up of the Body of Christ in accord with each one's own condition and function'; see, for example, c. 214 (right to worship) and c. 215 (right of association).

On the one hand, canonical declarations of fundamental human rights are most common in the African churches, with constitutional articles specially devoted to 'The Dignity and Rights of People',[76] or 'The Dignity and the Rights of Man',[77] or 'Issues Relating to Belief'.[78] Several principles are to be found in these documents. First, commonly laws declare the equality of all individuals before God: this is the case in Papua New Guinea,[79] Melanesia[80] and Tanzania.[81] The idea of equality is sometimes presented as a requirement of 'Christian doctrine', and sometimes it is rooted in the rights, value and dignity of the human person. For example, the constitution of the Province of Central Africa states: 'In conformity with Christian doctrine, the Church of this province proclaims the equal value of all men before the righteous Love of God';[82] and in Uganda the constitution provides that, in accordance with 'the established Christian doctrine, the Church of this Province shall proclaim and hold that all people have equal value, rights and dignity in the sight of God'.[83] Secondly, laws prescribe that the particular institutional church is responsible to provide for the needs, or special needs, of all those people who are committed to its charge; this is so in Melanesia,[84] Papua New Guinea,[85] Central Africa,[86] Uganda[87] and Tanzania.[88]

[76] See, for example, Uganda, Const. Art. 3.

[77] See, for example, Papua New Guinea, Const. Art. 3.

[78] Tanzania, Const. Art. 3. 5.

[79] Papua New Guinea, Const. Art. 3: 'all persons are of equal value in the sight of God'.

[80] Melanesia, Const. Art. 4.

[81] Tanzania, Const. Art. III. 5: 'the Church of this Province teaches that all human beings are equal before God'.

[82] Central Africa, Const., Fundamental Declarations, III; the same formula is used in Sudan, Const. Art. II(c).

[83] Uganda, Const. Art. 3; see also Jerusalem and the Middle East, Const. Art. 5(i); West Africa, Const. Art. 1, and Burundi, Const. Art. 4.

[84] Melanesia, Const. Art. 4: 'The Church of this Province declares that all persons are of equal value in the sight of God and will take care to provide for the needs of all people committed to its charge'.

[85] Papua New Guinea, Const. Art. 3.

[86] Const. Fundamental Declarations, III: the church must be 'careful to provide for the special needs of different peoples committed to its charge'.

[87] Uganda, Const. Art. 3: the church must be 'mindful to provide for the special needs of different people committed to its charge'.

[88] Tanzania, Const. Art. III. 5: the church must make 'a special effort to fulfil its duties to the faithful'.

Thirdly, laws of Anglican churches provide that there must be no discrimination in the membership and government of the Church. Discrimination is forbidden on grounds of, variously: *race alone*, as in Central Africa, Sudan, and Jerusalem and the Middle East;[89] *ethnicity*, as in the Indian Ocean,[90] and 'social discrimination' is prohibited in Zaire;[91] *nationality*, as in Tanzania,[92] *tribe*, as in Papua New Guinea,[93] or (occasionally) *region*, or combinations of these. The constitutional law of the Province of Uganda, for instance, provides that the church 'shall not allow discrimination in the membership and government of the Church solely on grounds of colour, sex, tribe or region'.[94] The canon law of ECUSA contains perhaps the fullest declaration of fundamental rights: 'No one shall be denied rights, status, or access to an equal place in the life, worship, and governance of this Church because of race, color, ethnic origin, national origin, marital status, sex, sexual orientation, disabilities or age, except as otherwise specified by Canon'.[95] A similar provision exists in the provincial laws of the churches in Burundi and the Philippines.[96] The laws of the majority of Anglican churches, including those in England, Wales, Scotland and Ireland, contain no formal equivalents to provisions of this sort.[97]

---

[89] Central Africa, Const. Fundamental Declarations, III: the church 'allows no discrimination on grounds of racial differences only, in the membership and government of the Church'; the same formula is used in Sudan, Const. Art. 2(c); a similar formula is to be found in Jerusalem and the Middle East, Const. Art. 5(I).

[90] Indian Ocean, Const. Art. 3: the church 'will not tolerate discrimination on grounds of "ethnicity" in membership and government of the church'.

[91] Zaire, Const. Art. 4.

[92] Tanzania, Const. III. 5.: the church 'will not allow any discrimination on grounds of nationality'.

[93] Papua New Guinea, Const. Art. 4 (race or tribe).

[94] Uganda, Const. Art. 3.

[95] ECUSA, Cans. I. 17. 5.

[96] Philippines, Cans. II. 2. 4; Burundi, Const. Art. 4: this prohibits 'sexual discrimination'.

[97] In relation to the United Kingdom, this may be attributable to the common law approach, particularly its influence on legal development within these churches, and the absence (before the Human Rights Act 1998) of a written secular constitution spelling out fundamental rights formally. For a comparison of the Church of England and the notion of fundamental rights in the Roman Catholic Church (operative under its Code of Canon Law 1983), see Doe, *Legal Framework*, 225–9.

On the other hand, there are those Anglican churches in which the concept of human rights surfaces not under a special canonical title, devoted to the dignity of the human person, but in a dispersed fashion amongst church laws dealing with discrete subjects. Canonical rights which may be understood as having the appearance of human rights include, for example: the provision that '[r]espect for the conscientious convictions of individual members shall be accorded by the Church, so long as they are in harmony with the mind of Christ and are not disruptive of the fellowship of His Body';[98] 'the right of every person to choose any particular cultural expression of the faith';[99] church doctrine 'may be assented to with a good conscience by all members';[100] and in one church the canon law provides that: 'No one shall be denied access to the selection process for ordination in this Church because of race, color, ethnic origin, sex, national origin, marital status, sexual orientation, disabilities or age, except as otherwise specified' in the law of the church.[101] Such provisions would seem to articulate an implicit notion of human rights implemented in the formal law.

By way of contrast, there is some evidence from the laws of Anglican churches that they seek to block access from within the church to facilities for the protection of human rights under secular law.[102] One area in which this appears to be the case is with regard to clerical discipline.[103] In this field, Anglican legal systems display no coherent set of shared principles dealing with the relationship between church tribunals or other quasi-judicial bodies and the secular courts of the states in which those churches exist. Only occasionally does formal church law treat the subject.

[98] North India, Const. I. I. II. 3–4, 9. Provisions of this sort are rare.

[99] New Zealand, Const. Preamble, 12.

[100] England, Can. A2.

[101] ECUSA, Cans. III. 4. 1.

[102] This, of course, may of itself simply be an exercise of the human right to freedom of religion.

[103] On the other hand, there is ample evidence in Anglican laws dealing with clerical discipline that every attempt is made to satisfy concepts of fair trial appearing in secular human rights instruments; see, for example, the discussions in M. Hill (ed.), *Faithful Discipleship: Clergy Discipline in Anglican and Roman Catholic Canon Law* (Cardiff, Centre for Law and Religion, 2001); see esp. 297: both communions share the principles that (for example) only certain breaches of canon law are actionable, and, in the disciplinary process, clergy are presumed innocent until proven guilty; also, that there ought to be no punishment without a distinct breach of church law.

On the one hand, alongside duties on clergy and others to undertake to be bound by church court decisions and sentences, some
churches operate a fundamental principle that recourse to the
secular courts ought not generally to be made: disputes should be
settled within the church. Two contrasting approaches are used in
North India and ECUSA. The constitution of the United Church of
North India states as an aspirational norm: 'No bishop, presbyter
or any other member of the Church . . . should go to a civil court,
for enforcing any of the spiritual and religious rights under the
Constitution . . . or the rules framed thereunder . . . but should seek
his remedy under this Constitution'.[104] The constitution of ECUSA,
which describes its own disciplinary proceedings as 'ecclesiastical in
nature', representing 'the polity and order of this hierarchical
church', presents the principle as a mandatory obligation: 'No
member of the Clergy of this Church may resort to the secular
courts for the purpose of delaying, hindering or reviewing any
proceeding' of the church's tribunals.[105]

However, the laws of other churches recognize the authority of
secular courts over ecclesiastical tribunals. The constitution of the
Church of Ireland provides that the General Synod must not
determine 'any matter or question which, in the opinion of the lay
judges, is within the jurisdiction and more proper to be submitted
to the consideration and decision of a civil tribunal'.[106]

The Dominant Regime of Juridical Relations
in Anglican Canon Laws

Needless to say, central to much contemporary human rights
discourse is the idea that they determine relations between human
beings, between individuals and the secular state, and, from a

---

[104] North India, Constitution. II. v. VII; see also Chile, Cans. E. 11: when there is
a conflict 'between Christians', and these propose to proceed in the civil courts, the
pastor must make every effort to resolve the case.

[105] ECUSA, Cans. IV. 14. 2: clergy may not claim 'constitutional guarantees
afforded to citizens in other contexts'. This has, of course, been the subject of consideration by the secular courts in the USA which operate a principle of deference to
hierarchical churches: see generally, for example, J. T. Noonan and E. M. Gaffney,
*Religious Freedom: History, Cases and Other Materials on the Interaction of
Religion and Government* (New York, Foundation Press, 2001), 609ff.

[106] Ireland, Const. VIII. 26. 4.

religious viewpoint, between the individual and God, when violation of human dignity is also seen as an offence to God.[107] These relationships, of course, become juridical relationships when incorporated in the laws of states and of churches. As seems to be the case from the legal evidence outlined in the previous two sections, in the Communion as a whole the explicit deployment of human rights concepts in Anglican canon laws is weak and uneven. This is in part the result of, and may best be understood from the perspective of, the dominant regimes of juridical relations within Anglican churches. The concept of human rights is not the usual inspiration behind juridical relations within Anglican churches. Rather than being rooted in a human rights outlook, juridical relations are instead based on two different fundamental approaches: one is positivist in appearance, the other theocratic.

On the one hand, juridical relations within Anglican churches are based on systems of duties and rights which are presented in canon law without reference to any obvious, more fundamental understanding of human relations in the ecclesial community. First, insofar as it exists to facilitate and to order the domestic life of churches, the purposes of canon law itself are spelt out in the legal texts of churches without mention of human rights: typically, laws function simply for 'the order, good government, and efficiency of the Church'.[108] Anglican jurisprudence generally is utilitarian.[109] Secondly, juridical relations, and with them ecclesial order, are fixed by positive duties rather than by human rights; this is perhaps

---

[107] Indeed, at the formal inauguration of the European Court of Human Rights at Strasbourg, on 20 April 1959, its first president Lord McNair stated that the words of Jesus Christ in Matthew 25: 40, 'inasmuch as ye have done it unto one of the least of these my brethren, ye have done it unto me', inspired such instruments as the Universal Declaration of Human Rights: *Yearbook of the European Convention on Human Rights: 1958–1959* (The Hague, 1960), 154.

[108] Southern Africa, Const. IX; the idea is not uncommon: see also, for example, Wales, Const. I. 33: laws are made 'for the general management and good government of the Church'.

[109] See, for example, *Re St Hilary, Cornwall* [1938] 4 All ER 147 at 152 *per* Stable, Deputy Dean of Arches: '[w]here a number of people are united in a community . . . such as the Anglican Church . . . the mutual rights, obligations and duties of the members of the community must be measured and determined by rules of some kind'; in this community 'when people are robbed of the rights which the law accords them, and which the law is supposed to protect, and, if necessary, enforce', the use of formal methods of control will be inevitable.

the most predominant juridical device in Anglican canon laws.[110] Thirdly, the vast majority of canonical rights in Anglican churches are correlative rights, their existence and enjoyment the indirect consequence of positive duties; as such, rights, enjoyed by individuals, derive from duties placed on others rather than from any notion of entitlement vested in the individual by virtue of their humanity, and these correlative rights may be based on preceptive duties,[111] or prohibitory duties.[112] Fourthly, as a matter of ecclesiastical practice, churches do not have a distinct compendium of laws spelling out the fundamental rights of church members.[113] Instead, positive rights are scattered throughout laws dealing with specific subjects, and normally they are framed and distributed according to an individual's ecclesial status, not according to the individual's inherent or God-given human dignity.[114] Finally, some laws focus on juridical relations relevant to church membership and life in terms of privileges rather than rights, a concept which may on the face of it be at odds with that of inherent human rights.[115]

[110]Typically: 'No person shall be admitted to officiate in sacred things in a congregation of this Church, except under the authority of the Bishop of the Diocese' (Southern Africa, Can. 33. 2).

[111]Typically: 'In each Parish there shall be a stated place of worship in which the Priest appointed by the Bishop regularly conducts Common Prayer, administers the Sacraments, and performs other Rites and Ceremonies of the Church with the participation of the Laity' (Japan, Const. Art. 2); this duty generates for others the facility of public worship.

[112]Typically: '[n]o minister may refuse or, except for the purpose of preparing or instructing the parents or guardians or godparents, delay baptizing a child who has a sponsoring parent, guardian or godparent who professes to be a Christian' (Australia, Can. P5 1992, 6); this ministerial duty generates a correlative right to infant baptism.

[113]See generally Doe, *Canon Law*, 166.

[114]See, for example, Wales, Const. VI. 2(2): 'The purpose of the [electoral] roll shall be the determination of eligibility to exercise voting rights'; and (under VI. 2(4)) 'A lay person who is over sixteen years of age shall be entitled to have his name entered on the roll if he [*inter alia*] . . . is a communicant'.

[115]See, for example, South India, Const. III. 2, 4, 8: '[t]he full privileges . . . of membership in the Church . . . belong to those who, having attained years of discretion and having gained some good measure of experience in the Christian life', and having received due instruction in Christian truth, 'make public profession of their faith and of their purpose, with God's help, to serve and to follow Christ as members of His Church'. The 'privilege of participation in the government of this Church is confined to adult communicant members of this Church'; the church's synod, or a diocesan council, have power 'to attach other conditions to the exercise of this privilege'. Moreover, '[i]t is the privilege of every

On the other hand, a study of actual laws seems to disclose the assumption that juridical relations, determined by rights and duties in the church, are founded more directly on ideas of divine law, formulated as a result of theological investigation and principle, not on a concept of human rights.[116] By way of example, first, unlike in civil jurisprudence, the primary limitation on the power of governance in churches, and the yardstick against which to measure the permissibility of action, is to be found in divine rights, rather than human rights enforceable against church authorities.[117] Generally, Anglican churches treat 'the Canonical Scriptures of the Old and New Testaments, given by inspiration of God, as containing all things necessary for salvation and *as being the ultimate rule and standard of the faith and life of the Church*'.[118] Secondly, duties are imposed on individuals not because of their own human status, nor because of their resultant relation with other church members as human beings, but by virtue of the office they hold within the particular church: for instance, clergy must obey the directions of their bishops,[119] not as a result of human dignity, but due to the inherent authority of the latter.[120] Thirdly, ministerial rights are enjoyed because of the prevailing theological understanding about the divine commission entrusted at ordination; for example, priests are treated as entitled to administer absolution through a divine commission not because

member of the Church to know himself to be a son in the family of God and to rejoice in the experience of his salvation'.

[116] Within these canonical ideas (that is, within the formal legal texts of churches), a concept of human rights either plays no obvious part (it is simply not expressly articulated), or else its place is hidden or, at best, implicit.

[117] See, for example, Thirty-Nine Articles of Religion, Art. 20: 'it is not lawful for the Church to ordain any thing that is contrary to God's Word written'; see also LC 1998, Res. III. 5: The 'Holy Scriptures are for us the "rule and ultimate standard" of faith and practice'.

[118] For this and similar formulae, see Doe, *Canon Law*, 198–9.

[119] For example: 'the inferior clergy who have received authority to minister in any diocese owe canonical obedience in all things lawful and honest to the bishop of the same' (England, Can. C1(3)). The usual form of the oath of canonical obedience, shared by most churches, is: 'I swear by Almighty God that I will pay true and canonical obedience to the Lord Bishop of C and his successors in all things lawful and honest' (England, Can. C14(3)). The bishop does not enjoy the correlative right of obedience qua human being, but qua bishop.

[120] Wales, Const. II. 32.

they are human persons.[121] Fourthly, correlative rights are enjoyed
by individuals not in virtue of their human value, but because the
duties from which they flow are inherent in a ministry to which its
bearer has been called by God; clergy, for example, must visit the
sick not because the latter have a human right to this, but because
it is a function of clergy having a cure of souls.[122]

   In sum: as a matter of ecclesiastical practice, juridical relations
within Anglican churches are dominated not by human rights
concepts but by a framework of positive duties, correlative rights,
and directly conferred rights – that is, rights and duties which exist
by virtue of individuals being Christian, or by virtue of offices
whose functions originate in divine commission or theocratic
legislation. The point here is not that such rights could not be
accommodated within a human rights framework, simply that
canonical systems do not articulate them as human rights. Indeed,
the idea that canon law is itself applied ecclesiology could readily
accommodate a human rights framework as the basis for some
juridical relations within churches.[123] Canon law seeks to put into
practice the revelation of God: God reveals the destiny of humankind; the church reflects on that revelation and formulates a
theology about humankind as created in the image of God; that
theology provides the church with an understanding of the values
and dignity of the human person; and each church implements
human rights, to free the faithful for the fulfilment of their destiny,
in the form of ecclesiastical human rights law.[124]

---

   [121]See, for example, Melanesia, Cans. A. 6. A. 1–5: 'the power to forgive sins is
given by God to a priest at his Ordination and the priest uses this power when he
forgives sins'.
   [122]England, Can. C24(6).
   [123]Some juridical relations may not be susceptible to expression as human rights
(for example, facultative rules about the manner in which proceedings and business
in church synods are transacted), while others are: for example, the canonical right
to a fair trial; again, the idea of a human right to marry could readily be
accommodated within the understanding of marriage in some churches as 'a
relationship which is part of God's fundamental purpose for the human race' (New
Zealand, Can. G. III).
   [124]For the purposes of church law, and its relation to theology, see N. Doe, 'The
Principles of Canon Law: A Focus of Legal Unity in Anglican–Roman Catholic
Relations', (1999) 5 Ecc.LJ, 221 at 226.

Conclusions

First, in global Anglican thought, illustrated by pronouncements of the Lambeth Conference, human rights exist as fundamental to, and of universal importance for, the dignity of the human person. Their foundation rests on the theological understanding of the equality of human beings, themselves created in the image of God. Human rights are necessary for humans to develop their personality, their relationship with God and with one another, and to ensure that their divine dignity is respected and divine destiny realized. Human rights include political rights and economic rights, and their fulfilment is related intimately to concepts of social justice. The church has a responsibility to promote human rights in civil society, by word and action, and in so doing acts out its witness to the gospel, though the Conference recognizes that there may be legitimate limitations on the exercise of human rights in prescribed circumstances. The duty to advance human rights falls on each church in its corporate capacity, on individual church members, as well as on secular governments and the international community. The Lambeth Conference has not, however, systematically articulated the idea that human rights also apply to life within, or are vested in members of, the church as a model community of reconciliation; its treatment of human rights has been confined to their recognition and protection only in civil society.

Second, there would seem to be a dissonance between the legal systems of Anglican churches and the pronouncements of the Lambeth Conference in relation to the promotion of human rights in civil society. While canonical lists of ecclesial activities sometimes include the transformation of unjust structures in civil society, most do not. Moreover, only a very small number of churches have canonical institutions charged specifically with the function of promoting human rights in civil society. The provinces of the West Indies and the Philippines are leading the way in this regard, though many churches have boards for social responsibility and social justice whose work may indirectly include the advancement of human rights. The specific Lambeth Conference call for individual church members to promote human rights in civil society finds no direct echo in the laws of any church, though church law in South India, exceptionally, requires members to participate in secular affairs to transform the structures of society.

Third, while the Lambeth Conference has not expressly applied its human rights standards to the internal life of churches, there is some canonical evidence to suggest that the language of human rights is beginning to surface in the laws of Anglican churches. In this respect, canon law is ahead of Lambeth Conference thought. On the one hand, the laws of some churches employ rudimentary declarations of human rights based on the equality and dignity of the human person. The laws of Anglican churches in Africa are playing a leading role in this respect with basic provisions which forbid discrimination in the membership and government of the church. (In the wider secular perspective, such charters would suggest that, in terms of Anglican polity and outlook, there is a presumption for some churches that human rights standards do apply in the private sphere of ecclesial life.) The vast majority of churches, however, do not have laws of this type, though there is evidence of provisions scattered throughout laws containing equivalents to, or articulating implicitly, human rights notions. Yet, in some churches, the law seeks to exclude the operation of secular human rights principles within the church.

Fourth, the absence of a general deployment of human rights concepts in Anglican canon law, itself apparently at odds with the rhetoric of Lambeth Conference resolutions, may be the result of, and may best be understood from the perspective of, the dominant regimes of juridical relations within Anglican churches. On the face of legal texts themselves, the idea of human rights currently plays no explicit part in the organization of juridical relations. The purposes of church law are presented without appeal to human rights. Juridical relations are mainly fixed by positive duties. Anglican laws do not contain compendia of fundamental rights. In other words, the dominant juridical regime in Anglican churches is that of duties. Within this, the dominant rights regime is that of correlative duties, not free-standing rights. If anything, correlative rights and directly conferred rights, dispersed among laws, are conceived as based on duties, rights and commissions of divine not human origin. In short, in practice the canon laws of Anglican churches do not systematically mirror theological ideas about human rights proposed by the Lambeth Conference.

Notes on Contributors

Mark Chopko has been General Counsel of the National Conference of Catholic Bishops in the United States since 1987. He is a graduate of the University of Scranton and Cornell Law School. He has written on church and state affairs in the *De Paul Law Review* and the *George Washington Law Review*. He is a Fellow in the International Academy of Freedom of Religion and Belief and was formerly Senior Attorney at the United States Nuclear Regulatory Commission.

Norman Doe is Professor of Law at Cardiff University and director of its Centre for Law and Religion. He is the author of *Fundamental Authority in Late Medieval English Law* (Cambridge, 1990), *The Legal Framework of the Church of England* (Oxford, 1996), *Canon Law in the Anglican Communion* (Oxford, 1998) and *The Law of the Church in Wales* (Cardiff, 2002); editor of *Essays in Canon Law* (Cardiff, 1992), and co-editor of *English Canon Law* (Cardiff, 1998). He is Deputy Chancellor of the Diocese of Manchester and a member of the European Consortium for Church and State Research.

David Harte is senior lecturer at Newcastle Law School in the University of Newcastle and a reader in the Diocese of Newcastle. He is a member of the editorial committee of the *Ecclesiastical Law Journal*. Recent publications include: 'Religious Education and Worship in State Schools', in N. Doe, M. Hill and R. Ombres (eds), *English Canon Law* (Cardiff, 1998); 'Legal Aspects of Development and the Church in the Countryside', in N. Herbert-Young (ed.), *Law, Policy and Development in the Rural Environment* (Cardiff, 1999); and 'Establishment and Autonomy:

The Church of England as a Voluntary Body', in A. Dunn (ed.), *The Voluntary Sector, the State and the Law* (Oxford, 2000).

Mark Hill, a practising barrister, is Chancellor of the Diocese of Chichester and Deputy Chancellor of the Diocese of Winchester. His publications include *Ecclesiastical Law*, 2nd edition (Oxford, 2001); *English Canon Law* (Cardiff, 1998), jointly edited with Professor Norman Doe and Dr Robert Ombres; and *Faithful Discipleship: Clergy Discipline in Anglican and Roman Catholic Canon Law* (Cardiff, 2001). Sometime Visiting Fellow of Emmanuel College, Cambridge, he is an Honorary Fellow of the Centre for Law and Religion at Cardiff University. He is editor of the *Ecclesiastical Law Journal* and a member of the Legal Advisory Commission of the General Synod of the Church of England.

Ian Leigh is Professor of Law at the University of Durham where he is a member of the Human Rights Unit in the European Law Institute. He is the author of *Law, Politics and Local Democracy* (Oxford, 2000) and contributed a chapter 'Towards a Christian Approach to Religious Liberty', in P. Beaumont (ed.), *Christian Perspectives on Human Rights and Legal Philosophy* (Carlisle, 1998). He has been involved in Human Rights Act training for the Judicial Studies Board and the police and has acted as a consultant for campaigning groups including Justice and the Christian Institute.

Javier Martínez-Torrón is Professor of Law at Complutense University, Madrid, and holds a doctorate *utroque iure* in law and canon law. He has been visiting professor and researcher in numerous universities in Europe, USA and Latin America. He is an associate member of the Spanish Royal Academy of Jurisprudence and Legislation (and Vice-President of its Canon Law section) and of the International Academy of Comparative Law. He is the author of *Anglo-American Law and Canon Law* (Berlin, 1998). He is a member of the Advisory Commission on Religious Freedom of the Spanish Ministry of Justice, of the International Advisory Council of the Oslo Coalition on Freedom of Religion and Belief, and of the International Academy for Freedom of Religion and Belief.

Roger Ruston taught theology at Blackfriars, Oxford during the 1970s and 1980s and Christian ethics at Bristol from 1991 to 1995.

He is the author of *A Say in the End of the World* (Oxford, 1989), on the ethics of British nuclear weapons policy, and has written many articles on religion and war. He is at present engaged on a project on Christianity and human rights at the Centre for Law and Religion at the University of Cardiff. This is sponsored by the English Dominican Province and funded by the Christendom Trust.

Stephen Sedley was called to the bar in 1964 and took silk in 1983. He was appointed to the High Court in 1992 and to the Court of Appeal in 1999. He is President of the British Institute of Human Rights and an *ad hoc* Judge of the European Court of Human Rights. He has delivered judgments in a number of church-related cases including *R v Archbishop of Canterbury ex parte Williamson* (15 March 1996); *R v Dean and Chapter of St Paul's Cathedral and the Church in Wales, ex parte Williamson* (1998) 5 *Ecc.LJ* 129; *Redmond-Bate v Director of Public Prosecutions* [1999] CLR 998; and *Aston Cantlow Parochial Church Council v Wallbank* [2001] 3 All ER 393. He is Honorary Professor of Law at Cardiff University.

Nicholas Sagovsky is Liverpool Professor of Theology and Public Life at Liverpool Hope University College. He is currently completing a study of Christian tradition and the practice of justice undertaken during his tenure of the William Leech Professorial Research Fellowship in Applied Christian Theology at Newcastle University (1997–2002). This will be published as a sequel to *Ecumenism, Christian Origins and the Practice of Justice* (Cambridge, 2000), which was an expanded version of the 1996 Hulsean Lectures at Cambridge University, where he was Dean of Clare College from 1986 to 1997. He has been a member of the Anglican–Roman Catholic International Commission (ARCIC) since 1992 and is a member of the newly established Inter-Anglican Theological and Doctrinal Commission.

Subscribers

The following have associated themselves with the publication of this volume through subscription:

Revd William Adam, Cambridge
J. R. Andrews, Exeter
Anthony W. Archer, Berkhamsted
Nicola Aries, Kingston-upon-Thames
Dr J. H. E. Baker, Cardiff
Stuart Barber, London
Revd Canon Derek G. Belcher, Cowbridge
Jonathan J. Bell, London
Revd Paul J. Benfield, Fleetwood
Christina Bennett, Henfield
Peter Birts QC, London
Professor Tony Bradney, Leicester
Monsignor Ralph Brown, London
Rupert D. H. Bursell, Winscombe
Revd Jeremy Caddick, Cambridge
Rt. Revd George Cassidy, Bishop of Southwell
Dominic Chambers, London
Revd Ian Chandler, Haywards Heath
Chancellor Peter Collier QC, York
Revd Irene Cowell, Liverpool
Frank Cranmer, London
Dr Clyde Croft SE, Geelong
David Cummings, Twickenham
Revd Dr John Dann, Cardiff
Eithne D'Auria, Didcot

Mark Dubbery, London
W. Cole Durham Jnr, Utah
Dr Peter W. Edge, Oxford
Revd Olubunmi A. Fagbemi, London
Clare Faulds, Isle of Man
Robert Forrest, Sheffield
Revd Jeffrey Gainer, Carmarthen
Justin Gau, London
Charles George QC, Sevenoaks
Rt. Revd J. W. Gladwin, Bishop of Guildford
Jonathan Goodchild, St Albans
Chancellor Michael Goodman, London
Revd K. Gresham, Oldham
Revd Canon Dr Mark N. Gretason, London
J. Andrew Grime, London
Jeremy Gunn, Washington DC
Dr Brian Hanson, Bolney
Nicola Harding, Ripon
Giles Harrap, London
Professor Richard Helmholz, Chicago
Raymond Hemingray, Peterborough
Rt. Revd Christopher Hill, Bishop of Stafford
Rt. Revd John Hind, Bishop of Chichester
Peter Edward Holden, Stalybridge
Andrew Johnson, Salisbury
Malcolm F. Jones, Ryde
S. M. S. Jones, London
Venerable Trevor Jones, Hertford
Rt. Revd Dr E. W. Kemp, Chichester
David Lambert, Cardiff
David J. Lamming, Sudbury
Rt. Hon. Lord Justice Laws, London
Damien H. R. Lochrane, London
Venerable Christopher Lowson, Southsea

Andrew McFarlane QC, London
Venerable Douglas McKittrick, Brighton
James Mannion, Headington
Lieutenant Colonel N. J. Mercer, Germany
Revd Mgr. Richard Moth, London
Rt. Revd Dr M. Nazir-Ali, Bishop of Rochester
Rubie Marie Nottage, Nassau
Revd B. M. M. O'Connor, Little Missenden
Robert Ombres OP, Cambridge
Revd Jeremy Paisey, Buckie
Revd D. W. Parrott, Rayleigh
Revd Kristian Paver, Totnes
Oliver Peirson, London
Ingvill Thorson Plesner, Oslo
Revd Gareth J. Powell, Cardiff
Rt. Revd Dr Geoffrey Rowell, Bishop of Gibraltar in
    Europe
Chancellor Philip Price QC, Cardiff
His Honour Judge Richard Price, Ryde
J. M. R. Prichard, Hove
Revd Canon John Rees, Oxford
James Rickards, London
Julian Rivers, Bristol
Andrew R. Robinson, Portsmouth
Rt. Revd David Rossdale, Bishop of Grimsby
Rt. Revd Michael Scott-Joynt, Bishop of Winchester
Very Revd John Seaford, Dean of Jersey
Stephen Slack, Taunton
N. D. W. Thomas, Wirral
David E. P. Turner QC, London
Rt. Revd Lindsay Urwin, Bishop of Horsham
Arthur D. Walker, Haworth
Rt. Revd Dominic Walker, Bishop of Reading
Ronald Watts, Edinburgh

D. West, Ipswich
Professor Sir David Williams QC, DL, Cambridge

The Athenæum, Pall Mall
College of the Resurrection, Mirfield
The Maughan Library, King's College, London
Llandaff Diocesan Registry, Cardiff
The Principal and Chapter, Pusey House, Oxford

Index